LIVING LITURGY™

SUNDAY MISSAL

2016

CELEBRATING THE EUCHARIST

LITURGICAL PRESS
Collegeville, Minnesota
www.litpress.org

Published with the approval of the
Committee on Divine Worship
United States Conference of Catholic Bishops

Nihil Obstat: Reverend Robert C. Harren, *Censor deputatus*

Imprimatur: ✠ Most Reverend Donald J. Kettler, J.C.D., Bishop of St. Cloud, Minnesota, February 17, 2015

Cover design by Ann Blattner. Art by Martin Erspamer, OSB, a monk of St. Meinrad Archabbey, Indiana.

ISSN 1949-1166
ISBN 978-0-8146-4971-8

Contents

The Order of Mass 1

Celebration of the Liturgy of the Word [with Holy Communion] 27

November 29 First Sunday of Advent 31

December 6 Second Sunday of Advent 35

December 8 The Immaculate Conception of the Blessed Virgin Mary 39

December 13 Third Sunday of Advent 44

December 20 Fourth Sunday of Advent 49

December 24 The Nativity of the Lord (Christmas)—At the Vigil Mass 53

December 25 The Nativity of the Lord—At the Mass during the Night 59

December 25 The Nativity of the Lord—At the Mass at Dawn 63

December 25 The Nativity of the Lord—At the Mass during the Day 66

December 27 The Holy Family of Jesus, Mary, and Joseph 71

January 1 Solemnity of Mary, the Holy Mother of God 76

January 2 The Epiphany of the Lord—At the Vigil Mass 80

January 3 The Epiphany of the Lord—At the Mass during the Day 81

January 10 The Baptism of the Lord 86

January 17 Second Sunday in Ordinary Time 90

January 24 Third Sunday in Ordinary Time 95

January 31 Fourth Sunday in Ordinary Time 101

February 7 Fifth Sunday in Ordinary Time 107

February 10 Ash Wednesday 112

February 14 First Sunday of Lent 118

February 21 Second Sunday of Lent 123

February 28 Third Sunday of Lent 129

March 6 Fourth Sunday of Lent 135

March 13 Fifth Sunday of Lent 141

March 20 Palm Sunday of the Lord's Passion 146

March 24 Thursday of the Lord's Supper (Holy Thursday)— At the Evening Mass 163

March 25 Friday of the Passion of the Lord (Good Friday) 169

March 26 Holy Saturday—The Easter Vigil in the Holy Night 188

March 27 Easter Sunday of the Resurrection of the Lord— At the Mass during the Day 226

April 3 Second Sunday of Easter (or of Divine Mercy) 232

April 10 Third Sunday of Easter 237

April 17 Fourth Sunday of Easter 243

April 24 Fifth Sunday of Easter 247

May 1 Sixth Sunday of Easter 251

May 4 or 7	The Ascension of the Lord—At the Vigil Mass	**256**
May 5 or 8	The Ascension of the Lord—At the Mass during the Day	**257**
May 8	Seventh Sunday of Easter	**263**
May 14	Pentecost Sunday—At the Vigil Mass	**267**
May 15	Pentecost Sunday—At the Mass during the Day	**272**
May 22	The Most Holy Trinity	**280**
May 29	The Most Holy Body and Blood of Christ	**284**
June 5	Tenth Sunday in Ordinary Time	**290**
June 12	Eleventh Sunday in Ordinary Time	**295**
June 19	Twelfth Sunday in Ordinary Time	**300**
June 26	Thirteenth Sunday in Ordinary Time	**304**
July 3	Fourteenth Sunday in Ordinary Time	**309**
July 10	Fifteenth Sunday in Ordinary Time	**314**
July 17	Sixteenth Sunday in Ordinary Time	**320**
July 24	Seventeenth Sunday in Ordinary Time	**324**
July 31	Eighteenth Sunday in Ordinary Time	**330**
August 7	Nineteenth Sunday in Ordinary Time	**334**
August 14	Twentieth Sunday in Ordinary Time	**340**
August 14	The Assumption of the Blessed Virgin Mary—At the Vigil Mass	**344**
August 15	The Assumption of the Blessed Virgin Mary—At the Mass during the Day	**348**
August 21	Twenty-First Sunday in Ordinary Time	**352**
August 28	Twenty-Second Sunday in Ordinary Time	**357**
September 4	Twenty-Third Sunday in Ordinary Time	**361**
September 11	Twenty-Fourth Sunday in Ordinary Time	**366**
September 18	Twenty-Fifth Sunday in Ordinary Time	**373**
September 25	Twenty-Sixth Sunday in Ordinary Time	**378**
October 2	Twenty-Seventh Sunday in Ordinary Time	**383**
October 9	Twenty-Eighth Sunday in Ordinary Time	**387**
October 16	Twenty-Ninth Sunday in Ordinary Time	**392**
October 23	Thirtieth Sunday in Ordinary Time	**397**
October 30	Thirty-First Sunday in Ordinary Time	**401**
November 1	All Saints	**406**
November 6	Thirty-Second Sunday in Ordinary Time	**411**
November 13	Thirty-Third Sunday in Ordinary Time	**416**
November 20	Our Lord Jesus Christ, King of the Universe	**421**
	Eucharistic Prayer for Reconciliation I	**425**

The Order of Mass

The Introductory Rites

Entrance Chant — STAND

Sign of the Cross

Priest: In the name of the Father, and of the Son, and of the Holy Spirit.

People: **Amen.**

Greeting

A Priest: The grace of our Lord Jesus Christ,
and the love of God,
and the communion of the Holy Spirit
be with you all.

People: **And with your spirit.**

B Priest: Grace to you and peace from God our Father
and the Lord Jesus Christ.

People: **And with your spirit.**

C Priest: The Lord be with you.

People: **And with your spirit.**

Penitential Act

A Priest: Brethren (brothers and sisters), let us acknowledge our sins,
and so prepare ourselves to celebrate the sacred mysteries. (Pause)

All: **I confess to almighty God**
and to you, my brothers and sisters,
that I have greatly sinned,
in my thoughts and in my words,
in what I have done and in what I have failed to do,

And, striking their breast, they say:

through my fault, through my fault,
through my most grievous fault;

Then they continue:

therefore I ask blessed Mary ever-Virgin,
all the Angels and Saints,
and you, my brothers and sisters,
to pray for me to the Lord our God.

Priest: May almighty God have mercy on us,
forgive us our sins,
and bring us to everlasting life.

People: **Amen.**

B Priest: Brethren (brothers and sisters), let us acknowledge our sins,
and so prepare ourselves to celebrate the sacred mysteries. (Pause)

Priest: Have mercy on us, O Lord.

People: **For we have sinned against you.**

Priest: Show us, O Lord, your mercy.

People: **And grant us your salvation.**

Priest: May almighty God have mercy on us,
forgive us our sins,
and bring us to everlasting life.

People: **Amen.**

C These or other invocations may be used:

Priest: Brethren (brothers and sisters), let us acknowledge our sins,
and so prepare ourselves to celebrate the sacred mysteries. (Pause)

Priest (Deacon or another minister):
You were sent to heal the contrite of heart:
Lord, have mercy. Or: Kyrie, eleison.

People: **Lord, have mercy.** Or: **Kyrie, eleison.**

Priest: You came to call sinners:
Christ, have mercy. Or: Christe, eleison.

People: **Christ, have mercy.** Or: **Christe, eleison.**

Priest: You are seated at the right hand of the Father to intercede for us:
Lord, have mercy. Or: Kyrie, eleison.
People: **Lord, have mercy.** Or: **Kyrie, eleison.**

Priest: May almighty God have mercy on us,
forgive us our sins,
and bring us to everlasting life.
People: **Amen.**

Kyrie

The Kyrie, eleison (Lord, have mercy) invocations follow, unless they have just occurred in a formula of the Penitential Act.

℣. Lord, have mercy. ℟. **Lord, have mercy.**
℣. Christ, have mercy. ℟. **Christ, have mercy.**
℣. Lord, have mercy. ℟. **Lord, have mercy.**

Or:

℣. Kyrie, eleison. ℟. **Kyrie, eleison.**
℣. Christe, eleison. ℟. **Christe, eleison.**
℣. Kyrie, eleison. ℟. **Kyrie, eleison.**

Gloria

All: **Glory to God in the highest,**
and on earth peace to people of good will.

We praise you,
we bless you,
we adore you,
we glorify you,
we give you thanks for your great glory,
Lord God, heavenly King,
O God, almighty Father.

Lord Jesus Christ, Only Begotten Son,
Lord God, Lamb of God, Son of the Father,
you take away the sins of the world,
have mercy on us;
you take away the sins of the world,
receive our prayer;
you are seated at the right hand of the Father,
have mercy on us.

For you alone are the Holy One,
you alone are the Lord,
you alone are the Most High,
Jesus Christ,
with the Holy Spirit,
in the glory of God the Father.
Amen.

Collect (Opening Prayer)

Priest: Let us pray.

All pray in silence with the Priest for a while.

Then the Priest, with hands extended, says the Collect prayer, at the end of which the people acclaim:

Amen.

The Liturgy of the Word

First Reading **SIT**

Then the reader goes to the ambo and reads the First Reading, while all sit and listen.

To indicate the end of the reading, the reader acclaims:

The word of the Lord.

All: **Thanks be to God.**

Responsorial Psalm

The psalmist or cantor sings or says the Psalm, with the people making the response.

Second Reading

After this, if there is to be a Second Reading, a reader reads it from the ambo, as above.

To indicate the end of the reading, the reader acclaims:

The word of the Lord.

All: **Thanks be to God.**

Gospel Acclamation **STAND**

There follows the Alleluia or another chant laid down by the rubrics, as the liturgical time requires.

Gospel Dialogue

Deacon or Priest: The Lord be with you.
People: **And with your spirit.**
Deacon or Priest: A reading from the holy Gospel according to N.
People: **Glory to you, O Lord.**

Gospel Reading

At the end of the Gospel, the Deacon, or the Priest, acclaims:
The Gospel of the Lord.
All: **Praise to you, Lord Jesus Christ.**

Homily — SIT

Profession of Faith — STAND

All: **I believe in one God,**
the Father almighty,
maker of heaven and earth,
of all things visible and invisible.

I believe in one Lord Jesus Christ,
the Only Begotten Son of God,
born of the Father before all ages.
God from God, Light from Light,
true God from true God,
begotten, not made, consubstantial with the Father;
through him all things were made.
For us men and for our salvation
he came down from heaven,

At the words that follow, up to and including and became man, all bow.

and by the Holy Spirit was incarnate of the Virgin Mary,
and became man.

For our sake he was crucified under Pontius Pilate,
he suffered death and was buried,
and rose again on the third day
in accordance with the Scriptures.

He ascended into heaven
and is seated at the right hand of the Father.
He will come again in glory
to judge the living and the dead
and his kingdom will have no end.

I believe in the Holy Spirit, the Lord, the giver of life,
who proceeds from the Father and the Son,
who with the Father and the Son is adored and glorified,
who has spoken through the prophets.

I believe in one, holy, catholic and apostolic Church.
I confess one Baptism for the forgiveness of sins
and I look forward to the resurrection of the dead
and the life of the world to come. Amen.

Instead of the Niceno-Constantinopolitan Creed, especially during Lent and Easter Time, the baptismal Symbol of the Roman Church, known as the Apostles' Creed, may be used.

All: **I believe in God,**
the Father almighty,
Creator of heaven and earth,
and in Jesus Christ, his only Son, our Lord,

At the words that follow, up to and including the Virgin Mary, all bow.

who was conceived by the Holy Spirit,
born of the Virgin Mary,
suffered under Pontius Pilate,
was crucified, died and was buried;
he descended into hell;
on the third day he rose again from the dead;
he ascended into heaven,
and is seated at the right hand of God the Father almighty;
from there he will come to judge the living and the dead.

I believe in the Holy Spirit,
the holy catholic Church,
the communion of saints,
the forgiveness of sins,
the resurrection of the body,
and life everlasting. Amen.

Universal Prayer
(*or* Prayer of the Faithful *or* Bidding Prayers)

The Liturgy of the Eucharist

Presentation and Preparation of the Gifts **SIT**

The Priest, standing at the altar, takes the paten with the bread and holds it slightly raised above the altar with both hands, saying in a low voice:

Blessed are you, Lord God of all creation,
for through your goodness we have received
the bread we offer you:
fruit of the earth and work of human hands,
it will become for us the bread of life.

If, however, the Offertory Chant is not sung, the Priest may speak these words aloud; at the end, the people may acclaim:

Blessed be God for ever.

The Deacon, or the Priest, pours wine and a little water into the chalice, saying quietly:

By the mystery of this water and wine
may we come to share in the divinity of Christ
who humbled himself to share in our humanity.

The Priest then takes the chalice and holds it slightly raised above the altar with both hands, saying in a low voice:

Blessed are you, Lord God of all creation,
for through your goodness we have received
the wine we offer you:
fruit of the vine and work of human hands,
it will become our spiritual drink.

If, however, the Offertory Chant is not sung, the Priest may speak these words aloud; at the end, the people may acclaim:

Blessed be God for ever.

After this, the Priest, bowing profoundly, says quietly:

With humble spirit and contrite heart
may we be accepted by you, O Lord,
and may our sacrifice in your sight this day
be pleasing to you, Lord God.

Then the Priest, standing at the side of the altar, washes his hands, saying quietly:

Wash me, O Lord, from my iniquity
and cleanse me from my sin.

Standing at the middle of the altar, facing the people, extending and then joining his hands, he says:

Pray, brethren (brothers and sisters),
that my sacrifice and yours
may be acceptable to God,
the almighty Father.

The people rise and reply: **STAND**

May the Lord accept the sacrifice at your hands
for the praise and glory of his name,
for our good
and the good of all his holy Church.

Prayer over the Offerings

Then the Priest, with hands extended, says the Prayer over the Offerings, at the end of which the people acclaim:

Amen.

The Eucharistic Prayer

Priest: The Lord be with you.
People: **And with your spirit.**
Priest: Lift up your hearts.
People: **We lift them up to the Lord.**
Priest: Let us give thanks to the Lord our God.
People: **It is right and just.**

Preface

Preface Acclamation

At the end of the Preface he joins his hands and concludes the Preface with the people, singing or saying aloud:

Holy, Holy, Holy Lord God of hosts.
Heaven and earth are full of your glory.
Hosanna in the highest.
Blessed is he who comes in the name of the Lord.
Hosanna in the highest.

Eucharistic Prayer I (The Roman Canon) **KNEEL**

Priest:

To you, therefore, most merciful Father,
we make humble prayer and petition
through Jesus Christ, your Son, our Lord:
that you accept
and bless ✠ these gifts, these offerings,
these holy and unblemished sacrifices,
which we offer you firstly
for your holy catholic Church.
Be pleased to grant her peace,
to guard, unite and govern her
throughout the whole world,
together with your servant N. our Pope
and N. our Bishop,*
and all those who, holding to the truth,
hand on the catholic and apostolic faith.

Commemoration of the Living

Remember, Lord, your servants N. and N.
and all gathered here,
whose faith and devotion are known to you.
For them, we offer you this sacrifice of praise
or they offer it for themselves
and all who are dear to them:
for the redemption of their souls,
in hope of health and well-being,
and paying their homage to you,
the eternal God, living and true.

In communion with those whose memory we venerate,
especially the glorious ever-Virgin Mary,

* Mention may be made here of the Coadjutor Bishop, or Auxiliary Bishops, as noted in the *General Instruction of the Roman Missal*, no. 149.

Mother of our God and Lord, Jesus Christ,
† and blessed Joseph, her Spouse,
your blessed Apostles and Martyrs,
Peter and Paul, Andrew,
(James, John,
Thomas, James, Philip,
Bartholomew, Matthew,
Simon and Jude;
Linus, Cletus, Clement, Sixtus,
Cornelius, Cyprian,
Lawrence, Chrysogonus,
John and Paul,
Cosmas and Damian)
and all your Saints;
we ask that through their merits and prayers,
in all things we may be defended
by your protecting help.
(Through Christ our Lord. Amen.)

On the Nativity of the Lord and throughout the Octave

Celebrating the most sacred night (day)
on which blessed Mary the immaculate Virgin
brought forth the Savior for this world,
and in communion with those whose memory we venerate,
especially the glorious ever-Virgin Mary,
Mother of our God and Lord, Jesus Christ, †

On the Epiphany of the Lord

Celebrating the most sacred day
on which your Only Begotten Son,
eternal with you in your glory,
appeared in a human body, truly sharing our flesh,
and in communion with those whose memory we venerate,
especially the glorious ever-Virgin Mary,
Mother of our God and Lord, Jesus Christ, †

From the Mass of the Easter Vigil until the Second Sunday of Easter

Celebrating the most sacred night (day)
of the Resurrection of our Lord Jesus Christ in the flesh,
and in communion with those whose memory we venerate,
especially the glorious ever-Virgin Mary,
Mother of our God and Lord, Jesus Christ, †

On the Ascension of the Lord

Celebrating the most sacred day
on which your Only Begotten Son, our Lord,
placed at the right hand of your glory

our weak human nature,
which he had united to himself,
and in communion with those whose memory we venerate,
especially the glorious ever-Virgin Mary,
Mother of our God and Lord, Jesus Christ, †

On Pentecost Sunday
Celebrating the most sacred day of Pentecost,
on which the Holy Spirit
appeared to the Apostles in tongues of fire,
and in communion with those whose memory we venerate,
especially the glorious ever-Virgin Mary,
Mother of our God and Lord, Jesus Christ, †

Therefore, Lord, we pray:
graciously accept this oblation of our service,
that of your whole family;
order our days in your peace,
and command that we be delivered from eternal damnation
and counted among the flock of those you have chosen.
(Through Christ our Lord. Amen.)

From the Mass of the Easter Vigil until the Second Sunday of Easter
Therefore, Lord, we pray:
graciously accept this oblation of our service,
that of your whole family,
which we make to you
also for those to whom you have been pleased to give
the new birth of water and the Holy Spirit,
granting them forgiveness of all their sins:
order our days in your peace,
and command that we be delivered from eternal damnation
and counted among the flock of those you have chosen.
(Through Christ our Lord. Amen.)

Be pleased, O God, we pray,
to bless, acknowledge,
and approve this offering in every respect;
make it spiritual and acceptable,
so that it may become for us
the Body and Blood of your most beloved Son,
our Lord Jesus Christ.

On the day before he was to suffer,
he took bread in his holy and venerable hands,
and with eyes raised to heaven

to you, O God, his almighty Father,
giving you thanks, he said the blessing,
broke the bread
and gave it to his disciples, saying:

TAKE THIS, ALL OF YOU, AND EAT OF IT,
FOR THIS IS MY BODY,
WHICH WILL BE GIVEN UP FOR YOU.

In a similar way, when supper was ended,
he took this precious chalice
in his holy and venerable hands,
and once more giving you thanks, he said the blessing
and gave the chalice to his disciples, saying:

TAKE THIS, ALL OF YOU, AND DRINK FROM IT,
FOR THIS IS THE CHALICE OF MY BLOOD,
THE BLOOD OF THE NEW AND ETERNAL COVENANT,
WHICH WILL BE POURED OUT FOR YOU AND FOR MANY
FOR THE FORGIVENESS OF SINS.

DO THIS IN MEMORY OF ME.

The mystery of faith.

And the people continue, acclaiming:

A **We proclaim your Death, O Lord,**
and profess your Resurrection
until you come again.

B **When we eat this Bread and drink this Cup,**
we proclaim your Death, O Lord,
until you come again.

C **Save us, Savior of the world,**
for by your Cross and Resurrection
you have set us free.

Priest:
Therefore, O Lord,
as we celebrate the memorial of the blessed Passion,
the Resurrection from the dead,
and the glorious Ascension into heaven
of Christ, your Son, our Lord,
we, your servants and your holy people,
offer to your glorious majesty
from the gifts that you have given us,
this pure victim,
this holy victim,

this spotless victim,
the holy Bread of eternal life
and the Chalice of everlasting salvation.

Be pleased to look upon these offerings
with a serene and kindly countenance,
and to accept them,
as once you were pleased to accept
the gifts of your servant Abel the just,
the sacrifice of Abraham, our father in faith,
and the offering of your high priest Melchizedek,
a holy sacrifice, a spotless victim.

In humble prayer we ask you, almighty God:
command that these gifts be borne
by the hands of your holy Angel
to your altar on high
in the sight of your divine majesty,
so that all of us, who through this participation at the altar
receive the most holy Body and Blood of your Son,
may be filled with every grace and heavenly blessing.
(Through Christ our Lord. Amen.)

Commemoration of the Dead

Remember also, Lord, your servants N. and N.,
who have gone before us with the sign of faith
and rest in the sleep of peace.

Grant them, O Lord, we pray,
and all who sleep in Christ,
a place of refreshment, light and peace.
(Through Christ our Lord. Amen.)

To us, also, your servants, who, though sinners,
hope in your abundant mercies,
graciously grant some share
and fellowship with your holy Apostles and Martyrs:
with John the Baptist, Stephen,
Matthias, Barnabas,
(Ignatius, Alexander,
Marcellinus, Peter,
Felicity, Perpetua,
Agatha, Lucy,
Agnes, Cecilia, Anastasia)
and all your Saints;
admit us, we beseech you,
into their company,
not weighing our merits,

but granting us your pardon,
through Christ our Lord.

Through whom
you continue to make all these good things, O Lord;
you sanctify them, fill them with life,
bless them, and bestow them upon us.

Through him, and with him, and in him,
O God, almighty Father,
in the unity of the Holy Spirit,
all glory and honor is yours,
for ever and ever.

People: **Amen.**

Then follows the Communion Rite, p. 23.

Eucharistic Prayer II

Preface

It is truly right and just, our duty and our salvation,
always and everywhere to give you thanks, Father most holy,
through your beloved Son, Jesus Christ,
your Word through whom you made all things,
whom you sent as our Savior and Redeemer,
incarnate by the Holy Spirit and born of the Virgin.

Fulfilling your will and gaining for you a holy people,
he stretched out his hands as he endured his Passion,
so as to break the bonds of death and manifest the resurrection.

And so, with the Angels and all the Saints
we declare your glory,
as with one voice we acclaim:

Holy, Holy, Holy Lord God of hosts.
Heaven and earth are full of your glory.
Hosanna in the highest.
Blessed is he who comes in the name of the Lord.
Hosanna in the highest.

Priest:
You are indeed Holy, O Lord,
the fount of all holiness.
Make holy, therefore, these gifts, we pray,
by sending down your Spirit upon them like the dewfall,
so that they may become for us
the Body and ✠ Blood of our Lord Jesus Christ.

At the time he was betrayed
and entered willingly into his Passion,

he took bread and, giving thanks, broke it,
and gave it to his disciples, saying:

TAKE THIS, ALL OF YOU, AND EAT OF IT,
FOR THIS IS MY BODY,
WHICH WILL BE GIVEN UP FOR YOU.

In a similar way, when supper was ended,
he took the chalice
and, once more giving thanks,
he gave it to his disciples, saying:

TAKE THIS, ALL OF YOU, AND DRINK FROM IT,
FOR THIS IS THE CHALICE OF MY BLOOD,
THE BLOOD OF THE NEW AND ETERNAL COVENANT,
WHICH WILL BE POURED OUT FOR YOU AND FOR MANY
FOR THE FORGIVENESS OF SINS.

DO THIS IN MEMORY OF ME.

The mystery of faith.

People:

A **We proclaim your Death, O Lord,
and profess your Resurrection
until you come again.**

B **When we eat this Bread and drink this Cup,
we proclaim your Death, O Lord,
until you come again.**

C **Save us, Savior of the world,
for by your Cross and Resurrection
you have set us free.**

Priest:

Therefore, as we celebrate
the memorial of his Death and Resurrection,
we offer you, Lord,
the Bread of life and the Chalice of salvation,
giving thanks that you have held us worthy
to be in your presence and minister to you.

Humbly we pray
that, partaking of the Body and Blood of Christ,
we may be gathered into one by the Holy Spirit.

Remember, Lord, your Church,
spread throughout the world,
and bring her to the fullness of charity,

together with N. our Pope and N. our Bishop*
and all the clergy.

In Masses for the Dead, the following may be added:
Remember your servant N.,
whom you have called (today)
from this world to yourself.
Grant that he (she) who was united with your Son in a death like his,
may also be one with him in his Resurrection.

Remember also our brothers and sisters
who have fallen asleep in the hope of the resurrection,
and all who have died in your mercy:
welcome them into the light of your face.
Have mercy on us all, we pray,
that with the Blessed Virgin Mary, Mother of God,
with blessed Joseph, her Spouse,
with the blessed Apostles,
and all the Saints who have pleased you throughout the ages,
we may merit to be coheirs to eternal life,
and may praise and glorify you
through your Son, Jesus Christ.

Through him, and with him, and in him,
O God, almighty Father,
in the unity of the Holy Spirit,
all glory and honor is yours,
for ever and ever.

People: **Amen.**

Then follows the Communion Rite, p. 23.

Eucharistic Prayer III

Priest:
You are indeed Holy, O Lord,
and all you have created
rightly gives you praise,
for through your Son our Lord Jesus Christ,
by the power and working of the Holy Spirit,
you give life to all things and make them holy,
and you never cease to gather a people to yourself,
so that from the rising of the sun to its setting
a pure sacrifice may be offered to your name.

* Mention may be made here of the Coadjutor Bishop, or Auxiliary Bishops, as noted in the *General Instruction of the Roman Missal*, no. 149.

Therefore, O Lord, we humbly implore you:
by the same Spirit graciously make holy
these gifts we have brought to you for consecration,
that they may become the Body and ✠ Blood
of your Son our Lord Jesus Christ,
at whose command we celebrate these mysteries.

For on the night he was betrayed
he himself took bread,
and, giving you thanks, he said the blessing,
broke the bread and gave it to his disciples, saying:

TAKE THIS, ALL OF YOU, AND EAT OF IT,
FOR THIS IS MY BODY,
WHICH WILL BE GIVEN UP FOR YOU.

In a similar way, when supper was ended,
he took the chalice,
and, giving you thanks, he said the blessing,
and gave the chalice to his disciples, saying:

TAKE THIS, ALL OF YOU, AND DRINK FROM IT,
FOR THIS IS THE CHALICE OF MY BLOOD,
THE BLOOD OF THE NEW AND ETERNAL COVENANT,
WHICH WILL BE POURED OUT FOR YOU AND FOR MANY
FOR THE FORGIVENESS OF SINS.

DO THIS IN MEMORY OF ME.

The mystery of faith.

People:

A **We proclaim your Death, O Lord,
and profess your Resurrection
until you come again.**

B **When we eat this Bread and drink this Cup,
we proclaim your Death, O Lord,
until you come again.**

C **Save us, Savior of the world,
for by your Cross and Resurrection
you have set us free.**

Priest:
Therefore, O Lord, as we celebrate the memorial
of the saving Passion of your Son,
his wondrous Resurrection
and Ascension into heaven,
and as we look forward to his second coming,

we offer you in thanksgiving
this holy and living sacrifice.

Look, we pray, upon the oblation of your Church
and, recognizing the sacrificial Victim by whose death
you willed to reconcile us to yourself,
grant that we, who are nourished
by the Body and Blood of your Son
and filled with his Holy Spirit,
may become one body, one spirit in Christ.

May he make of us
an eternal offering to you,
so that we may obtain an inheritance with your elect,
especially with the most Blessed Virgin Mary, Mother of God,
with blessed Joseph, her Spouse,
with your blessed Apostles and glorious Martyrs
(with Saint N.: the Saint of the day or Patron Saint)
and with all the Saints,
on whose constant intercession in your presence
we rely for unfailing help.

May this Sacrifice of our reconciliation,
we pray, O Lord,
advance the peace and salvation of all the world.
Be pleased to confirm in faith and charity
your pilgrim Church on earth,
with your servant N. our Pope and N. our Bishop,*
the Order of Bishops, all the clergy,
and the entire people you have gained for your own.

Listen graciously to the prayers of this family,
whom you have summoned before you:
in your compassion, O merciful Father,
gather to yourself all your children
scattered throughout the world.

† To our departed brothers and sisters
and to all who were pleasing to you
at their passing from this life,
give kind admittance to your kingdom.
There we hope to enjoy for ever the fullness of your glory
through Christ our Lord,
through whom you bestow on the world all that is good. †

* Mention may be made here of the Coadjutor Bishop, or Auxiliary Bishops, as noted in the *General Instruction of the Roman Missal*, no. 149.

When this Eucharistic Prayer is used in Masses for the Dead, the following may be said:

† Remember your servant N.
whom you have called (today)
from this world to yourself.
Grant that he (she) who was united with your Son in a death like his,
may also be one with him in his Resurrection,
when from the earth
he will raise up in the flesh those who have died,
and transform our lowly body
after the pattern of his own glorious body.
To our departed brothers and sisters, too,
and to all who were pleasing to you
at their passing from this life,
give kind admittance to your kingdom.
There we hope to enjoy for ever the fullness of your glory,
when you will wipe away every tear from our eyes.
For seeing you, our God, as you are,
we shall be like you for all the ages
and praise you without end,
through Christ our Lord,
through whom you bestow on the world all that is good. †

Through him, and with him, and in him,
O God, almighty Father,
in the unity of the Holy Spirit,
all glory and honor is yours,
for ever and ever.

People: **Amen.**

Then follows the Communion Rite, p. 23.

Eucharistic Prayer IV

Preface

It is truly right to give you thanks,
truly just to give you glory, Father most holy,
for you are the one God living and true,
existing before all ages and abiding for all eternity,
dwelling in unapproachable light;
yet you, who alone are good, the source of life,
have made all that is,
so that you might fill your creatures with blessings
and bring joy to many of them by the glory of your light.

And so, in your presence are countless hosts of Angels,
who serve you day and night

and, gazing upon the glory of your face,
glorify you without ceasing.

With them we, too, confess your name in exultation,
giving voice to every creature under heaven,
as we acclaim:

Holy, Holy, Holy Lord God of hosts.
Heaven and earth are full of your glory.
Hosanna in the highest.
Blessed is he who comes in the name of the Lord.
Hosanna in the highest.

Priest:
We give you praise, Father most holy,
for you are great
and you have fashioned all your works
in wisdom and in love.
You formed man in your own image
and entrusted the whole world to his care,
so that in serving you alone, the Creator,
he might have dominion over all creatures.
And when through disobedience he had lost your friendship,
you did not abandon him to the domain of death.
For you came in mercy to the aid of all,
so that those who seek might find you.
Time and again you offered them covenants
and through the prophets
taught them to look forward to salvation.

And you so loved the world, Father most holy,
that in the fullness of time
you sent your Only Begotten Son to be our Savior.
Made incarnate by the Holy Spirit
and born of the Virgin Mary,
he shared our human nature
in all things but sin.
To the poor he proclaimed the good news of salvation,
to prisoners, freedom,
and to the sorrowful of heart, joy.
To accomplish your plan,
he gave himself up to death,
and, rising from the dead,
he destroyed death and restored life.

And that we might live no longer for ourselves
but for him who died and rose again for us,
he sent the Holy Spirit from you, Father,

as the first fruits for those who believe,
so that, bringing to perfection his work in the world,
he might sanctify creation to the full.

Therefore, O Lord, we pray:
may this same Holy Spirit
graciously sanctify these offerings,
that they may become
the Body and ✠ Blood of our Lord Jesus Christ
for the celebration of this great mystery,
which he himself left us
as an eternal covenant.

For when the hour had come
for him to be glorified by you, Father most holy,
having loved his own who were in the world,
he loved them to the end:
and while they were at supper,
he took bread, blessed and broke it,
and gave it to his disciples, saying:

TAKE THIS, ALL OF YOU, AND EAT OF IT,
FOR THIS IS MY BODY,
WHICH WILL BE GIVEN UP FOR YOU.

In a similar way,
taking the chalice filled with the fruit of the vine,
he gave thanks,
and gave the chalice to his disciples, saying:

TAKE THIS, ALL OF YOU, AND DRINK FROM IT,
FOR THIS IS THE CHALICE OF MY BLOOD,
THE BLOOD OF THE NEW AND ETERNAL COVENANT,
WHICH WILL BE POURED OUT FOR YOU AND FOR MANY
FOR THE FORGIVENESS OF SINS.

DO THIS IN MEMORY OF ME.

The mystery of faith.

People:

A **We proclaim your Death, O Lord,
and profess your Resurrection
until you come again.**

B **When we eat this Bread and drink this Cup,
we proclaim your Death, O Lord,
until you come again.**

C **Save us, Savior of the world,**
for by your Cross and Resurrection
you have set us free.

Priest:
Therefore, O Lord,
as we now celebrate the memorial of our redemption,
we remember Christ's Death
and his descent to the realm of the dead,
we proclaim his Resurrection
and his Ascension to your right hand,
and, as we await his coming in glory,
we offer you his Body and Blood,
the sacrifice acceptable to you
which brings salvation to the whole world.

Look, O Lord, upon the Sacrifice
which you yourself have provided for your Church,
and grant in your loving kindness
to all who partake of this one Bread and one Chalice
that, gathered into one body by the Holy Spirit,
they may truly become a living sacrifice in Christ
to the praise of your glory.

Therefore, Lord, remember now
all for whom we offer this sacrifice:
especially your servant N. our Pope,
N. our Bishop,* and the whole Order of Bishops,
all the clergy,
those who take part in this offering,
those gathered here before you,
your entire people,
and all who seek you with a sincere heart.

Remember also
those who have died in the peace of your Christ
and all the dead,
whose faith you alone have known.

To all of us, your children,
grant, O merciful Father,
that we may enter into a heavenly inheritance
with the Blessed Virgin Mary, Mother of God,
with blessed Joseph, her Spouse,
and with your Apostles and Saints in your kingdom.

* Mention may be made here of the Coadjutor Bishop, or Auxiliary Bishops, as noted in the *General Instruction of the Roman Missal*, no. 149.

There, with the whole of creation,
freed from the corruption of sin and death,
may we glorify you through Christ our Lord,
through whom you bestow on the world all that is good.

Through him, and with him, and in him,
O God, almighty Father,
in the unity of the Holy Spirit,
all glory and honor is yours,
for ever and ever.

People: **Amen.**

THE COMMUNION RITE **STAND**

THE LORD'S PRAYER

Priest: At the Savior's command
and formed by divine teaching,
we dare to say:

All: **Our Father, who art in heaven,
hallowed be thy name;
thy kingdom come,
thy will be done
on earth as it is in heaven.
Give us this day our daily bread,
and forgive us our trespasses,
as we forgive those who trespass against us;
and lead us not into temptation,
but deliver us from evil.**

Priest: Deliver us, Lord, we pray, from every evil,
graciously grant peace in our days,
that, by the help of your mercy,
we may be always free from sin
and safe from all distress,
as we await the blessed hope
and the coming of our Savior, Jesus Christ.

All: **For the kingdom,
the power and the glory are yours
now and for ever.**

Sign of Peace

Priest: Lord Jesus Christ,
who said to your Apostles:
Peace I leave you, my peace I give you,
look not on our sins,
but on the faith of your Church,
and graciously grant her peace and unity
in accordance with your will.
Who live and reign for ever and ever.

People: **Amen.**

Priest: The peace of the Lord be with you always.

People: **And with your spirit.**

Then, if appropriate, the Deacon, or the Priest, adds:

Let us offer each other the sign of peace.

Fraction of the Bread

The Priest says quietly:

Priest: May this mingling of the Body and Blood
of our Lord Jesus Christ
bring eternal life to us who receive it.

All: **Lamb of God, you take away the sins of the world,**
have mercy on us.
Lamb of God, you take away the sins of the world,
have mercy on us.
Lamb of God, you take away the sins of the world,
grant us peace.

The Priest says quietly: **KNEEL**

Lord Jesus Christ, Son of the living God,
who, by the will of the Father
and the work of the Holy Spirit,
through your Death gave life to the world,
free me by this, your most holy Body and Blood,
from all my sins and from every evil;
keep me always faithful to your commandments,
and never let me be parted from you.

Or:

May the receiving of your Body and Blood,
Lord Jesus Christ,
not bring me to judgment and condemnation,
but through your loving mercy
be for me protection in mind and body
and a healing remedy.

Invitation to Communion

Priest: Behold the Lamb of God,
behold him who takes away the sins of the world.
Blessed are those called to the supper of the Lamb.

All: **Lord, I am not worthy**
that you should enter under my roof,
but only say the word
and my soul shall be healed.

Communion

The Priest says quietly: May the Body of Christ
keep me safe for eternal life.

The Priest says quietly: May the Blood of Christ
keep me safe for eternal life. **STAND**

The Priest says to each of the communicants: The Body of Christ.

The communicant replies: **Amen.**

Priest says quietly: What has passed our lips as food, O Lord,
may we possess in purity of heart,
that what has been given to us in time
may be our healing for eternity.

Prayer after Communion **STAND**

The Priest says: Let us pray.

At the end the people acclaim: **Amen.**

The Concluding Rites

Final Blessing

Priest: The Lord be with you.

People: **And with your spirit.**

Priest: May almighty God bless you,
the Father, and the Son, ✠ and the Holy Spirit.

People: **Amen.**

Dismissal

The Deacon, or the Priest himself:

Go forth, the Mass is ended.

Or:

Go and announce the Gospel of the Lord.

Or:

Go in peace, glorifying the Lord by your life.

Or:

Go in peace.

People: **Thanks be to God.**

A Prayer for Vocations

"O Lord, send us chosen messengers and teachers,
lovers of worship and of art
who will restore with chaste and noble works
the beauty of your house!
May they teach us to see with pure heart
the splendor of your Son Jesus Christ
and to express what we have seen
in images worthy of so great a vision."

Thomas Merton, OCSO

Celebration of the Liturgy of the Word

[With Holy Communion]

Introductory Rites

Introduction

Deacon or lay leader:

We gather here to celebrate the Lord's Day.
Sunday has been called the Lord's Day because
it was on this day
that Jesus conquered sin and death and rose to new life.
Unfortunately, we are not able to celebrate the Mass today
because we do not have a Priest.
Let us be united in the spirit of Christ with
the Church around the world
and celebrate our redemption in Christ's suffering,
Death and Resurrection.

Sign of the Cross

STAND

Deacon or lay leader:

In the name of the Father, and of the Son, and of the Holy Spirit.

All respond: **Amen.**

Greeting

Deacon or lay leader:

Grace to you and peace from God our Father
and the Lord Jesus Christ.
Blessed be God for ever.

All: **Blessed be God for ever.**

Collect

Liturgy of the Word

SIT

First Reading

Responsorial Psalm

Second Reading

Gospel Acclamation **STAND**

Gospel

Homily or Reflection on the Readings **SIT**

Period of Silence

Profession of Faith **STAND**

[The Nicene Creed can be found on page 5]

Apostles' Creed

I believe in God,
the Father almighty,
Creator of heaven and earth,
and in Jesus Christ, his only Son, our Lord,

At the words that follow, up to and including the Virgin Mary, all bow.

who was conceived by the Holy Spirit,
born of the Virgin Mary,
suffered under Pontius Pilate,
was crucified, died and was buried;
he descended into hell;
on the third day he rose again from the dead;
he ascended into heaven,
and is seated at the right hand of God the Father almighty;
from there he will come to judge the living and the dead.

I believe in the Holy Spirit,
the holy catholic Church,
the communion of saints,
the forgiveness of sins,
the resurrection of the body,
and life everlasting. Amen.

Prayer of the Faithful

Communion Rite

Lord's Prayer

Deacon or lay leader:

The Father provides us with food
for eternal life.
Let us pray for nourishment
and strength.

All say:

**Our Father, who art in heaven,
hallowed be thy name;
thy kingdom come,
thy will be done
on earth as it is in heaven.
Give us this day our daily bread,
and forgive us our trespasses,
as we forgive those who trespass against us;
and lead us not into temptation,
but deliver us from evil.
Amen.**

Invitation to Communion — KNEEL

Deacon or lay leader:

Behold the Lamb of God,
behold him who takes away the sins of the world.
Blessed are those called to the supper of the Lamb.

All say:

**Lord, I am not worthy
that you should enter under my roof,
but only say the word
and my soul shall be healed.**

Communion

Act of Thanksgiving — STAND

Concluding Rites

Invitation to Pray for Vocations to the Priesthood

Deacon or lay leader:

Mindful of the Lord's word, "Ask the Master of the harvest to send out laborers for the harvest," let us pray for an increase of vocations to the Priesthood. May our prayer hasten the day when we will be able to take part in the celebration of the Holy Eucharist every Sunday.

Blessing

Sign of Peace

A Prayer for Generosity

Dear Lord, teach me to be generous,
teach me to serve you as you deserve,
to give and not to count the cost,
to fight and not to heed the wound,
to toil and not to seek for rest,
to labor and not to seek reward,
save that of knowing that I do your will.

St. Ignatius Loyola

First Sunday of Advent

November 29, 2015

Reflection on the Gospel

At first reading, it seems as though the gospel is only about tribulations and calamities and fear. Yes, right now, today, tribulations, wars, natural calamities are upon us. We can cringe in fear or "stand erect" in hope. Jesus tells us not to fear what calamities might do to us, but to be "vigilant" for his coming. He comes with redemption not only in glory at the end of time, but right now, today.

- *I prepare for the Son of Man's return when I . . .*

—Living Liturgy™, *First Sunday of Advent 2015*

Entrance Antiphon (Cf. Psalm 25[24]:1-3)

To you, I lift up my soul, O my God.
In you, I have trusted; let me not be put to shame.
Nor let my enemies exult over me;
and let none who hope in you be put to shame.

Collect

Grant your faithful, we pray, almighty God,
the resolve to run forth to meet your Christ
with righteous deeds at his coming,
so that, gathered at his right hand,
they may be worthy to possess the heavenly Kingdom.
Through our Lord Jesus Christ, your Son,
who lives and reigns with you in the unity of the Holy Spirit,
one God, for ever and ever. All: **Amen.**

Reading I (L 3) (Jeremiah 33:14-16)

A reading from the Book of the Prophet Jeremiah

I will raise up for David a just shoot.

The days are coming, says the Lord,
when I will fulfill the promise
I made to the house of Israel and Judah.

In those days, in that time,
I will raise up for David a just shoot;
he shall do what is right and just in the land.
In those days Judah shall be safe
and Jerusalem shall dwell secure;
this is what they shall call her:
"The LORD our justice."

The word of the Lord. All: **Thanks be to God.**

RESPONSORIAL PSALM 25

P-486

Psalm 25:4-5, 8-9, 10, 14

℟. (1b) **To you, O Lord, I lift my soul.**

Your ways, O LORD, make known to me;
teach me your paths,
guide me in your truth and teach me,
for you are God my savior,
and for you I wait all the day. ℟.

Good and upright is the LORD;
thus he shows sinners the way.
He guides the humble to justice,
and teaches the humble his way. ℟.

All the paths of the LORD are kindness and constancy
toward those who keep his covenant and his decrees.
The friendship of the LORD is with those who fear him,
and his covenant, for their instruction. ℟.

READING II (1 Thessalonians 3:12—4:2)

A reading from the first Letter of Saint Paul to the Thessalonians

May the Lord strengthen your hearts at the coming of our Lord Jesus.

Brothers and sisters:
May the Lord make you increase and abound in love
for one another and for all,
just as we have for you,
so as to strengthen your hearts,
to be blameless in holiness before our God and Father
at the coming of our Lord Jesus with all his holy ones.
Amen.

Finally, brothers and sisters,
we earnestly ask and exhort you in the Lord Jesus that,
as you received from us
how you should conduct yourselves to please God
—and as you are conducting yourselves—
you do so even more.
For you know what instructions we gave you through the Lord Jesus.

The word of the Lord. All: **Thanks be to God.**

GOSPEL (Luke 21:25-28, 34-36)
ALLELUIA (Psalm 85:8)
℣. Alleluia, alleluia. ℟. **Alleluia, alleluia.**
℣. Show us, Lord, your love;
and grant us your salvation. ℟.

✠ **A reading from the holy Gospel according to Luke**

All: **Glory to you, O Lord.**

Your redemption is at hand.

Jesus said to his disciples:
"There will be signs in the sun, the moon, and the stars,
and on earth nations will be in dismay,
perplexed by the roaring of the sea and the waves.
People will die of fright
in anticipation of what is coming upon the world,
for the powers of the heavens will be shaken.
And then they will see the Son of Man
coming in a cloud with power and great glory.

But when these signs begin to happen,
stand erect and raise your heads
because your redemption is at hand.

"Beware that your hearts do not become drowsy
from carousing and drunkenness
and the anxieties of daily life,
and that day catch you by surprise like a trap.
For that day will assault everyone
who lives on the face of the earth.
Be vigilant at all times
and pray that you have the strength
to escape the tribulations that are imminent
and to stand before the Son of Man."

The Gospel of the Lord. All: **Praise to you, Lord Jesus Christ.**

Prayer over the Offerings

Accept, we pray, O Lord, these offerings we make,
gathered from among your gifts to us,
and may what you grant us to celebrate devoutly here below
gain for us the prize of eternal redemption.
Through Christ our Lord. All: **Amen.**

Communion Antiphon (Psalm 85[84]:13)

The Lord will bestow his bounty, and our earth shall yield its increase.

Prayer after Communion

May these mysteries, O Lord,
in which we have participated,
profit us, we pray,
for even now, as we walk amid passing things,
you teach us by them to love the things of heaven
and hold fast to what endures.
Through Christ our Lord. All: **Amen.**

Second Sunday of Advent

December 6, 2015

Reflection on the Gospel

The meandering paths and winding roads of our lives are straightened and the valleys filled and mountains brought low when our lives are characterized by attitudes of repentance. Our work of repentance is a matter of turning ourselves toward the God who embraces us in mercy and forgiveness and welcomes us home. Our work of repentance is our response to the word-invitation to "see the salvation of God." We are to hear the "word of God" and act on it. Do we? How well?

- *I turn to God by . . .*

—Living Liturgy™, *Second Sunday of Advent 2015*

Entrance Antiphon (Cf. Isaiah 30:19, 30)

O people of Sion, behold,
the Lord will come to save the nations,
and the Lord will make the glory of his voice heard
in the joy of your heart.

Collect

Almighty and merciful God,
may no earthly undertaking hinder those
who set out in haste to meet your Son,
but may our learning of heavenly wisdom
gain us admittance to his company.
Who lives and reigns with you in the unity of the Holy Spirit,
one God, for ever and ever. All: **Amen.**

Reading I (L 6) (Baruch 5:1-9)

A reading from the Book of the Prophet Baruch

Jerusalem, God will show your splendor.

Jerusalem, take off your robe of mourning and misery;
put on the splendor of glory from God forever:
wrapped in the cloak of justice from God,
bear on your head the mitre

that displays the glory of the eternal name.
For God will show all the earth your splendor:
you will be named by God forever
the peace of justice, the glory of God's worship.

Up, Jerusalem! stand upon the heights;
look to the east and see your children
gathered from the east and the west
at the word of the Holy One,
rejoicing that they are remembered by God.
Led away on foot by their enemies they left you:
but God will bring them back to you
borne aloft in glory as on royal thrones.
For God has commanded
that every lofty mountain be made low,
and that the age-old depths and gorges
be filled to level ground,
that Israel may advance secure in the glory of God.
The forests and every fragrant kind of tree
have overshadowed Israel at God's command;
for God is leading Israel in joy
by the light of his glory,
with his mercy and justice for company.

The word of the Lord. All: **Thanks be to God.**

Responsorial Psalm 126

P-487

Psalm 126:1-2, 2-3, 4-5, 6

℟. (3) **The Lord has done great things for us; we are filled with joy.**

When the LORD brought back the captives of Zion,
  we were like men dreaming.
Then our mouth was filled with laughter,
  and our tongue with rejoicing. ℟.

Then they said among the nations,
  "The LORD has done great things for them."
The LORD has done great things for us;
  we are glad indeed. ℟.

Restore our fortunes, O LORD,
  like the torrents in the southern desert.
Those who sow in tears
  shall reap rejoicing. ℟.

Although they go forth weeping,
  carrying the seed to be sown,
they shall come back rejoicing,
  carrying their sheaves. ℟.

READING II (Philippians 1:4-6, 8-11)

A reading from the Letter of Saint Paul to the Philippians

Show yourselves pure and blameless for the day of Christ.

Brothers and sisters:
I pray always with joy in my every prayer for all of you,
  because of your partnership for the gospel
  from the first day until now.
I am confident of this,
  that the one who began a good work in you
  will continue to complete it
  until the day of Christ Jesus.
God is my witness,
  how I long for all of you with the affection of Christ Jesus.
And this is my prayer:
  that your love may increase ever more and more
  in knowledge and every kind of perception,
  to discern what is of value,
  so that you may be pure and blameless for the day of Christ,

filled with the fruit of righteousness
that comes through Jesus Christ
for the glory and praise of God.

The word of the Lord. All: **Thanks be to God.**

GOSPEL (Luke 3:1-6)
ALLELUIA (Luke 3:4, 6)

℣. Alleluia, alleluia. ℟. **Alleluia, alleluia.**
℣. Prepare the way of the Lord, make straight his paths:
all flesh shall see the salvation of God. ℟.

✠ **A reading from the holy Gospel according to Luke**

All: **Glory to you, O Lord.**

All flesh shall see the salvation of God.

In the fifteenth year of the reign of Tiberius Caesar,
when Pontius Pilate was governor of Judea,
and Herod was tetrarch of Galilee,
and his brother Philip tetrarch of the region
of Ituraea and Trachonitis,
and Lysanias was tetrarch of Abilene,
during the high priesthood of Annas and Caiaphas,
the word of God came to John the son of Zechariah in the desert.
John went throughout the whole region of the Jordan,
proclaiming a baptism of repentance for the forgiveness of sins,
as it is written in the book of the words of the prophet Isaiah:
A voice of one crying out in the desert:
"Prepare the way of the Lord,
make straight his paths.
Every valley shall be filled
and every mountain and hill shall be made low.
The winding roads shall be made straight,
and the rough ways made smooth,
and all flesh shall see the salvation of God."

The Gospel of the Lord. All: **Praise to you, Lord Jesus Christ.**

Prayer over the Offerings

Be pleased, O Lord, with our humble prayers and offerings,
and, since we have no merits to plead our cause,
come, we pray, to our rescue
with the protection of your mercy.
Through Christ our Lord. All: **Amen.**

Communion Antiphon (Baruch 5:5; 4:36)

Jerusalem, arise and stand upon the heights,
and behold the joy which comes to you from God.

Prayer after Communion

Replenished by the food of spiritual nourishment,
we humbly beseech you, O Lord,
that, through our partaking in this mystery,
you may teach us to judge wisely the things of earth
and hold firm to the things of heaven.
Through Christ our Lord. All: **Amen.**

The Immaculate Conception of the Blessed Virgin Mary

December 8, 2015

Reflection on the Gospel

Mary responded to God's call to salvation by saying yes to the mystery of being overshadowed by the Holy Spirit and giving birth to the Son of God. We, too, respond to God's call to salvation by listening to the Spirit who dwells within us, by bearing Christ in the world today, by speaking an ongoing yes to whatever God asks of us. The mystery we live is the mystery of God's loving, saving, incarnate Presence.

- *Like Mary, I respond to God when I . . .*

—Living Liturgy™, *Immaculate Conception 2015*

ENTRANCE ANTIPHON (Isaiah 61:10)

I rejoice heartily in the Lord,
in my God is the joy of my soul;
for he has clothed me with a robe of salvation,
and wrapped me in a mantle of justice,
like a bride adorned with her jewels.

COLLECT

O God, who by the Immaculate Conception of the Blessed Virgin
prepared a worthy dwelling for your Son,
grant, we pray,
that, as you preserved her from every stain
by virtue of the Death of your Son, which you foresaw,
so, through her intercession,
we, too, may be cleansed and admitted to your presence.
Through our Lord Jesus Christ, your Son,
who lives and reigns with you in the unity of the Holy Spirit,
one God, for ever and ever. All: **Amen.**

READING I (L 689) (Genesis 3:9-15, 20)

A reading from the Book of Genesis

I will put enmity between your offspring and hers.

**After the man, Adam, had eaten of the tree,
the LORD God called to the man and asked him,
"Where are you?"
He answered, "I heard you in the garden;
but I was afraid, because I was naked,
so I hid myself."
Then he asked, "Who told you that you were naked?
You have eaten, then,
from the tree of which I had forbidden you to eat!"
The man replied, "The woman whom you put here
with me—
she gave me fruit from the tree, and so I ate it."
The LORD God then asked the woman,
"Why did you do such a thing?"
The woman answered, "The serpent tricked me into it,
so I ate it."**

Then the LORD God said to the serpent:
"Because you have done this, you shall be banned
from all the animals
and from all the wild creatures;
on your belly shall you crawl,
and dirt shall you eat
all the days of your life.
I will put enmity between you and the woman,
and between your offspring and hers;
he will strike at your head,
while you strike at his heel."

The man called his wife Eve,
because she became the mother of all the living.

The word of the Lord. All: **Thanks be to God.**

RESPONSORIAL PSALM 98

P-189

Psalm 98:1, 2-3ab, 3cd-4

℟. (1a) **Sing to the Lord a new song, for he has done marvelous deeds.**

Sing to the LORD a new song,
for he has done wondrous deeds;
His right hand has won victory for him,
his holy arm. ℟.

The LORD has made his salvation known:
in the sight of the nations he has revealed his justice.
He has remembered his kindness and his faithfulness
toward the house of Israel. ℟.

(continued)

All the ends of the earth have seen
the salvation by our God.
Sing joyfully to the LORD, all you lands;
break into song; sing praise. ℟.

READING II (Ephesians 1:3-6, 11-12)

A reading from the Letter of Saint Paul to the Ephesians

He chose us in Christ before the foundation of the world.

Brothers and sisters:
Blessed be the God and Father of our Lord Jesus Christ,
who has blessed us in Christ
with every spiritual blessing in the heavens,
as he chose us in him, before the foundation of the world,
to be holy and without blemish before him.
In love he destined us for adoption to himself through Jesus Christ,
in accord with the favor of his will,
for the praise of the glory of his grace
that he granted us in the beloved.

In him we were also chosen,
destined in accord with the purpose of the One
who accomplishes all things according to the intention of his will,
so that we might exist for the praise of his glory,
we who first hoped in Christ.

The word of the Lord. All: **Thanks be to God.**

GOSPEL (Luke 1:26-38)

ALLELUIA (*See* Luke 1:28)

℣. Alleluia, alleluia. ℟. **Alleluia, alleluia.**
℣. Hail, Mary, full of grace, the Lord is with you;
blessed are you among women. ℟.

✠ **A reading from the holy Gospel according to Luke**

All: **Glory to you, O Lord.**

Hail, full of grace! The Lord is with you.

The angel Gabriel was sent from God
to a town of Galilee called Nazareth,
to a virgin betrothed to a man named Joseph,
of the house of David,
and the virgin's name was Mary.
And coming to her, he said,
"Hail, full of grace! The Lord is with you."
But she was greatly troubled at what was said
and pondered what sort of greeting this might be.
Then the angel said to her,
"Do not be afraid, Mary,
for you have found favor with God.
Behold, you will conceive in your womb and bear a son,
and you shall name him Jesus.
He will be great and will be called Son of the Most High,
and the Lord God will give him the throne of David his father,
and he will rule over the house of Jacob forever,
and of his Kingdom there will be no end."
But Mary said to the angel,
"How can this be,
since I have no relations with a man?"
And the angel said to her in reply,
"The Holy Spirit will come upon you,
and the power of the Most High will overshadow you.
Therefore the child to be born
will be called holy, the Son of God.
And behold, Elizabeth, your relative,
has also conceived a son in her old age,
and this is the sixth month for her who was called barren;
for nothing will be impossible for God."
Mary said, "Behold, I am the handmaid of the Lord.
May it be done to me according to your word."
Then the angel departed from her.

The Gospel of the Lord. All: **Praise to you, Lord Jesus Christ.**

Prayer over the Offerings

Graciously accept the saving sacrifice
which we offer you, O Lord,
on the Solemnity of the Immaculate Conception
of the Blessed Virgin Mary,
and grant that, as we profess her,
on account of your prevenient grace,
to be untouched by any stain of sin,
so, through her intercession,
we may be delivered from all our faults.
Through Christ our Lord. All: **Amen.**

Communion Antiphon

Glorious things are spoken of you, O Mary,
for from you arose the sun of justice,
Christ our God.

Prayer after Communion

May the Sacrament we have received,
O Lord our God,
heal in us the wounds of that fault
from which in a singular way
you preserved Blessed Mary in her Immaculate Conception.
Through Christ our Lord. All: **Amen.**

Third Sunday of Advent

December 13, 2015

Reflection on the Gospel

John the Baptist challenged the people who asked him, "What should we do?" by admonishing them to far exceed their present way of acting toward others. Yet even such "good news" does not measure up to what the "one mightier" than John will ask of us: to live a Gospel that exacts the gift of our very selves. If we ask, "What should we do?" we must be prepared for an answer that challenges us. Are we willing even to ask the question?

- *I can exceed expectations when I . . .*

—Living Liturgy™, *Third Sunday of Advent 2015*

Entrance Antiphon (Philippians 4:4-5)

Rejoice in the Lord always; again I say, rejoice.
Indeed, the Lord is near.

Collect

O God, who see how your people
faithfully await the feast of the Lord's Nativity,
enable us, we pray,
to attain the joys of so great a salvation
and to celebrate them always
with solemn worship and glad rejoicing.
Through our Lord Jesus Christ, your Son,
who lives and reigns with you in the unity of the Holy Spirit,
one God, for ever and ever. All: **Amen.**

Reading I (L 9) (Zephaniah 3:14-18a)

A reading from the Book of the Prophet Zephaniah

The Lord will rejoice over you with gladness.

Shout for joy, O daughter Zion!
Sing joyfully, O Israel!
Be glad and exult with all your heart,
O daughter Jerusalem!
The Lord has removed the judgment against you
he has turned away your enemies;
the King of Israel, the Lord, is in your midst,
you have no further misfortune to fear.
On that day, it shall be said to Jerusalem:
Fear not, O Zion, be not discouraged!
The Lord, your God, is in your midst,
a mighty savior;
he will rejoice over you with gladness,
and renew you in his love,
he will sing joyfully because of you,
as one sings at festivals.

The word of the Lord. All: **Thanks be to God.**

Responsorial Psalm

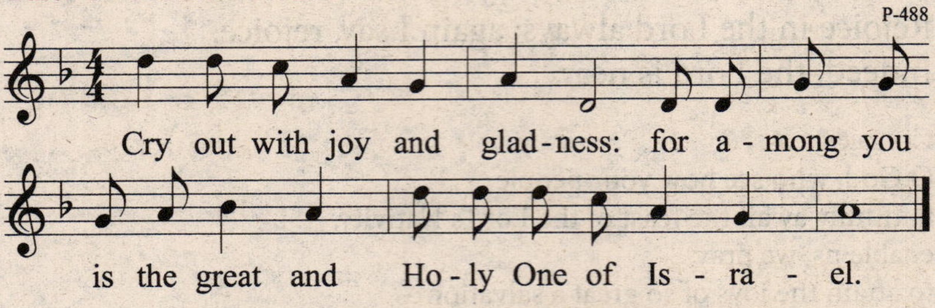

Music: Jay F. Hunstiger, © 1991, administered by Liturgical Press.

Isaiah 12:2-3, 4, 5-6

℟. (6) **Cry out with joy and gladness: for among you is the great and Holy One of Israel.**

God indeed is my savior;
I am confident and unafraid.
My strength and my courage is the LORD,
and he has been my savior.
With joy you will draw water
at the fountain of salvation. ℟.

Give thanks to the LORD, acclaim his name;
among the nations make known his deeds,
proclaim how exalted is his name. ℟.

Sing praise to the LORD for his glorious achievement;
let this be known throughout all the earth.
Shout with exultation, O city of Zion,
for great in your midst
is the Holy One of Israel! ℟.

Reading II (Philippians 4:4-7)

A reading from the Letter of Saint Paul to the Philippians

The Lord is near.

Brothers and sisters:
Rejoice in the Lord always.
I shall say it again: rejoice!
Your kindness should be known to all.
The Lord is near.
Have no anxiety at all, but in everything,

by prayer and petition, with thanksgiving,
make your requests known to God.
Then the peace of God that surpasses all understanding
will guard your hearts and minds in Christ Jesus.

The word of the Lord. All: **Thanks be to God.**

GOSPEL (Luke 3:10-18)

ALLELUIA (Isaiah 61:1; see Luke 4:18)

℣. Alleluia, alleluia. ℟. **Alleluia, alleluia.**
℣. The Spirit of the Lord is upon me,
because he has anointed me
to bring glad tidings to the poor. ℟.

✠ **A reading from the holy Gospel according to Luke**

All: **Glory to you, O Lord.**

What should we do?

The crowds asked John the Baptist,
"What should we do?"
He said to them in reply,
"Whoever has two cloaks
should share with the person who has none.
And whoever has food should do likewise."
Even tax collectors came to be baptized and they said to him,
"Teacher, what should we do?"
He answered them,
"Stop collecting more than what is prescribed."
Soldiers also asked him,
"And what is it that we should do?"
He told them,
"Do not practice extortion,
do not falsely accuse anyone,
and be satisfied with your wages."

Now the people were filled with expectation,
and all were asking in their hearts
whether John might be the Christ.

John answered them all, saying,
"I am baptizing you with water,
but one mightier than I is coming.
I am not worthy to loosen the thongs of his sandals.
He will baptize you with the Holy Spirit and fire.
His winnowing fan is in his hand to clear his threshing floor
and to gather the wheat into his barn,
but the chaff he will burn with unquenchable fire."
Exhorting them in many other ways,
he preached good news to the people.

The Gospel of the Lord. All: **Praise to you, Lord Jesus Christ.**

Prayer over the Offerings

May the sacrifice of our worship, Lord, we pray,
be offered to you unceasingly,
to complete what was begun in sacred mystery
and powerfully accomplish for us your saving work.
Through Christ our Lord. All: **Amen.**

Communion Antiphon (Cf. Isaiah 35:4)

Say to the faint of heart: Be strong and do not fear.
Behold, our God will come, and he will save us.

Prayer after Communion

We implore your mercy, Lord,
that this divine sustenance may cleanse us of our faults
and prepare us for the coming feasts.
Through Christ our Lord. All: **Amen.**

Fourth Sunday of Advent

December 20, 2015

Reflection on the Gospel

Salvation is the convergence of God's will and our own will. Like Mary and Elizabeth, we must always say yes to what God asks of us. Mary and Elizabeth show us the way to our being overshadowed by the Spirit, for they offered their own bodies in cooperating with God's plan of salvation. So must we offer ourselves with the same willingness, with the same love response, with the same eager desire for divine Presence within and among us.

- *I accept what God asks of me when I . . .*

—Living Liturgy™, *Fourth Sunday of Advent 2015*

Entrance Antiphon (Cf. Isaiah 45:8)

Drop down dew from above, you heavens,
and let the clouds rain down the Just One;
let the earth be opened and bring forth a Savior.

Collect

Pour forth, we beseech you, O Lord,
your grace into our hearts,
that we, to whom the Incarnation of Christ your Son
was made known by the message of an Angel,
may by his Passion and Cross
be brought to the glory of his Resurrection.
Who lives and reigns with you in the unity of the Holy Spirit,
one God, for ever and ever. All: **Amen.**

Reading I (L 12) (Micah 5:1-4a)

A reading from the Book of the Prophet Micah

From you shall come forth the ruler of Israel.

Thus says the Lord:
You, Bethlehem-Ephrathah
too small to be among the clans of Judah,

from you shall come forth for me
one who is to be ruler in Israel;
whose origin is from of old,
from ancient times.
Therefore the Lord will give them up, until the time
when she who is to give birth has borne,
and the rest of his kindred shall return
to the children of Israel.
He shall stand firm and shepherd his flock
by the strength of the LORD,
in the majestic name of the LORD, his God;
and they shall remain, for now his greatness
shall reach to the ends of the earth;
he shall be peace.

The word of the Lord. All: **Thanks be to God.**

RESPONSORIAL PSALM 80

Psalm 80:2-3, 15-16, 18-19

℟. (4) **Lord, make us turn to you; let us see your face and we shall be saved.**

O shepherd of Israel, hearken,
from your throne upon the cherubim, shine forth.
Rouse your power,
and come to save us. ℟.

Once again, O LORD of hosts,
look down from heaven, and see;
take care of this vine,
and protect what your right hand has planted,
the son of man whom you yourself made strong. ℟.

May your help be with the man of your right hand,
with the son of man whom you yourself made strong.
Then we will no more withdraw from you;
give us new life, and we will call upon your name. ℟.

READING II (Hebrews 10:5-10)

A reading from the Letter to the Hebrews

Behold, I come to do your will.

Brothers and sisters:
When Christ came into the world, he said:
"Sacrifice and offering you did not desire,
but a body you prepared for me;
in holocausts and sin offerings you took no delight.
Then I said, 'As is written of me in the scroll,
behold, I come to do your will, O God.'"

First he says, "Sacrifices and offerings,
holocausts and sin offerings,
you neither desired nor delighted in."
These are offered according to the law.
Then he says, "Behold, I come to do your will."
He takes away the first to establish the second.
By this "will," we have been consecrated
through the offering of the body of Jesus Christ once for all.

The word of the Lord. All: **Thanks be to God.**

GOSPEL (Luke 1:39-45)

ALLELUIA (Luke 1:38)

℣. Alleluia, alleluia. ℟. **Alleluia, alleluia.**
℣. Behold, I am the handmaid of the Lord.
May it be done to me according to your word. ℟.

✠ **A reading from the holy Gospel according to Luke**

All: **Glory to you, O Lord.**

And how does this happen to me, that the mother of my Lord should come to me?

Mary set out
and traveled to the hill country in haste
to a town of Judah,
where she entered the house of Zechariah
and greeted Elizabeth.
When Elizabeth heard Mary's greeting,
the infant leaped in her womb,
and Elizabeth, filled with the Holy Spirit,
cried out in a loud voice and said,
"Blessed are you among women,
and blessed is the fruit of your womb.
And how does this happen to me,
that the mother of my Lord should come to me?
For at the moment the sound of your greeting reached my ears,
the infant in my womb leaped for joy.
Blessed are you who believed
that what was spoken to you by the Lord
would be fulfilled."

The Gospel of the Lord. All: **Praise to you, Lord Jesus Christ.**

Prayer over the Offerings

May the Holy Spirit, O Lord,
sanctify these gifts laid upon your altar,
just as he filled with his power the womb of the Blessed Virgin Mary.
Through Christ our Lord. All: **Amen.**

Communion Antiphon (Isaiah 7:14)

Behold, a Virgin shall conceive and bear a son;
and his name will be called Emmanuel.

Prayer after Communion

Having received this pledge of eternal redemption,
we pray, almighty God,
that, as the feast day of our salvation draws ever nearer,
so we may press forward all the more eagerly
to the worthy celebration of the mystery of your Son's Nativity.
Who lives and reigns for ever and ever. All: **Amen.**

The Nativity of the Lord (Christmas)

AT THE VIGIL MASS

December 24, 2015

The Mass of the Vigil of Christmas is to be used on Thursday evening in those places where the Sunday (holy day of) obligation may be fulfilled on Thursday evening.

Reflection on the Gospel

Mary gave birth "to her firstborn son." This birth, however, is more than about one life; it is about the life of all. Mary gave birth to a God-Man who from the very beginning wishes to seek us, to encounter us, to love us. While contained in human flesh, this newborn babe is still the infinite God who is the "savior . . . born" for us. This newborn babe is still the One who loves beyond compare. This newborn babe is still the One to whom we sing "Glory to God."

- *I give glory to God when I . . .*

—Living Liturgy™, *Christmas 2015*

ENTRANCE ANTIPHON (Cf. Exodus 16:6-7)

Today you will know that the Lord will come, and he will save us,
and in the morning you will see his glory.

COLLECT

O God, who gladden us year by year
as we wait in hope for our redemption,
grant that, just as we joyfully welcome
your Only Begotten Son as our Redeemer,
we may also merit to face him confidently
when he comes again as our Judge.
Who lives and reigns with you in the unity of the Holy Spirit,
one God, for ever and ever. All: **Amen.**

READING I (L 13) (Isaiah 62:1-5)

A reading from the Book of the Prophet Isaiah

The Lord delights in you.

For Zion's sake I will not be silent,
for Jerusalem's sake I will not be quiet,
until her vindication shines forth like the dawn
and her victory like a burning torch.

Nations shall behold your vindication,
and all the kings your glory;
you shall be called by a new name
pronounced by the mouth of the Lord.
You shall be a glorious crown in the hand of the Lord,
a royal diadem held by your God.
No more shall people call you "Forsaken,"
or your land "Desolate,"
but you shall be called "My Delight,"
and your land "Espoused."
For the Lord delights in you
and makes your land his spouse.
As a young man marries a virgin,
your Builder shall marry you;
and as a bridegroom rejoices in his bride
so shall your God rejoice in you.

The word of the Lord. All: **Thanks be to God.**

Responsorial Psalm 89

P-102

Psalm 89:4-5, 16-17, 27, 29

℟. (2a) **For ever I will sing the goodness of the Lord.**

I have made a covenant with my chosen one,
I have sworn to David my servant:
forever will I confirm your posterity
and establish your throne for all generations. ℟.

Blessed the people who know the joyful shout;
in the light of your countenance, O Lord, they walk.

At your name they rejoice all the day,
and through your justice they are exalted. ℟.

He shall say of me, "You are my father,
my God, the Rock, my savior."
Forever I will maintain my kindness toward him,
and my covenant with him stands firm. ℟.

READING II (Acts of the Apostles 13:16-17, 22-25)

A reading from the Acts of the Apostles

Paul bears witness to Christ, the Son of David.

When Paul reached Antioch in Pisidia and entered the synagogue,
he stood up, motioned with his hand, and said,
"Fellow Israelites and you others who are God-fearing, listen.
The God of this people Israel chose our ancestors
and exalted the people during their sojourn in the land of Egypt.
With uplifted arm he led them out of it.
Then he removed Saul and raised up David as king;
of him he testified,
'I have found David, son of Jesse, a man after my own heart;
he will carry out my every wish.'
From this man's descendants God, according to his promise,
has brought to Israel a savior, Jesus.
John heralded his coming by proclaiming a baptism of repentance
to all the people of Israel;
and as John was completing his course, he would say,
'What do you suppose that I am? I am not he.
Behold, one is coming after me;
I am not worthy to unfasten the sandals of his feet.'"

The word of the Lord. All: **Thanks be to God.**

GOSPEL (Matthew 1:1-25) *or* Shorter Form [ ] (Matthew 1:18-25)

ALLELUIA

℣. Alleluia, alleluia. ℟. **Alleluia, alleluia.**

℣. Tomorrow the wickedness of the earth will be destroyed:
the Savior of the world will reign over us. ℟.

✠ **A reading from the beginning of the holy Gospel according to Matthew**

All: **Glory to you, O Lord.**

The genealogy of Jesus Christ, the Son of David.

**The book of the genealogy of Jesus Christ,
the son of David, the son of Abraham.**

**Abraham became the father of Isaac,
Isaac the father of Jacob,
Jacob the father of Judah and his brothers.
Judah became the father of Perez and Zerah,
whose mother was Tamar.
Perez became the father of Hezron,
Hezron the father of Ram,
Ram the father of Amminadab.
Amminadab became the father of Nahshon,
Nahshon the father of Salmon,
Salmon the father of Boaz,
whose mother was Rahab.
Boaz became the father of Obed,
whose mother was Ruth.
Obed became the father of Jesse,
Jesse the father of David the king.**

**David became the father of Solomon,
whose mother had been the wife of Uriah.
Solomon became the father of Rehoboam,
Rehoboam the father of Abijah,
Abijah the father of Asaph.
Asaph became the father of Jehoshaphat,
Jehoshaphat the father of Joram,
Joram the father of Uzziah.**

Uzziah became the father of Jotham,
Jotham the father of Ahaz,
Ahaz the father of Hezekiah.
Hezekiah became the father of Manasseh,
Manasseh the father of Amos,
Amos the father of Josiah.
Josiah became the father of Jechoniah and his brothers
at the time of the Babylonian exile.

After the Babylonian exile,
Jechoniah became the father of Shealtiel,
Shealtiel the father of Zerubbabel,
Zerubbabel the father of Abiud.
Abiud became the father of Eliakim,
Eliakim the father of Azor,
Azor the father of Zadok.
Zadok became the father of Achim,
Achim the father of Eliud,
Eliud the father of Eleazar.
Eleazar became the father of Matthan,
Matthan the father of Jacob,
Jacob the father of Joseph, the husband of Mary.
Of her was born Jesus who is called the Christ.

Thus the total number of generations
from Abraham to David
is fourteen generations;
from David to the Babylonian exile,
fourteen generations;
from the Babylonian exile to the Christ,
fourteen generations.

Now [this is how the birth of Jesus Christ came about.
When his mother Mary was betrothed to Joseph,
but before they lived together,
she was found with child through the Holy Spirit.
Joseph her husband, since he was a righteous man,
yet unwilling to expose her to shame,

decided to divorce her quietly.
Such was his intention when, behold,
the angel of the Lord appeared to him in a dream
and said,
"Joseph, son of David,
do not be afraid to take Mary your wife into your home.
For it is through the Holy Spirit
that this child has been conceived in her.
She will bear a son and you are to name him Jesus,
because he will save his people from their sins."
All this took place to fulfill
what the Lord had said through the prophet:
Behold, the virgin shall conceive and bear a son,
and they shall name him Emmanuel,
which means "God is with us."
When Joseph awoke,
he did as the angel of the Lord had commanded him
and took his wife into his home.
He had no relations with her until she bore a son,
and he named him Jesus.]

The Gospel of the Lord. All: **Praise to you, Lord Jesus Christ.**

Prayer over the Offerings

As we look forward, O Lord,
to the coming festivities,
may we serve you all the more eagerly
for knowing that in them
you make manifest the beginnings of our redemption.
Through Christ our Lord. All: **Amen.**

Communion Antiphon (Cf. Isaiah 40:5)

The glory of the Lord will be revealed,
and all flesh will see the salvation of our God.

Prayer after Communion

Grant, O Lord, we pray,
that we may draw new vigor
from celebrating the Nativity of your Only Begotten Son,
by whose heavenly mystery we receive both food and drink.
Who lives and reigns for ever and ever. All: **Amen.**

The Nativity of the Lord

AT THE MASS DURING THE NIGHT

December 25, 2015

ENTRANCE ANTIPHON (Psalm 2:7)

The Lord said to me: You are my Son.
It is I who have begotten you this day.

Or:

Let us all rejoice in the Lord, for our Savior has been born in the world.
Today true peace has come down to us from heaven.

COLLECT

O God, who have made this most sacred night
radiant with the splendor of the true light,
grant, we pray, that we, who have known the mysteries of his light on earth,
may also delight in his gladness in heaven.
Who lives and reigns with you in the unity of the Holy Spirit,
one God, for ever and ever. All: **Amen.**

READING I (L 14) (Isaiah 9:1-6)

A reading from the Book of the Prophet Isaiah

A son is given us.

The people who walked in darkness
have seen a great light;
upon those who dwelt in the land of gloom
a light has shone.
You have brought them abundant joy
and great rejoicing,
as they rejoice before you as at the harvest,
as people make merry when dividing spoils.

For the yoke that burdened them,
the pole on their shoulder,
and the rod of their taskmaster
you have smashed, as on the day of Midian.
For every boot that tramped in battle,
every cloak rolled in blood,
will be burned as fuel for flames.
For a child is born to us, a son is given us;
upon his shoulder dominion rests.
They name him Wonder-Counselor, God-Hero,
Father-Forever, Prince of Peace.
His dominion is vast
and forever peaceful,
from David's throne, and over his kingdom,
which he confirms and sustains
by judgment and justice,
both now and forever.
The zeal of the Lord of hosts will do this!

The word of the Lord. All: **Thanks be to God.**

Responsorial Psalm 96

Psalm 96:1-2, 2-3, 11-12, 13

℟. (Luke 2:11) **Today is born our Savior, Christ the Lord.**

Sing to the Lord a new song;
sing to the Lord, all you lands.
Sing to the Lord; bless his name. ℟.

Announce his salvation, day after day.
Tell his glory among the nations;
among all peoples, his wondrous deeds. ℟.

Let the heavens be glad and the earth rejoice;
let the sea and what fills it resound;

let the plains be joyful and all that is in them!
Then shall all the trees of the forest exult. ℟.

They shall exult before the LORD, for he comes;
for he comes to rule the earth.
He shall rule the world with justice
and the peoples with his constancy. ℟.

READING II (Titus 2:11-14)

A reading from the Letter of Saint Paul to Titus

The grace of God has appeared to all.

Beloved:
The grace of God has appeared, saving all
and training us to reject godless ways and worldly desires
and to live temperately, justly, and devoutly in this age,
as we await the blessed hope,
the appearance of the glory of our great God
and savior Jesus Christ,
who gave himself for us to deliver us from all lawlessness
and to cleanse for himself a people as his own,
eager to do what is good.

The word of the Lord. All: **Thanks be to God.**

GOSPEL (Luke 2:1-14)

ALLELUIA (Luke 2:10-11)

℣. Alleluia, alleluia. ℟. **Alleluia, alleluia.**
℣. I proclaim to you good news of great joy:
today a Savior is born for us,
Christ the Lord. ℟.

✠ **A reading from the holy Gospel according to Luke**

All: **Glory to you, O Lord.**

Today a Savior has been born for you.

In those days a decree went out from Caesar Augustus
that the whole world should be enrolled.
This was the first enrollment,
when Quirinius was governor of Syria.

So all went to be enrolled, each to his own town.
And Joseph too went up from Galilee from the town of Nazareth
to Judea, to the city of David that is called Bethlehem,
because he was of the house and family of David,
to be enrolled with Mary, his betrothed, who was with child.
While they were there,
the time came for her to have her child,
and she gave birth to her firstborn son.
She wrapped him in swaddling clothes and laid him in a manger,
because there was no room for them in the inn.

Now there were shepherds in that region living in the fields
and keeping the night watch over their flock.
The angel of the Lord appeared to them
and the glory of the Lord shone around them,
and they were struck with great fear.
The angel said to them,
"Do not be afraid;
for behold, I proclaim to you good news of great joy
that will be for all the people.
For today in the city of David
a savior has been born for you who is Christ and Lord.
And this will be a sign for you:
you will find an infant wrapped in swaddling clothes
and lying in a manger."
And suddenly there was a multitude of the heavenly host with the angel,
praising God and saying:
"Glory to God in the highest
and on earth peace to those on whom his favor rests."

The Gospel of the Lord. All: **Praise to you, Lord Jesus Christ.**

Prayer over the Offerings

May the oblation of this day's feast
be pleasing to you, O Lord, we pray,
that through this most holy exchange
we may be found in the likeness of Christ,
in whom our nature is united to you.
Who lives and reigns for ever and ever. All: **Amen.**

Communion Antiphon (John 1:14)

The Word became flesh, and we have seen his glory.

Prayer after Communion

Grant us, we pray, O Lord our God,
that we, who are gladdened by participation
in the feast of our Redeemer's Nativity,
may through an honorable way of life become worthy of union with him.
Who lives and reigns for ever and ever. All: **Amen.**

AT THE MASS AT DAWN

Entrance Antiphon
(Cf. Isaiah 9:1, 5; Luke 1:33)

Today a light will shine upon us,
for the Lord is born for us;
and he will be called Wondrous God,
Prince of peace, Father of future ages:
and his reign will be without end.

Collect

Grant, we pray, almighty God,
that, as we are bathed in the new radiance of your incarnate Word,
the light of faith, which illumines our minds,
may also shine through in our deeds.
Through our Lord Jesus Christ, your Son,
who lives and reigns with you in the unity of the Holy Spirit,
one God, for ever and ever. All: **Amen.**

Reading I (L 15) (Isaiah 62:11-12)

A reading from the Book of the Prophet Isaiah

Behold, your Savior comes!

See, the Lord proclaims
to the ends of the earth:
say to daughter Zion,
your savior comes!
Here is his reward with him,
his recompense before him.
They shall be called the holy people,
the redeemed of the Lord,
and you shall be called "Frequented,"
a city that is not forsaken.

The word of the Lord. All: **Thanks be to God.**

Responsorial Psalm 97

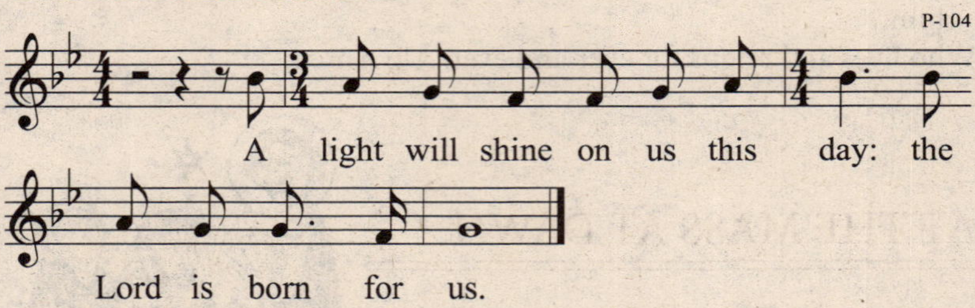

Psalm 97:1, 6, 11-12

℟. **A light will shine on us this day: the Lord is born for us.**

The Lord is king; let the earth rejoice;
let the many isles be glad.
The heavens proclaim his justice,
and all peoples see his glory. ℟.

Light dawns for the just;
and gladness, for the upright of heart.
Be glad in the Lord, you just,
and give thanks to his holy name. ℟.

Reading II (Titus 3:4-7)

A reading from the Letter of Saint Paul to Titus

Because of his mercy, he saved us.

Beloved:
When the kindness and generous love
of God our savior appeared,
not because of any righteous deeds we had done
but because of his mercy,
he saved us through the bath of rebirth
and renewal by the Holy Spirit,
whom he richly poured out on us
through Jesus Christ our savior,
so that we might be justified by his grace
and become heirs in hope of eternal life.

The word of the Lord. All: **Thanks be to God.**

GOSPEL (Luke 2:15-20)
ALLELUIA (Luke 2:14)

℣. Alleluia, alleluia. ℟. **Alleluia, alleluia.**
℣. Glory to God in the highest,
and on earth peace to those
on whom his favor rests. ℟.

✠ **A reading from the holy Gospel according to Luke**

All: **Glory to you, O Lord.**

The shepherds found Mary and Joseph and the infant.

When the angels went away from them to heaven,
the shepherds said to one another,
"Let us go, then, to Bethlehem
to see this thing that has taken place,
which the Lord has made known to us."
So they went in haste and found Mary and Joseph,
and the infant lying in the manger.
When they saw this,
they made known the message
that had been told them about this child.
All who heard it were amazed
by what had been told them by the shepherds.
And Mary kept all these things,
reflecting on them in her heart.

Then the shepherds returned,
glorifying and praising God
for all they had heard and seen,
just as it had been told to them.

The Gospel of the Lord. All: **Praise to you, Lord Jesus Christ.**

Prayer over the Offerings

May our offerings be worthy, we pray, O Lord,
of the mysteries of the Nativity this day,
that, just as Christ was born a man and also shone forth as God,
so these earthly gifts may confer on us what is divine.
Through Christ our Lord. All: **Amen.**

Communion Antiphon (Cf. Zechariah 9:9)

Rejoice, O Daughter Sion; lift up praise, Daughter Jerusalem:
Behold, your King will come, the Holy One and Savior of the world.

Prayer after Communion

Grant us, Lord, as we honor with joyful devotion
the Nativity of your Son,
that we may come to know with fullness of faith
the hidden depths of this mystery
and to love them ever more and more.
Through Christ our Lord. All: **Amen.**

AT THE MASS DURING THE DAY

Entrance Antiphon (Cf. Isaiah 9:5)

A child is born for us, and a son is given to us;
his scepter of power rests upon his shoulder,
and his name will be called Messenger of great counsel.

Collect

O God, who wonderfully created the dignity of human nature
and still more wonderfully restored it,
grant, we pray,
that we may share in the divinity of Christ,
who humbled himself to share in our humanity.
Who lives and reigns with you in the unity of the Holy Spirit,
one God, for ever and ever. All: **Amen.**

READING I (L 16) (Isaiah 52:7-10)

A reading from the Book of the Prophet Isaiah

All the ends of the earth will behold the salvation of our God.

How beautiful upon the mountains
are the feet of him who brings glad tidings,
announcing peace, bearing good news,
announcing salvation, and saying to Zion,
"Your God is King!"

Hark! Your sentinels raise a cry,
together they shout for joy,
for they see directly, before their eyes,
the LORD restoring Zion.
Break out together in song,
O ruins of Jerusalem!
For the LORD comforts his people,
he redeems Jerusalem.
The LORD has bared his holy arm
in the sight of all the nations;
all the ends of the earth will behold
the salvation of our God.

The word of the Lord. All: **Thanks be to God.**

RESPONSORIAL PSALM 98

P-105

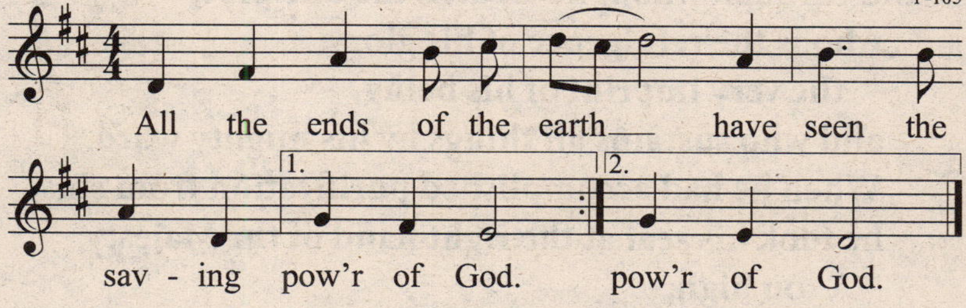

Psalm 98:1, 2-3, 3-4, 5-6

℟. (3c) **All the ends of the earth have seen the saving power of God.**

Sing to the LORD a new song,
for he has done wondrous deeds;

(continued)

his right hand has won victory for him,
his holy arm. ℟.

The LORD has made his salvation known:
in the sight of the nations he has revealed his justice.
He has remembered his kindness and his faithfulness
toward the house of Israel. ℟.

All the ends of the earth have seen
the salvation by our God.
Sing joyfully to the LORD, all you lands;
break into song; sing praise. ℟.

Sing praise to the LORD with the harp,
with the harp and melodious song.
With trumpets and the sound of the horn
sing joyfully before the King, the LORD. ℟.

READING II (Hebrews 1:1-6)

A reading from the beginning of the Letter to the Hebrews

God has spoken to us through the Son.

Brothers and sisters:
In times past, God spoke in partial and various ways
to our ancestors through the prophets;
in these last days, he has spoken to us through the Son,
whom he made heir of all things
and through whom he created the universe,
who is the refulgence of his glory,
the very imprint of his being,
and who sustains all things by his mighty word.
When he had accomplished purification from sins,
he took his seat at the right hand of the Majesty on high,
as far superior to the angels
as the name he has inherited is more excellent than theirs.

For to which of the angels did God ever say:
You are my son; this day I have begotten you?
Or again:

I will be a father to him, and he shall be a son to me?
And again, when he leads the firstborn into the world,
he says:
Let all the angels of God worship him.

The word of the Lord. All: **Thanks be to God.**

GOSPEL (John 1:1-18) *or* Shorter Form [ ] (John 1:1-5, 9-14)
ALLELUIA

℣. Alleluia, alleluia. ℟. **Alleluia, alleluia.**
℣. A holy day has dawned upon us.
Come, you nations, and adore the Lord.
For today a great light has come upon the earth. ℟.

✠ **A reading from the holy Gospel according to John**

All: **Glory to you, O Lord.**

The Word became flesh and made his dwelling among us.

[In the beginning was the Word,
and the Word was with God,
and the Word was God.
He was in the beginning with God.
All things came to be through him,
and without him nothing came to be.
What came to be through him was life,
and this life was the light of the human race;
the light shines in the darkness,
and the darkness has not overcome it.]
A man named John was sent from God.
He came for testimony, to testify to the light,
so that all might believe through him.
He was not the light,
but came to testify to the light.
[The true light, which enlightens everyone,
was coming into the world.
He was in the world,
and the world came to be through him,
but the world did not know him.

He came to what was his own,
but his own people did not accept him.

But to those who did accept him
he gave power to become children of God,
to those who believe in his name,
who were born not by natural generation
nor by human choice nor by a man's decision
but of God.
And the Word became flesh
and made his dwelling among us,
and we saw his glory,
the glory as of the Father's only Son,
full of grace and truth.]
John testified to him and cried out, saying,
"This was he of whom I said,
'The one who is coming after me ranks ahead of me
because he existed before me.'"
From his fullness we have all received,
grace in place of grace,
because while the law was given through Moses,
grace and truth came through Jesus Christ.
No one has ever seen God.
The only Son, God, who is at the Father's side,
has revealed him.

The Gospel of the Lord. All: **Praise to you, Lord Jesus Christ.**

Prayer over the Offerings

Make acceptable, O Lord, our oblation on this solemn day,
when you manifested the reconciliation
that makes us wholly pleasing in your sight
and inaugurated for us the fullness of divine worship.
Through Christ our Lord. All: **Amen.**

Communion Antiphon (Cf. Psalm 98[97]:3)

All the ends of the earth have seen the salvation of our God.

Prayer after Communion

Grant, O merciful God,
that, just as the Savior of the world, born this day,

is the author of divine generation for us,
so he may be the giver even of immortality.
Who lives and reigns for ever and ever. All: **Amen.**

The Holy Family of Jesus, Mary, and Joseph

SUNDAY WITHIN THE OCTAVE OF THE NATIVITY OF THE LORD (Christmas)

December 27, 2015

Reflection on the Gospel

So much tradition shapes the event in this gospel: Passover in Jerusalem, significance of being twelve years old, traveling in caravan, being in the temple, obedience to parents. A surprising interruption of tradition also shapes this event: "the boy Jesus" astounded the teachers "at his understanding and his answers." Each family—the Holy Family, our own families—must find a way to keep worthy traditions alive while at the same time remain open to something astoundingly new. Holiness consists in finding that way.

- *When I . . ., I remain true to tradition.*

—Living Liturgy™, *Holy Family 2015*

Entrance Antiphon (Luke 2:16)

The shepherds went in haste,
and found Mary and Joseph and the Infant lying in a manger.

Collect

O God, who were pleased to give us
the shining example of the Holy Family,
graciously grant that we may imitate them
in practicing the virtues of family life and in the bonds of charity,
and so, in the joy of your house,
delight one day in eternal rewards.
Through our Lord Jesus Christ, your Son,
who lives and reigns with you in the unity of the Holy Spirit,
one God, for ever and ever. All: **Amen.**

Reading I (L 17) (Sirach 3:2-6, 12-14) *for this year additional options can be found in the Lectionary*

A reading from the Book of Sirach

Those who fear the Lord honor their parents.

God sets a father in honor over his children;
a mother's authority he confirms over her sons.
Whoever honors his father atones for sins,
and preserves himself from them.
When he prays, he is heard;
he stores up riches who reveres his mother.
Whoever honors his father is gladdened by children,
and, when he prays, is heard.
Whoever reveres his father will live a long life;
he who obeys his father brings comfort to his mother.

My son, take care of your father when he is old;
grieve him not as long as he lives.
Even if his mind fail, be considerate of him;
revile him not all the days of his life;
kindness to a father will not be forgotten,
firmly planted against the debt of your sins
—a house raised in justice to you.

The word of the Lord. All: **Thanks be to God.**

Responsorial Psalm 128

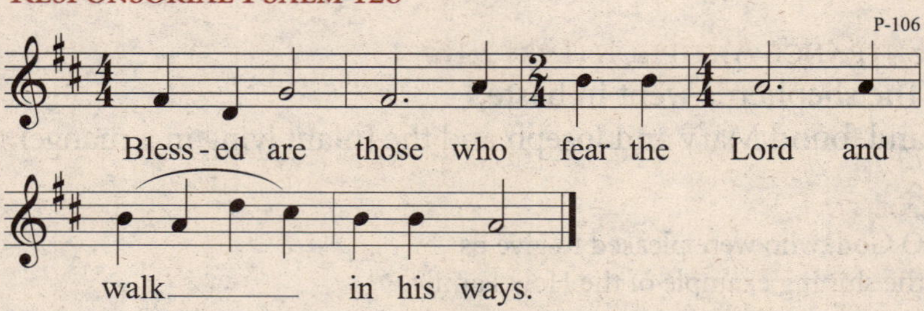

Psalm 128:1-2, 3, 4-5

℟. (*See* 1) **Blessed are those who fear the Lord and walk in his ways.**

Blessed is everyone who fears the LORD,
who walks in his ways!
For you shall eat the fruit of your handiwork;
blessed shall you be, and favored. ℟.

Your wife shall be like a fruitful vine
in the recesses of your home;
your children like olive plants
around your table. ℟.

Behold, thus is the man blessed
who fears the LORD.
The LORD bless you from Zion:
may you see the prosperity of Jerusalem
all the days of your life. ℟.

READING II (Colossians 3:12-21) *or* Shorter Form [ ] (Colossians 3:12-17) *for this year additional options can be found in the Lectionary*

A reading from the Letter of Saint Paul to the Colossians

Family life in the Lord.

[Brothers and sisters:
Put on, as God's chosen ones, holy and beloved,
heartfelt compassion, kindness, humility, gentleness,
and patience,
bearing with one another and forgiving one another,
if one has a grievance against another;
as the Lord has forgiven you, so must you also do.
And over all these put on love,
that is, the bond of perfection.
And let the peace of Christ control your hearts,
the peace into which you were also called in one body.
And be thankful.
Let the word of Christ dwell in you richly,
as in all wisdom you teach and admonish one another,
singing psalms, hymns, and spiritual songs
with gratitude in your hearts to God.

And whatever you do, in word or in deed,
do everything in the name of the Lord Jesus,
giving thanks to God the Father through him.]

Wives, be subordinate to your husbands,
as is proper in the Lord.
Husbands, love your wives,
and avoid any bitterness toward them.
Children, obey your parents in everything,
for this is pleasing to the Lord.
Fathers, do not provoke your children,
so they may not become discouraged.

The word of the Lord. All: **Thanks be to God.**

GOSPEL (Luke 2:41-52)

ALLELUIA (Colossians 3:15a, 16a)

℣. Alleluia, alleluia. ℟. **Alleluia, alleluia.**
℣. Let the peace of Christ control your hearts;
let the word of Christ dwell in you richly. ℟.

Or:

ALLELUIA (*See* Acts of the Apostles 16:14b)

℣. Alleluia, alleluia. ℟. **Alleluia, alleluia.**
℣. Open our hearts, O Lord,
to listen to the words of your Son. ℟.

✠ **A reading from the holy Gospel according to Luke**

All: **Glory to you, O Lord.**

His parents found Jesus sitting in the midst of the teachers.

Each year Jesus' parents went to Jerusalem for the feast of Passover,
and when he was twelve years old,
they went up according to festival custom.
After they had completed its days, as they were returning,
the boy Jesus remained behind in Jerusalem,
but his parents did not know it.
Thinking that he was in the caravan,
they journeyed for a day

and looked for him among their relatives and acquaintances,
but not finding him,
they returned to Jerusalem to look for him.
After three days they found him in the temple,
sitting in the midst of the teachers,
listening to them and asking them questions,
and all who heard him were astounded
at his understanding and his answers.
When his parents saw him,
they were astonished,
and his mother said to him,
"Son, why have you done this to us?
Your father and I have been looking for you with great anxiety."
And he said to them,
"Why were you looking for me?
Did you not know that I must be in my Father's house?"
But they did not understand what he said to them.
He went down with them and came to Nazareth,
and was obedient to them;
and his mother kept all these things in her heart.
And Jesus advanced in wisdom and age and favor before God and man.

The Gospel of the Lord. All: **Praise to you, Lord Jesus Christ.**

Prayer over the Offerings

We offer you, Lord, the sacrifice of conciliation,
humbly asking that,
through the intercession of the Virgin Mother of God and Saint Joseph,
you may establish our families firmly in your grace and your peace.
Through Christ our Lord. All: **Amen.**

Communion Antiphon (Baruch 3:38)

Our God has appeared on the earth, and lived among us.

Prayer after Communion

Bring those you refresh with this heavenly Sacrament,
most merciful Father,

to imitate constantly the example of the Holy Family,
so that, after the trials of this world,
we may share their company for ever.
Through Christ our Lord. All: **Amen.**

Solemnity of Mary, the Holy Mother of God

OCTAVE DAY OF THE NATIVITY OF THE LORD (Christmas)

January 1, 2016

World Day of Peace

Reflection on the Gospel

The shepherds obeyed the angel's revelation and searched for the newborn babe, the Savior, the Messiah. Mary, the Mother of this wondrous Child, also had a message made known to her by an angel. She heard, accepted, and said yes to what God revealed to her. She is the Mother of God. She is our Mother who helps us hear this same message. When do we go "in haste," like the shepherds, and tell everyone we meet what has been told to us?

- *I make haste to spread the message of the Savior when I . . .*

—Living Liturgy™, *Mary, Mother of God 2016*

Entrance Antiphon

Hail, Holy Mother, who gave birth to the King
who rules heaven and earth for ever.

Or:

(Cf. Isaiah 9:1, 5; Luke 1:33)
Today a light will shine upon us, for the Lord is born for us;
and he will be called Wondrous God,
Prince of peace, Father of future ages:
and his reign will be without end.

Collect

O God, who through the fruitful virginity of Blessed Mary
bestowed on the human race
the grace of eternal salvation,
grant, we pray,
that we may experience the intercession of her,
through whom we were found worthy
to receive the author of life,
our Lord Jesus Christ, your Son.
Who lives and reigns with you in the unity of the Holy Spirit,
one God, for ever and ever. All: **Amen.**

Reading I (L 18) (Numbers 6:22-27)

A reading from the Book of Numbers

They shall invoke my name upon the Israelites, and I will bless them.

The Lord said to Moses:
"Speak to Aaron and his sons and tell them:
This is how you shall bless the Israelites.
Say to them:
The Lord bless you and keep you!
The Lord let his face shine upon
you, and be gracious to you!
The Lord look upon you kindly and
give you peace!
So shall they invoke my name upon the Israelites,
and I will bless them."

The word of the Lord. All: **Thanks be to God.**

Responsorial Psalm 67

P-107

Psalm 67:2-3, 5, 6, 8

℟. (2a) **May God bless us in his mercy.**

May God have pity on us and bless us;
may he let his face shine upon us.

(continued)

So may your way be known upon earth;
among all nations, your salvation. ℟.

May the nations be glad and exult
because you rule the peoples in equity;
the nations on the earth you guide. ℟.

May the peoples praise you, O God;
may all the peoples praise you!
May God bless us,
and may all the ends of the earth fear him! ℟.

READING II (Galatians 4:4-7)

A reading from the Letter of Saint Paul to the Galatians

God sent his Son, born of a woman.

Brothers and sisters:
When the fullness of time had come, God sent his Son,
born of a woman, born under the law,
to ransom those under the law,
so that we might receive adoption as sons.
As proof that you are sons,
God sent the Spirit of his Son into our hearts,
crying out, "Abba, Father!"
So you are no longer a slave but a son,
and if a son then also an heir, through God.

The word of the Lord. All: **Thanks be to God.**

GOSPEL (Luke 2:16-21)

ALLELUIA (Hebrews 1:1-2)

℣. Alleluia, alleluia. ℟. **Alleluia, alleluia.**
℣. In the past God spoke to our ancestors through the prophets;
in these last days, he has spoken to us through the Son. ℟.

✠ **A reading from the holy Gospel according to Luke**

All: **Glory to you, O Lord.**

They found Mary and Joseph and the infant. When the eight days were completed, he was named Jesus.

The shepherds went in haste to Bethlehem and found
Mary and Joseph,
and the infant lying in the manger.
When they saw this,
they made known the message
that had been told them about this child.
All who heard it were amazed
by what had been told them by the shepherds.
And Mary kept all these things,
reflecting on them in her heart.
Then the shepherds returned,
glorifying and praising God
for all they had heard and seen,
just as it had been told to them.

When eight days were completed for his circumcision,
he was named Jesus, the name given him by the angel
before he was conceived in the womb.

The Gospel of the Lord. All: **Praise to you, Lord Jesus Christ.**

Prayer over the Offerings

O God, who in your kindness begin all good things
and bring them to fulfillment,
grant to us, who find joy in the Solemnity of the holy Mother of God,
that, just as we glory in the beginnings of your grace,
so one day we may rejoice in its completion.
Through Christ our Lord. All: **Amen.**

Communion Antiphon (Hebrews 13:8)

Jesus Christ is the same yesterday, today, and for ever.

Prayer after Communion

We have received this heavenly Sacrament with joy, O Lord:
grant, we pray,
that it may lead us to eternal life,
for we rejoice to proclaim the blessed ever-Virgin Mary
Mother of your Son and Mother of the Church.
Through Christ our Lord. All: **Amen.**

The Epiphany of the Lord

AT THE VIGIL MASS

January 2, 2016

This Mass is used on the evening of the day before the Solemnity, either before or after First Vespers (Evening Prayer I) of the Epiphany.

Reflection on the Gospel

The "magi from the east" followed the light of a star. A light of heaven that guided them. A light of revelation that manifested "the newborn king of the Jews" to Gentile wise men. A light of warning that protected this Child from harm until his time had come. Like the magi, we must follow this light to the *Light. Like the magi, we must offer "the child" homage—the gift of our very selves become the Light of his Presence.*

- *I am guided by the Light when I . . .*

—Living Liturgy™, *Epiphany 2016*

Entrance Antiphon (Cf. Baruch 5:5)

Arise, Jerusalem, and look to the East
and see your children gathered from the rising to the setting of the sun.

Collect

May the splendor of your majesty, O Lord, we pray,
shed its light upon our hearts,
that we may pass through the shadows of this world
and reach the brightness of our eternal home.
Through our Lord Jesus Christ, your Son,
who lives and reigns with you in the unity of the Holy Spirit,
one God, for ever and ever. All: **Amen.**

(Note readings are those of the day.)

Prayer over the Offerings

Accept we pray, O Lord, our offerings,
in honor of the appearing of your Only Begotten Son
and the first fruits of the nations,

that to you praise may be rendered
and eternal salvation be ours.
Through Christ our Lord. All: **Amen.**

Communion Antiphon (Cf. Revelation 21:23)

The brightness of God illumined the holy city Jerusalem,
and the nations will walk by its light.

Prayer after Communion

Renewed by sacred nourishment,
we implore your mercy, O Lord,
that the star of your justice
may shine always bright in our minds
and that our true treasure may ever consist in our confession of you.
Through Christ our Lord. All. **Amen.**

January 3

AT THE MASS DURING THE DAY

Entrance Antiphon (Cf. Malachi 3:1; 1 Chronicles 29:12)

Behold, the Lord, the Mighty One, has come;
and kingship is in his grasp, and power and dominion.

Collect

O God, who on this day
revealed your Only Begotten Son to the nations
by the guidance of a star,
grant in your mercy
that we, who know you already by faith,
may be brought to behold the beauty of your sublime glory.
Through our Lord Jesus Christ, your Son,
who lives and reigns with you in the unity of the Holy Spirit,
one God, for ever and ever. All: **Amen.**

Reading I (L 20) (Isaiah 60:1-6)

A reading from the Book of the Prophet Isaiah

The glory of the Lord shines upon you.

Rise up in splendor, Jerusalem! Your light has come,
the glory of the Lord shines upon you.
See, darkness covers the earth,
and thick clouds cover the peoples;

but upon you the LORD shines,
and over you appears his glory.
Nations shall walk by your light,
and kings by your shining radiance.
Raise your eyes and look about;
they all gather and come to you:
your sons come from afar,
and your daughters in the arms of their nurses.

Then you shall be radiant at what you see,
your heart shall throb and overflow,
for the riches of the sea shall be emptied out before you,
the wealth of nations shall be brought to you.
Caravans of camels shall fill you,
dromedaries from Midian and Ephah;
all from Sheba shall come
bearing gold and frankincense,
and proclaiming the praises of the LORD.

The word of the Lord. All: **Thanks be to God.**

RESPONSORIAL PSALM 72

P-108

Psalm 72:1-2, 7-8, 10-11, 12-13

℟. (*See* 11) **Lord, every nation on earth will adore you.**

O God, with your judgment endow the king,
and with your justice, the king's son;
he shall govern your people with justice
and your afflicted ones with judgment. ℟.

Justice shall flower in his days,
and profound peace, till the moon be no more.
May he rule from sea to sea,
and from the River to the ends of the earth. ℟.

The kings of Tarshish and the Isles shall offer gifts;
the kings of Arabia and Seba shall bring tribute.
All kings shall pay him homage,
all nations shall serve him. ℟.

For he shall rescue the poor when he cries out,
and the afflicted when he has no one to help him.
He shall have pity for the lowly and the poor;
the lives of the poor he shall save. ℟.

READING II (Ephesians 3:2-3a, 5-6)

A reading from the Letter of Saint Paul to the Ephesians

Now it has been revealed that the Gentiles are coheirs of the promise.

Brothers and sisters:
You have heard of the stewardship of God's grace
that was given to me for your benefit,
namely, that the mystery was made known to me by revelation.
It was not made known to people in other generations
as it has now been revealed
to his holy apostles and prophets by the Spirit:
that the Gentiles are coheirs, members of the same body,
and copartners in the promise in Christ Jesus through the gospel.

The word of the Lord. All: **Thanks be to God.**

GOSPEL (Matthew 2:1-12)

ALLELUIA (Matthew 2:2)

℣. Alleluia, alleluia. ℟. **Alleluia, alleluia.**
℣. We saw his star at its rising
and have come to do him homage. ℟.

✠ **A reading from the holy Gospel according to Matthew**

All: **Glory to you, O Lord.**

We saw his star at its rising and have come to do him homage.

When Jesus was born in Bethlehem of Judea,
in the days of King Herod,

behold, magi from the east arrived in Jerusalem,
saying,
"Where is the newborn king of the Jews?
We saw his star at its rising
and have come to do him homage."
When King Herod heard this,
he was greatly troubled,
and all Jerusalem with him.
Assembling all the chief priests and the scribes of the people,
he inquired of them where the Christ was to be born.
They said to him, "In Bethlehem of Judea,
for thus it has been written through the prophet:
And you, Bethlehem, land of Judah,
are by no means least among the rulers of Judah;
since from you shall come a ruler,
***who is to shepherd my people Israel.*"**
Then Herod called the magi secretly
and ascertained from them the time of the star's appearance.
He sent them to Bethlehem and said,
"Go and search diligently for the child.
When you have found him, bring me word,
that I too may go and do him homage."
After their audience with the king they set out.
And behold, the star that they had seen at its rising preceded them,
until it came and stopped over the place where the child was.
They were overjoyed at seeing the star,
and on entering the house
they saw the child with Mary his mother.
They prostrated themselves and did him homage.
Then they opened their treasures
and offered him gifts of gold, frankincense, and myrrh.

And having been warned in a dream not to return to Herod,
they departed for their country by another way.

The Gospel of the Lord. All: **Praise to you, Lord Jesus Christ.**

Prayer over the Offerings

Look with favor, Lord, we pray,
on these gifts of your Church,
in which are offered now not gold or frankincense or myrrh,
but he who by them is proclaimed,
sacrificed and received, Jesus Christ.
Who lives and reigns for ever and ever. All: **Amen.**

Communion Antiphon (Cf. Matthew 2:2)

We have seen his star in the East,
and have come with gifts to adore the Lord.

Prayer after Communion

Go before us with heavenly light, O Lord,
always and everywhere,
that we may perceive with clear sight
and revere with true affection
the mystery in which you have willed us to participate.
Through Christ our Lord. All: **Amen.**

The Baptism of the Lord

January 10, 2016

Reflection on the Gospel

The people in the gospel looked to John the Baptist to be the long-awaited Messiah. It was precisely their expectation—misdirected though it was—that kept them looking for the Messiah. John redirected them from himself to the person of Jesus, the "beloved Son" of God. Our own baptism with "the Holy Spirit and fire" initiates us on a journey of discovery not only of who Jesus is, but also who we are in him: the beloved of God.

- *I follow the "beloved Son" by . . .*

—Living Liturgy™, *Baptism of the Lord 2016*

ENTRANCE ANTIPHON (Cf. Matthew 3:16-17)

After the Lord was baptized, the heavens were opened,
and the Spirit descended upon him like a dove,
and the voice of the Father thundered:
This is my beloved Son, with whom I am well pleased.

COLLECT

Almighty ever-living God,
who, when Christ had been baptized in the River Jordan
and as the Holy Spirit descended upon him,
solemnly declared him your beloved Son,
grant that your children by adoption,
reborn of water and the Holy Spirit,
may always be well pleasing to you.
Through our Lord Jesus Christ, your Son,
who lives and reigns with you in the unity of the Holy Spirit,
one God, for ever and ever. All: **Amen.**

Or:

O God, whose Only Begotten Son
has appeared in our very flesh,
grant, we pray, that we may be inwardly transformed
through him whom we recognize as outwardly like ourselves.
Who lives and reigns with you in the unity of the Holy Spirit,
one God, for ever and ever. All: **Amen.**

READING I (L 21) (Isaiah 42:1-4, 6-7) *for this year additional options can be found in the Lectionary*

A reading from the Book of the Prophet Isaiah

Behold my servant with whom I am well pleased.

Thus says the LORD:
Here is my servant whom I uphold,
my chosen one with whom I am pleased,
upon whom I have put my spirit;
he shall bring forth justice to the nations,
not crying out, not shouting,
not making his voice heard in the street.
A bruised reed he shall not break,
and a smoldering wick he shall not quench,
until he establishes justice on the earth;
the coastlands will wait for his teaching.

I, the LORD, have called you for the victory of justice,
I have grasped you by the hand;
I formed you, and set you
as a covenant of the people,
a light for the nations,
to open the eyes of the blind,
to bring out prisoners from confinement,
and from the dungeon, those who live in darkness.

The word of the Lord. All: **Thanks be to God.**

RESPONSORIAL PSALM 29

P-109

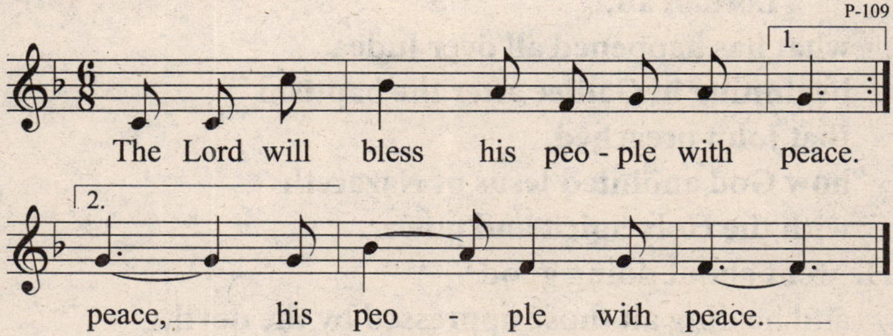

Psalm 29:1-2, 3-4, 3, 9-10

℟. (11b) **The Lord will bless his people with peace.**

Give to the LORD, you sons of God,
give to the LORD glory and praise,
give to the LORD the glory due his name;
adore the LORD in holy attire. ℟.

The voice of the LORD is over the waters,
the LORD, over vast waters.
The voice of the LORD is mighty;
the voice of the LORD is majestic. ℟.

The God of glory thunders,
and in his temple all say, "Glory!"
The LORD is enthroned above the flood;
the LORD is enthroned as king forever. ℟.

READING II (Acts of the Apostles 10:34-38) *for this year additional options can be found in the Lectionary*

A reading from the Acts of the Apostles

God anointed him with the Holy Spirit.

Peter proceeded to speak to those gathered
in the house of Cornelius, saying:
"In truth, I see that God shows no partiality.
Rather, in every nation whoever fears him and acts uprightly
is acceptable to him.
You know the word that he sent to the Israelites
as he proclaimed peace through Jesus Christ, who is Lord of all,
what has happened all over Judea,
beginning in Galilee after the baptism
that John preached,
how God anointed Jesus of Nazareth
with the Holy Spirit and power.
He went about doing good
and healing all those oppressed by the devil,
for God was with him."

The word of the Lord. All: **Thanks be to God.**

Gospel (Luke 3:15-16, 21-22)

Alleluia (*See* Mark 9:7)

℣. Alleluia, alleluia. ℟. **Alleluia, alleluia.**
℣. The heavens were opened and the voice of the Father thundered:
This is my beloved Son, listen to him. ℟.

Or:

Alleluia (*See* Luke 3:16)

℣. Alleluia, alleluia. ℟. **Alleluia, alleluia.**
℣. John said: One mightier than I is coming;
he will baptize you with the Holy Spirit and with fire. ℟.

✠ **A reading from the holy Gospel according to Luke**

All: **Glory to you, O Lord.**

When Jesus had been baptized and was praying, heaven was opened.

The people were filled with expectation,
and all were asking in their hearts
whether John might be the Christ.
John answered them all, saying,
"I am baptizing you with water,
but one mightier than I is coming.
I am not worthy to loosen the thongs of his sandals.
He will baptize you with the Holy Spirit and fire."

After all the people had been baptized
and Jesus also had been baptized and was praying,
heaven was opened and the Holy Spirit descended upon him
in bodily form like a dove.
And a voice came from heaven,
"You are my beloved Son;
with you I am well pleased."

The Gospel of the Lord. All: **Praise to you, Lord Jesus Christ.**

Prayer over the Offerings

Accept, O Lord, the offerings
we have brought to honor the revealing of your beloved Son,
so that the oblation of your faithful

may be transformed into the sacrifice of him
who willed in his compassion
to wash away the sins of the world.
Who lives and reigns for ever and ever. All: **Amen.**

Communion Antiphon (John 1:32, 34)

Behold the One of whom John said:
I have seen and testified that this is the Son of God.

Prayer after Communion

Nourished with these sacred gifts,
we humbly entreat your mercy, O Lord,
that, faithfully listening to your Only Begotten Son,
we may be your children in name and in truth.
Through Christ our Lord. All: **Amen.**

Second Sunday in Ordinary Time

January 17, 2016

Reflection on the Gospel

What is Jesus' "hour"? It is a time of the revelation of God's immense gift of abundance. In this gospel, not one jar of water became wine, but six. Not partially filled jars, but "to the brim." Not inferior wine, but "good wine." Not just one sign, but "the beginning of his signs." God's glory is revealed in many signs of abundance. Most fully in Jesus himself. Most fully in us, the Body of Christ, as we come to deeper belief and continue his ministry.

- *I am filled to the brim with "good wine" when I . . .*

—Living Liturgy™, *Second Sunday in Ordinary Time 2016*

Entrance Antiphon (Psalm 66[65]:4)

All the earth shall bow down before you, O God,
and shall sing to you,
shall sing to your name, O Most High!

Collect

Almighty ever-living God,
who govern all things,
both in heaven and on earth,
mercifully hear the pleading of your people
and bestow your peace on our times.
Through our Lord Jesus Christ, your Son,
who lives and reigns with you in the unity of the Holy Spirit,
one God, for ever and ever. All: **Amen.**

Reading I (L 66) (Isaiah 62:1-5)

A reading from the Book of the Prophet Isaiah

The bridegroom rejoices in his bride.

For Zion's sake I will not be silent,
for Jerusalem's sake I will not be quiet,
until her vindication shines forth like the dawn
and her victory like a burning torch.

Nations shall behold your vindication,
and all the kings your glory;
you shall be called by a new name
pronounced by the mouth of the Lord.
You shall be a glorious crown in the hand of the Lord,
a royal diadem held by your God.
No more shall people call you "Forsaken,"
or your land "Desolate,"
but you shall be called "My Delight,"
and your land "Espoused."
For the Lord delights in you
and makes your land his spouse.
As a young man marries a virgin,
your Builder shall marry you;
and as a bridegroom rejoices in his bride
so shall your God rejoice in you.

The word of the Lord. All: **Thanks be to God.**

Responsorial Psalm 96

P-501

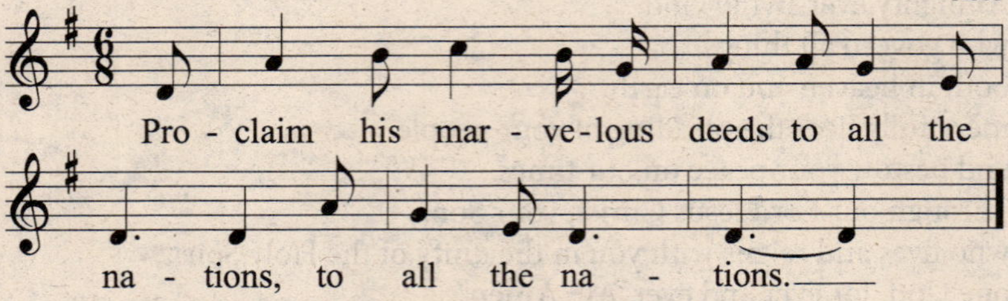

Psalm 96:1-2, 2-3, 7-8, 9-10

℟. (3) **Proclaim his marvelous deeds to all the nations.**

Sing to the LORD a new song;
sing to the LORD, all you lands.
Sing to the LORD; bless his name. ℟.

Announce his salvation, day after day.
Tell his glory among the nations;
among all peoples, his wondrous deeds. ℟.

Give to the LORD, you families of nations,
give to the LORD glory and praise;
give to the LORD the glory due his name! ℟.

Worship the LORD in holy attire.
Tremble before him, all the earth;
say among the nations: The LORD is king.
He governs the peoples with equity. ℟.

Reading II (1 Corinthians 12:4-11)

A reading from the first Letter of Saint Paul to the Corinthians

One and the same Spirit distributing them individually to each person as he wishes.

Brothers and sisters:
There are different kinds of spiritual gifts but the same Spirit;
there are different forms of service but the same Lord;
there are different workings but the same God
who produces all of them in everyone.

To each individual the manifestation of the Spirit
is given for some benefit.
To one is given through the Spirit the expression of wisdom;
to another, the expression of knowledge according to the same Spirit;
to another, faith by the same Spirit;
to another, gifts of healing by the one Spirit;
to another, mighty deeds;
to another, prophecy;
to another, discernment of spirits;
to another, varieties of tongues;
to another, interpretation of tongues.
But one and the same Spirit produces all of these,
distributing them individually to each person as he wishes.

The word of the Lord. All: **Thanks be to God.**

GOSPEL (John 2:1-11)
ALLELUIA (*See* 2 Thessalonians 2:14)

℣. Alleluia, alleluia. ℟. **Alleluia, alleluia.**
℣. God has called us through the Gospel
to possess the glory of our Lord Jesus Christ. ℟.

✠ **A reading from the holy Gospel according to John**

All: **Glory to you, O Lord.**

Jesus did this as the beginning of his signs at Cana in Galilee.

There was a wedding at Cana in Galilee,
and the mother of Jesus was there.
Jesus and his disciples were also invited to the wedding.
When the wine ran short,
the mother of Jesus said to him,
"They have no wine."
And Jesus said to her,
"Woman, how does your concern affect me?
My hour has not yet come."

His mother said to the servers,
"Do whatever he tells you."
Now there were six stone water jars there for Jewish ceremonial washings,
each holding twenty to thirty gallons.
Jesus told them,
"Fill the jars with water."
So they filled them to the brim.
Then he told them,
"Draw some out now and take it to the headwaiter."
So they took it.
And when the headwaiter tasted the water that had become wine,
without knowing where it came from
—although the servers who had drawn the water knew—,
the headwaiter called the bridegroom and said to him,
"Everyone serves good wine first,
and then when people have drunk freely, an inferior one;
but you have kept the good wine until now."
Jesus did this as the beginning of his signs at Cana in Galilee
and so revealed his glory,
and his disciples began to believe in him.

The Gospel of the Lord. All: **Praise to you, Lord Jesus Christ.**

Prayer over the Offerings

Grant us, O Lord, we pray,
that we may participate worthily in these mysteries,
for whenever the memorial of this sacrifice is celebrated
the work of our redemption is accomplished.
Through Christ our Lord. All: **Amen.**

Communion Antiphon (Cf. Psalm 23[22]:5)

You have prepared a table before me,
and how precious is the chalice that quenches my thirst.

Or:

(1 John 4:16)
We have come to know and to believe
in the love that God has for us.

Prayer after Communion
Pour on us, O Lord, the Spirit of your love,
and in your kindness
make those you have nourished
by this one heavenly Bread
one in mind and heart.
Through Christ our Lord. All: **Amen.**

Third Sunday in Ordinary Time

January 24, 2016

Reflection on the Gospel

In this gospel Jesus clearly proclaims who he is and what he comes to bring. He is One who lives "in the power of the Spirit"; he comes to bring a new teaching. He is God's anointed; he comes to bring the human community glad tidings, liberty, sight, freedom, favor. He is the long-awaited Messiah; he comes to bring manifest signs of salvation. The "eyes of all . . . looked intently at him." Do our own eyes look intently upon him?

- *When I . . . , I look intently on Jesus.*

—Living Liturgy™, *Third Sunday in Ordinary Time 2016*

Entrance Antiphon (Cf. Psalm 96[95]:1, 6)
O sing a new song to the Lord;
sing to the Lord, all the earth.
In his presence are majesty and splendor,
strength and honor in his holy place.

Collect
Almighty ever-living God,
direct our actions according to your good pleasure,
that in the name of your beloved Son
we may abound in good works.

Through our Lord Jesus Christ, your Son,
who lives and reigns with you in the unity of the Holy Spirit,
one God, for ever and ever. All: **Amen.**

READING I (L 69) (Nehemiah 8:2-4a, 5-6, 8-10)

A reading from the Book of Nehemiah

They read from the book of the Law and they understood what was read.

Ezra the priest brought the law before the assembly,
which consisted of men, women,
and those children old enough to understand.
Standing at one end of the open place that was before the Water Gate,
he read out of the book from daybreak till midday,
in the presence of the men, the women,
and those children old enough to understand;
and all the people listened attentively to the book of the law.
Ezra the scribe stood on a wooden platform
that had been made for the occasion.
He opened the scroll
so that all the people might see it
—for he was standing higher up than any of the people—;
and, as he opened it, all the people rose.
Ezra blessed the LORD, the great God,
and all the people, their hands raised high, answered,
"Amen, amen!"
Then they bowed down and prostrated themselves before the LORD,
their faces to the ground.
Ezra read plainly from the book of the law of God,
interpreting it so that all could understand what was read.
Then Nehemiah, that is, His Excellency, and Ezra the priest-scribe
and the Levites who were instructing the people

said to all the people:
"Today is holy to the LORD your God.
Do not be sad, and do not weep"—
for all the people were weeping as they heard the words of the law.
He said further: "Go, eat rich foods and drink sweet drinks,
and allot portions to those who had nothing prepared;
for today is holy to our LORD.
Do not be saddened this day,
for rejoicing in the LORD must be your strength!"

The word of the Lord. All: **Thanks be to God.**

RESPONSORIAL PSALM 19

Psalm 19:8, 9, 10, 15

℟. (*See* John 6:63c) **Your words, Lord, are Spirit and life.**

The law of the LORD is perfect,
refreshing the soul;
the decree of the LORD is trustworthy,
giving wisdom to the simple. ℟.

The precepts of the LORD are right,
rejoicing the heart;
the command of the LORD is clear,
enlightening the eye. ℟.

The fear of the LORD is pure,
enduring forever;
the ordinances of the LORD are true,
all of them just. ℟.

(continued)

Let the words of my mouth and the thought of my heart
find favor before you,
O Lord, my rock and my redeemer. R.

Reading II (1 Corinthians 12:12-30) *or* Shorter Form [ ]
(1 Corinthians 12:12-14, 27)

A reading from the first Letter of Saint Paul to the Corinthians

You are Christ's body and individually parts of it.

[Brothers and sisters:
As a body is one though it has many parts,
and all the parts of the body, though many, are one body,
so also Christ.
For in one Spirit we were all baptized into one body,
whether Jews or Greeks, slaves or free persons,
and we were all given to drink of one Spirit.

Now the body is not a single part, but many.]
If a foot should say,
"Because I am not a hand I do not belong to the body,"
it does not for this reason belong any less to the body.
Or if an ear should say,
"Because I am not an eye I do not belong to the body,"
it does not for this reason belong any less to the body.
If the whole body were an eye, where would the hearing be?
If the whole body were hearing, where would the sense of smell be?
But as it is, God placed the parts,
each one of them, in the body as he intended.
If they were all one part, where would the body be?
But as it is, there are many parts, yet one body.
The eye cannot say to the hand, "I do not need you,"
nor again the head to the feet, "I do not need you."
Indeed, the parts of the body that seem to be weaker
are all the more necessary,

and those parts of the body that we consider less honorable
we surround with greater honor,
and our less presentable parts are treated with greater propriety,
whereas our more presentable parts do not need this.
But God has so constructed the body
as to give greater honor to a part that is without it,
so that there may be no division in the body,
but that the parts may have the same concern for one another.
If one part suffers, all the parts suffer with it;
if one part is honored, all the parts share its joy.

Now [you are Christ's body, and individually parts of it.]
Some people God has designated in the church
to be, first, apostles; second, prophets; third, teachers;
then, mighty deeds;
then gifts of healing, assistance, administration,
and varieties of tongues.
Are all apostles? Are all prophets? Are all teachers?
Do all work mighty deeds? Do all have gifts of healing?
Do all speak in tongues? Do all interpret?

The word of the Lord. All: **Thanks be to God.**

Gospel (Luke 1:1-4; 4:14-21)
Alleluia (*See* Luke 4:18)

℣. Alleluia, alleluia. ℟. **Alleluia, alleluia.**
℣. The Lord sent me to bring glad tidings to the poor,
and to proclaim liberty to captives. ℟.

✠ **A reading from the holy Gospel according to Luke**

All: **Glory to you, O Lord.**

Today this Scripture passage is fulfilled.

Since many have undertaken to compile a narrative of the events
that have been fulfilled among us,

just as those who were eyewitnesses from the beginning
and ministers of the word have handed them down
to us,
I too have decided,
after investigating everything accurately anew,
to write it down in an orderly sequence for you,
most excellent Theophilus,
so that you may realize the certainty of the teachings
you have received.

Jesus returned to Galilee in the power of the Spirit,
and news of him spread throughout the whole region.
He taught in their synagogues and was praised by all.

He came to Nazareth, where he had grown up,
and went according to his custom
into the synagogue on the sabbath day.
He stood up to read and was handed a scroll of the
prophet Isaiah.
He unrolled the scroll and found the passage where it
was written:
The Spirit of the Lord is upon me,
because he has anointed me
to bring glad tidings to the poor.
He has sent me to proclaim liberty to captives
and recovery of sight to the blind,
to let the oppressed go free,
and to proclaim a year acceptable to the Lord.
Rolling up the scroll, he handed it back to the attendant
and sat down,
and the eyes of all in the synagogue looked intently
at him.
He said to them,
"Today this Scripture passage is fulfilled in your
hearing."

The Gospel of the Lord. All: Praise to you, Lord Jesus Christ.

Prayer over the Offerings

Accept our offerings, O Lord, we pray,
and in sanctifying them
grant that they may profit us for salvation.
Through Christ our Lord. All: **Amen.**

Communion Antiphon (Cf. Psalm 34[33]:6)

Look toward the Lord and be radiant;
let your faces not be abashed.

Or:

(John 8:12)
I am the light of the world, says the Lord;
whoever follows me will not walk in darkness,
but will have the light of life.

Prayer after Communion

Grant, we pray, almighty God,
that, receiving the grace
by which you bring us to new life,
we may always glory in your gift.
Through Christ our Lord. All: **Amen.**

Fourth Sunday in Ordinary Time

January 31, 2016

Reflection on the Gospel

More than one Scripture passage is being fulfilled in this gospel. The words and deeds of Jesus fulfill the Scripture passage from Isaiah about the coming of salvation: glad tidings for the poor, liberty for captives, sight for the blind, freedom for the oppressed. The words and deeds of the people fulfill the Scripture passages about rejecting and killing God's prophets: they question Jesus' origins, become furious at his words, and act to destroy him. Which Scripture passages do we hear?

- *I hear Jesus when I . . . , and I will . . .*

—Living Liturgy™, *Fourth Sunday in Ordinary Time 2016*

ENTRANCE ANTIPHON (Psalm 106[105]:47)
Save us, O Lord our God!
And gather us from the nations,
to give thanks to your holy name,
and make it our glory to praise you.

COLLECT
Grant us, Lord our God,
that we may honor you with all our mind,
and love everyone in truth of heart.
Through our Lord Jesus Christ, your Son,
who lives and reigns with you in the unity of the Holy Spirit,
one God, for ever and ever. All: **Amen.**

READING I (L 72) (Jeremiah 1:4-5, 17-19)
A reading from the Book of the Prophet Jeremiah

A prophet to the nations I appointed you.

The word of the LORD came to me, saying:
Before I formed you in the womb I knew you,
before you were born I dedicated you,
a prophet to the nations I appointed you.

But do you gird your loins;
stand up and tell them
all that I command you.
Be not crushed on their account,
as though I would leave you crushed before them;
for it is I this day
who have made you a fortified city,
a pillar of iron, a wall of brass,
against the whole land:
against Judah's kings and princes,
against its priests and people.
They will fight against you but not prevail over you,
for I am with you to deliver you, says the LORD.

The word of the Lord. All: **Thanks be to God.**

RESPONSORIAL PSALM 71

P-503

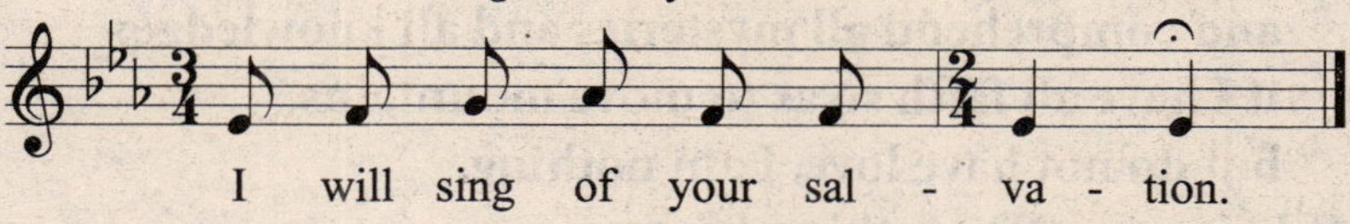

Psalm 71:1-2, 3-4, 5-6, 15, 17

℟. (*See* 15ab) **I will sing of your salvation.**

In you, O LORD, I take refuge;
  let me never be put to shame.
In your justice rescue me, and deliver me;
  incline your ear to me, and save me. ℟.

Be my rock of refuge,
  a stronghold to give me safety,
  for you are my rock and my fortress.
O my God, rescue me from the hand of the wicked. ℟.

For you are my hope, O Lord;
  my trust, O God, from my youth.
On you I depend from birth;
  from my mother's womb you are my strength. ℟.

My mouth shall declare your justice,
  day by day your salvation.
O God, you have taught me from my youth,
  and till the present I proclaim your wondrous deeds. ℟.

READING II (1 Corinthians 12:31—13:13) *or* Shorter Form [ ] (1 Corinthians 13:4-13)

A reading from the first Letter of Saint Paul to the Corinthians

So faith, hope, love remain, these three; but the greatest of these is love.

[Brothers and sisters:]
Strive eagerly for the greatest spiritual gifts.
But I shall show you a still more excellent way.

If I speak in human and angelic tongues,
but do not have love,
I am a resounding gong or a clashing cymbal.
And if I have the gift of prophecy,
and comprehend all mysteries and all knowledge;
if I have all faith so as to move mountains,
but do not have love, I am nothing.
If I give away everything I own,
and if I hand my body over so that I may boast,
but do not have love, I gain nothing.

[**Love is patient, love is kind.**
It is not jealous, it is not pompous,
it is not inflated, it is not rude,
it does not seek its own interests,
it is not quick-tempered, it does not brood over injury,
it does not rejoice over wrongdoing
but rejoices with the truth.
It bears all things, believes all things,
hopes all things, endures all things.

Love never fails.
If there are prophecies, they will be brought to nothing;
if tongues, they will cease;
if knowledge, it will be brought to nothing.
For we know partially and we prophesy partially,
but when the perfect comes, the partial will pass away.
When I was a child, I used to talk as a child,
think as a child, reason as a child;
when I became a man, I put aside childish things.
At present we see indistinctly, as in a mirror,
but then face to face.
At present I know partially;
then I shall know fully, as I am fully known.
So faith, hope, love remain, these three;
but the greatest of these is love.]

The word of the Lord. All: **Thanks be to God.**

Gospel (Luke 4:21-30)

Alleluia (Luke 4:18)

℣. Alleluia, alleluia. ℟. **Alleluia, alleluia.**
℣. The Lord sent me to bring glad tidings to the poor,
to proclaim liberty to captives. ℟.

✠ **A reading from the holy Gospel according to Luke**

All: **Glory to you, O Lord.**

Like Elijah and Elisha, Jesus was not sent only to the Jews.

Jesus began speaking in the synagogue, saying:
"Today this Scripture passage is fulfilled in your hearing."
And all spoke highly of him
and were amazed at the gracious words that came from his mouth.
They also asked, "Isn't this the son of Joseph?"
He said to them, "Surely you will quote me this proverb,
'Physician, cure yourself,' and say,
'Do here in your native place
the things that we heard were done in Capernaum.' "
And he said, "Amen, I say to you,
no prophet is accepted in his own native place.
Indeed, I tell you,
there were many widows in Israel in the days of Elijah
when the sky was closed for three and a half years
and a severe famine spread over the entire land.
It was to none of these that Elijah was sent,
but only to a widow in Zarephath in the land of Sidon.
Again, there were many lepers in Israel
during the time of Elisha the prophet;
yet not one of them was cleansed, but only Naaman the Syrian."
When the people in the synagogue heard this,
they were all filled with fury.
They rose up, drove him out of the town,
and led him to the brow of the hill

on which their town had been built,
to hurl him down headlong.
But Jesus passed through the midst of them and went away.

The Gospel of the Lord. All: **Praise to you, Lord Jesus Christ.**

Prayer over the Offerings

O Lord, we bring to your altar
these offerings of our service:
be pleased to receive them, we pray,
and transform them
into the Sacrament of our redemption.
Through Christ our Lord. All: **Amen.**

Communion Antiphon (Cf. Psalm 31[30]:17-18)

Let your face shine on your servant.
Save me in your merciful love.
O Lord, let me never be put to shame, for I call on you.

Or:

(Matthew 5:3-4)
Blessed are the poor in spirit,
for theirs is the Kingdom of Heaven.
Blessed are the meek, for they shall possess the land.

Prayer after Communion

Nourished by these redeeming gifts,
we pray, O Lord,
that through this help to eternal salvation
true faith may ever increase.
Through Christ our Lord. All: **Amen.**

Fifth Sunday in Ordinary Time

February 7, 2016

Reflection on the Gospel

After fishing all night and catching nothing, Peter obeys Jesus, putting out his boat and nets once again. He makes a great catch of fish. Even more, he comes to a great insight about himself. Encounter with Jesus leads Peter to see himself as he really is ("I am a sinful man"), and to become what he is not yet: a follower of Jesus participating in his saving mission. Jesus "caught" Peter. He will "catch" us, too. Will he?

- *I have learned . . . from Jesus.*

—Living Liturgy™, *Fifth Sunday in Ordinary Time 2016*

Entrance Antiphon (Psalm 95[94]:6-7)

O come, let us worship God
and bow low before the God who made us,
for he is the Lord our God.

Collect

Keep your family safe, O Lord, with unfailing care,
that, relying solely on the hope of heavenly grace,
they may be defended always by your protection.
Through our Lord Jesus Christ, your Son,
who lives and reigns with you in the unity of the Holy Spirit,
one God, for ever and ever. All: **Amen.**

Reading I (L 75) (Isaiah 6:1-2a, 3-8)

A reading from the Book of the Prophet Isaiah

Here I am! Send me.

In the year King Uzziah died,
I saw the Lord seated on a high and lofty throne,
with the train of his garment filling the temple.
Seraphim were stationed above.

They cried one to the other,
"Holy, holy, holy is the LORD of hosts!
All the earth is filled with his glory!"
At the sound of that cry, the frame of the door shook
and the house was filled with smoke.

Then I said, "Woe is me, I am doomed!
For I am a man of unclean lips,
living among a people of unclean lips;
yet my eyes have seen the King, the LORD of hosts!"
Then one of the seraphim flew to me,
holding an ember that he had taken with tongs from the altar.

He touched my mouth with it, and said,
"See, now that this has touched your lips,
your wickedness is removed, your sin purged."

Then I heard the voice of the LORD saying,
"Whom shall I send? Who will go for us?"
"Here I am," I said; "send me!"

The word of the Lord. All: **Thanks be to God.**

RESPONSORIAL PSALM 138

P-504

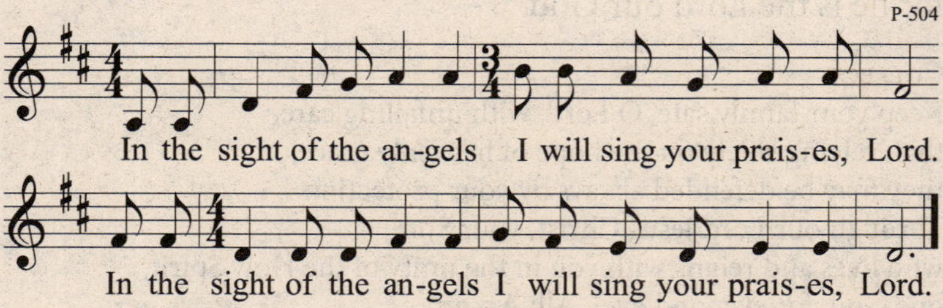

Music: Jay F. Hunstiger, © 1991, administered by Liturgical Press.

Psalm 138:1-2, 2-3, 4-5, 7-8

℟. (1c) **In the sight of the angels I will sing your praises, Lord.**

I will give thanks to you, O LORD, with all my heart,
for you have heard the words of my mouth;
in the presence of the angels I will sing your praise;

I will worship at your holy temple
and give thanks to your name. ℟.

Because of your kindness and your truth;
for you have made great above all things
your name and your promise.
When I called, you answered me;
you built up strength within me. ℟.

All the kings of the earth shall give thanks to you,
O LORD,
when they hear the words of your mouth;
and they shall sing of the ways of the LORD:
"Great is the glory of the LORD." ℟.

Your right hand saves me.
The LORD will complete what he has done for me;
your kindness, O LORD, endures forever;
forsake not the work of your hands. ℟.

READING II (1 Corinthians 15:1-11) *or* Shorter Form [ ]
(1 Corinthians 15:3-8, 11)

A reading from the first Letter of Saint Paul to the Corinthians

So we preached and so you believe.

I am reminding you, [brothers and sisters,]
of the gospel I preached to you,
which you indeed received and in which you also stand.
Through it you are also being saved,
if you hold fast to the word I preached to you,
unless you believed in vain.
For [I handed on to you as of first importance what I also received:
that Christ died for our sins
in accordance with the Scriptures;
that he was buried;
that he was raised on the third day
in accordance with the Scriptures;
that he appeared to Cephas, then to the Twelve.

After that, he appeared to more
than five hundred brothers at once,
most of whom are still living,
though some have fallen asleep.
After that he appeared to James,
then to all the apostles.
Last of all, as to one born abnormally,
he appeared to me.]
For I am the least of the apostles,
not fit to be called an apostle,
because I persecuted the church of God.
But by the grace of God I am what I am,
and his grace to me has not been ineffective.
Indeed, I have toiled harder than all of them;
not I, however, but the grace of God that is with me.
[Therefore, whether it be I or they,
so we preach and so you believed.]

The word of the Lord. All: **Thanks be to God.**

GOSPEL (Luke 5:1-11)

ALLELUIA (Matthew 4:19)

℣. Alleluia, alleluia. ℟. **Alleluia, alleluia.**
℣. Come after me
and I will make you fishers of men. ℟.

✠ **A reading from the holy Gospel according to Luke**

All: **Glory to you, O Lord.**

They left everything and followed Jesus.

While the crowd was pressing in on Jesus and listening
to the word of God,
he was standing by the Lake of Gennesaret.
He saw two boats there alongside the lake;
the fishermen had disembarked and were washing
their nets.
Getting into one of the boats, the one belonging to Simon,
he asked him to put out a short distance from the
shore.

Then he sat down and taught the crowds from the boat.
After he had finished speaking, he said to Simon,
"Put out into deep water and lower your nets for a catch."
Simon said in reply,
"Master, we have worked hard all night and have caught nothing,
but at your command I will lower the nets."
When they had done this, they caught a great number of fish
and their nets were tearing.
They signaled to their partners in the other boat
to come to help them.
They came and filled both boats
so that the boats were in danger of sinking.
When Simon Peter saw this, he fell at the knees of Jesus and said,
"Depart from me, Lord, for I am a sinful man."
For astonishment at the catch of fish they had made seized him
and all those with him,
and likewise James and John, the sons of Zebedee,
who were partners of Simon.
Jesus said to Simon, "Do not be afraid;
from now on you will be catching men."
When they brought their boats to the shore,
they left everything and followed him.

The Gospel of the Lord. All: **Praise to you, Lord Jesus Christ.**

Prayer over the Offerings

O Lord our God,
who once established these created things
to sustain us in our frailty,
grant, we pray,
that they may become for us now
the Sacrament of eternal life.
Through Christ our Lord. All: **Amen.**

Communion Antiphon (Cf. Psalm 107[106]:8-9)
Let them thank the Lord for his mercy,
his wonders for the children of men,
for he satisfies the thirsty soul,
and the hungry he fills with good things.

Or:

(Matthew 5:5-6)
Blessed are those who mourn, for they shall be consoled.
Blessed are those who hunger and thirst for righteousness,
for they shall have their fill.

Prayer after Communion
O God, who have willed that we be partakers
in the one Bread and the one Chalice,
grant us, we pray, so to live
that, made one in Christ,
we may joyfully bear fruit
for the salvation of the world.
Through Christ our Lord. All: **Amen.**

Ash Wednesday

February 10, 2016

Reflection on the Gospel

The spirit in which we do penance—and, indeed, the purpose of all of Lent—is openness to God's work *in us leading to conversion of heart. Lenten penance that transforms us and makes a difference in our ongoing daily living and deepens our relationship with God and each other is our response to God's overture of Presence and grace. The outward signs of Lenten penance are indications that God is at work in us. Even our choice to do penance is a response to God.*

- *God transforms and converts me . . .*

—Living Liturgy™, *Ash Wednesday 2016*

Entrance Antiphon (Wisdom 11:24, 25, 27)

You are merciful to all, O Lord,
and despise nothing that you have made.
You overlook people's sins, to bring them to repentance,
and you spare them, for you are the Lord our God.

Collect

Grant, O Lord, that we may begin with holy fasting
this campaign of Christian service,
so that, as we take up battle against spiritual evils,
we may be armed with weapons of self-restraint.
Through our Lord Jesus Christ, your Son,
who lives and reigns with you in the unity of the Holy Spirit,
one God, for ever and ever. All: **Amen.**

Reading I (L 219) (Joel 2:12-18)

A reading from the Book of the Prophet Joel

Rend your hearts, not your garments.

Even now, says the Lord,
return to me with your whole heart,
with fasting, and weeping, and mourning;
Rend your hearts, not your garments,
and return to the Lord, your God.
For gracious and merciful is he,
slow to anger, rich in kindness,
and relenting in punishment.
Perhaps he will again relent
and leave behind him a blessing,
Offerings and libations
for the Lord, your God.

Blow the trumpet in Zion!
proclaim a fast,
call an assembly;
Gather the people,
notify the congregation;
Assemble the elders,
gather the children
and the infants at the breast;

Let the bridegroom quit his room
and the bride her chamber.
Between the porch and the altar
let the priests, the ministers of the Lord, weep,
And say, "Spare, O Lord, your people,
and make not your heritage a reproach,
with the nations ruling over them!
Why should they say among the peoples,
'Where is their God?' "

Then the Lord was stirred to concern for his land
and took pity on his people.

The word of the Lord. All: **Thanks be to God.**

Responsorial Psalm 51

P-174

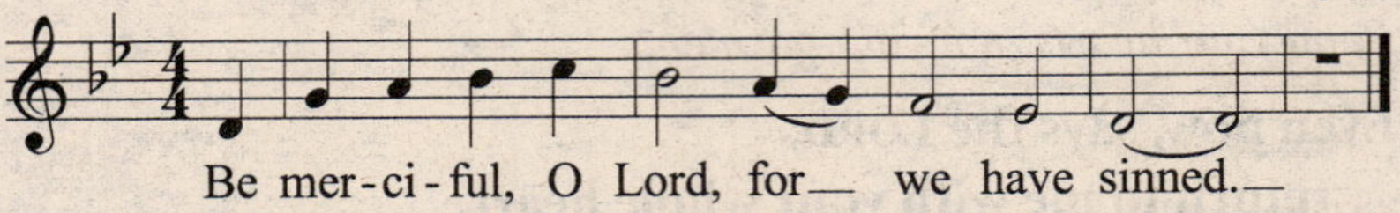

Psalm 51:3-4, 5-6ab, 12-13, 14 and 17

℟. (*See* 3a) **Be merciful, O Lord, for we have sinned.**

Have mercy on me, O God, in your goodness;
in the greatness of your compassion wipe out my offense.
Thoroughly wash me from my guilt
and of my sin cleanse me. ℟.

For I acknowledge my offense,
and my sin is before me always:
"Against you only have I sinned,
and done what is evil in your sight." ℟.

A clean heart create for me, O God,
and a steadfast spirit renew within me.
Cast me not out from your presence,
and your Holy Spirit take not from me. ℟.

Give me back the joy of your salvation,
and a willing spirit sustain in me.

O Lord, open my lips,
and my mouth shall proclaim your praise. ℟.

READING II (2 Corinthians 5:20—6:2)

A reading from the second Letter of Saint Paul to the Corinthians

Be reconciled to God. Behold, now is the acceptable time.

Brothers and sisters:
We are ambassadors for Christ,
as if God were appealing through us.
We implore you on behalf of Christ,
be reconciled to God.
For our sake he made him to be sin who did not know sin,
so that we might become the righteousness of God in him.

Working together, then,
we appeal to you not to receive the grace of God in vain.
For he says:

In an acceptable time I heard you,
and on the day of salvation I helped you.

Behold, now is a very acceptable time;
behold, now is the day of salvation.

The word of the Lord. All: **Thanks be to God.**

GOSPEL (Matthew 6:1-6, 16-18)

VERSE BEFORE THE GOSPEL (*See* Psalm 95:8)

℣. Praise to you, Lord Jesus Christ, King of endless glory!
℟. **Praise to you, Lord Jesus Christ, King of endless glory!**
℣. If today you hear his voice,
harden not your hearts. ℟.

✠ **A reading from the holy Gospel according to Matthew**

All: **Glory to you, O Lord.**

Your Father who sees in secret will repay you.

Jesus said to his disciples:
"Take care not to perform righteous deeds

in order that people may see them;
otherwise, you will have no recompense from your heavenly Father.
When you give alms,
do not blow a trumpet before you,
as the hypocrites do in the synagogues and in the streets
to win the praise of others.
Amen, I say to you,
they have received their reward.
But when you give alms,
do not let your left hand know what your right is doing,
so that your almsgiving may be secret.
And your Father who sees in secret will repay you.

"When you pray,
do not be like the hypocrites,
who love to stand and pray in the synagogues and on street corners
so that others may see them.
Amen, I say to you,
they have received their reward.
But when you pray, go to your inner room,
close the door, and pray to your Father in secret.
And your Father who sees in secret will repay you.

"When you fast,
do not look gloomy like the hypocrites.
They neglect their appearance,
so that they may appear to others to be fasting.
Amen, I say to you, they have received their reward.
But when you fast,
anoint your head and wash your face,
so that you may not appear to be fasting,
except to your Father who is hidden.
And your Father who sees what is hidden will repay you."

The Gospel of the Lord. All: **Praise to you, Lord Jesus Christ.**

Blessing and Distribution of Ashes

Dear brethren (brothers and sisters), let us humbly ask God our Father that he be pleased to bless with the abundance of his grace these ashes, which we will put on our heads in penitence.

O God, who are moved by acts of humility
and respond with forgiveness to works of penance,
lend your merciful ear to our prayers
and in your kindness pour out the grace of your ✠ blessing
on your servants who are marked with these ashes,
that, as they follow the Lenten observances,
they may be worthy to come with minds made pure
to celebrate the Paschal Mystery of your Son.
Through Christ our Lord. All: **Amen.**

Or:

O God, who desire not the death of sinners,
but their conversion,
mercifully hear our prayers
and in your kindness be pleased to bless ✠ these ashes,
which we intend to receive upon our heads,
that we, who acknowledge we are but ashes
and shall return to dust,
may, through a steadfast observance of Lent,
gain pardon for sins and newness of life
after the likeness of your Risen Son.
Who lives and reigns for ever and ever. All: **Amen.**

To each who receives the ashes:

Repent, and believe in the Gospel.

or:

Remember that you are dust, and to dust you shall return.

The rite concludes with the Prayer of the Faithful.

Prayer over the Offerings

As we solemnly offer
the annual sacrifice for the beginning of Lent,
we entreat you, O Lord,
that, through works of penance and charity,
we may turn away from harmful pleasures
and, cleansed from our sins, may become worthy
to celebrate devoutly the Passion of your Son.
Who lives and reigns for ever and ever. All: **Amen.**

Communion Antiphon (Cf. Psalm 1:2-3)
He who ponders the law of the Lord day and night
will yield fruit in due season.

Prayer after Communion
May the Sacrament we have received sustain us, O Lord,
that our Lenten fast may be pleasing to you
and be for us a healing remedy.
Through Christ our Lord. All: **Amen.**

First Sunday of Lent

February 14, 2016

Reflection on the Gospel

The encounter of Jesus with "the devil" parallels our own encounters with "the devil." None of us—not even the God-Man—is exempt from temptation. By resisting the devil's temptations to act as "the Son of God," Jesus fully embraces his human identity. By resisting the devil's temptations to act against who God created us to be, we fully embrace our own human identity: graced beings created in the image of God.

- *Like Jesus, I resist temptation . . .*

—Living Liturgy™, *First Sunday of Lent 2016*

Entrance Antiphon (Cf. Psalm 91[90]:15-16)
When he calls on me, I will answer him;
I will deliver him and give him glory,
I will grant him length of days.

Collect
Grant, almighty God,
through the yearly observances of holy Lent,
that we may grow in understanding

of the riches hidden in Christ
and by worthy conduct pursue their effects.
Through our Lord Jesus Christ, your Son,
who lives and reigns with you in the unity of the Holy Spirit,
one God, for ever and ever. All: **Amen.**

Reading I (L 24-C) (Deuteronomy 26:4-10)

A reading from the Book of Deuteronomy

The confession of faith of the chosen people.

Moses spoke to the people, saying:
"The priest shall receive the basket from you
and shall set it in front of the altar of the Lord,
your God.
Then you shall declare before the Lord, your God,
'My father was a wandering Aramean
who went down to Egypt with a small household
and lived there as an alien.
But there he became a nation
great, strong, and numerous.
When the Egyptians maltreated and oppressed us,
imposing hard labor upon us,
we cried to the Lord, the God of our fathers,
and he heard our cry
and saw our affliction, our toil, and our oppression.
He brought us out of Egypt
with his strong hand and outstretched arm,
with terrifying power, with signs and wonders;
and bringing us into this country,
he gave us this land flowing with milk and honey.
Therefore, I have now brought you the firstfruits
of the products of the soil
which you, O Lord, have given me.'
And having set them before the Lord, your God,
you shall bow down in his presence."

The word of the Lord. All: **Thanks be to God.**

Responsorial Psalm 91

Psalm 91:1-2, 10-11, 12-13, 14-15

℟. (*See* 15b) **Be with me, Lord, when I am in trouble.**

You who dwell in the shelter of the Most High,
 who abide in the shadow of the Almighty,
say to the LORD, "My refuge and fortress,
 my God in whom I trust." ℟.

No evil shall befall you,
 nor shall affliction come near your tent,
for to his angels he has given command about you,
 that they guard you in all your ways. ℟.

Upon their hands they shall bear you up,
 lest you dash your foot against a stone.
You shall tread upon the asp and the viper;
 you shall trample down the lion and the dragon. ℟.

Because he clings to me, I will deliver him;
 I will set him on high because he acknowledges my name.
He shall call upon me, and I will answer him;
 I will be with him in distress;
I will deliver him and glorify him. ℟.

Reading II (Romans 10:8-13)

A reading from the Letter of Saint Paul to the Romans

The confession of faith of all believers in Christ.

Brothers and sisters:
What does Scripture say?
The word is near you,
in your mouth and in your heart
—that is, the word of faith that we preach—,
for, if you confess with your mouth that Jesus is Lord
and believe in your heart that God raised him from the dead,
you will be saved.
For one believes with the heart and so is justified,
and one confesses with the mouth and so is saved.
For the Scripture says,
No one who believes in him will be put to shame.
For there is no distinction between Jew and Greek;
the same Lord is Lord of all,
enriching all who call upon him.
For "everyone who calls on the name of the Lord will be saved."

The word of the Lord. All: **Thanks be to God.**

GOSPEL (Luke 4:1-13)

VERSE BEFORE THE GOSPEL (Matthew 4:4b)

℣. Praise to you, Lord Jesus Christ, king of endless glory!
℟. **Praise to you, Lord Jesus Christ, king of endless glory!**
℣. One does not live on bread alone,
but on every word that comes forth from the mouth of God. ℟.

✠ **A reading from the holy Gospel according to Luke**

All: **Glory to you, O Lord.**

Jesus was led by the Spirit into the desert and was tempted.

Filled with the Holy Spirit, Jesus returned from the Jordan
and was led by the Spirit into the desert for forty days,
to be tempted by the devil.
He ate nothing during those days,
and when they were over he was hungry.

The devil said to him,
"If you are the Son of God,
command this stone to become bread."
Jesus answered him,
"It is written, *One does not live on bread alone.*"
Then he took him up and showed him
all the kingdoms of the world in a single instant.
The devil said to him,
"I shall give to you all this power and glory;
for it has been handed over to me,
and I may give it to whomever I wish.
All this will be yours, if you worship me."
Jesus said to him in reply,
"It is written:
You shall worship the Lord, your God,
***and him alone shall you serve.*"**
Then he led him to Jerusalem,
made him stand on the parapet of the temple, and said to him,
"If you are the Son of God,
throw yourself down from here, for it is written:
He will command his angels concerning you,
to guard you,
and:
With their hands they will support you,
***lest you dash your foot against a stone.*"**
Jesus said to him in reply,
"It also says,
***You shall not put the Lord, your God, to the test.*"**
When the devil had finished every temptation,
he departed from him for a time.

The Gospel of the Lord. All: **Praise to you, Lord Jesus Christ.**

Prayer over the Offerings

Give us the right dispositions, O Lord, we pray,
to make these offerings,
for with them we celebrate the beginning

of this venerable and sacred time.
Through Christ our Lord. All: **Amen.**

Communion Antiphon (Matthew 4:4)

One does not live by bread alone,
but by every word that comes forth from the mouth of God.

Or:

(Cf. Psalm 91[90]:4)
The Lord will conceal you with his pinions,
and under his wings you will trust.

Prayer after Communion

Renewed now with heavenly bread,
by which faith is nourished, hope increased,
and charity strengthened,
we pray, O Lord,
that we may learn to hunger for Christ,
the true and living Bread,
and strive to live by every word
which proceeds from your mouth.
Through Christ our Lord. All: **Amen.**

Second Sunday of Lent

February 21, 2016

Reflection on the Gospel

Moses and Elijah speak of exodus, of going forth to Jerusalem; by contrast, Peter speaks of pitching tents, of staying on the mountain in the moment of glory. He chooses to stay with the beauty and wonder of the glory he sees, but by doing so he would deny his own share in this same glory. Are we to stay or to go? Both! Disciples must stay in Jesus' Presence and "listen to him," and go to their own Jerusalem to pass over from death to new Life.

- *I, like Jesus, am transformed to new life . . .*

—Living Liturgy™, *Second Sunday of Lent 2016*

ENTRANCE ANTIPHON (Cf. Psalm 27[26]:8-9)
Of you my heart has spoken: Seek his face.
It is your face, O Lord, that I seek;
hide not your face from me.

Or:

(Cf. Psalm 25[24]:6, 2, 22)
Remember your compassion, O Lord,
and your merciful love, for they are from of old.
Let not our enemies exult over us.
Redeem us, O God of Israel, from all our distress.

COLLECT
O God, who have commanded us
to listen to your beloved Son,
be pleased, we pray,
to nourish us inwardly by your word,
that, with spiritual sight made pure,
we may rejoice to behold your glory.
Through our Lord Jesus Christ, your Son,
who lives and reigns with you in the unity of the Holy Spirit,
one God, for ever and ever. All: **Amen.**

READING I (L 27-C) (Genesis 15:5-12, 17-18)
A reading from the Book of Genesis

God made a covenant with Abraham, his faithful servant.

The Lord God took Abram outside and said,
"Look up at the sky and count the stars, if you can.
Just so," he added, "shall your descendants be."
Abram put his faith in the LORD,
who credited it to him as an act of righteousness.

He then said to him,
"I am the LORD who brought you from Ur of the Chaldeans
to give you this land as a possession."
"O Lord GOD," he asked,
"how am I to know that I shall possess it?"

He answered him,
"Bring me a three-year-old heifer, a three-year-old she-goat,
a three-year-old ram, a turtledove, and a young pigeon."
Abram brought him all these, split them in two,
and placed each half opposite the other;
but the birds he did not cut up.
Birds of prey swooped down on the carcasses,
but Abram stayed with them.
As the sun was about to set, a trance fell upon Abram,
and a deep, terrifying darkness enveloped him.

When the sun had set and it was dark,
there appeared a smoking fire pot and a flaming torch,
which passed between those pieces.
It was on that occasion that the LORD made a covenant with Abram,
saying: "To your descendants I give this land,
from the Wadi of Egypt to the Great River, the Euphrates."

The word of the Lord. All: **Thanks be to God.**

RESPONSORIAL PSALM 27

P-491

Psalm 27:1, 7-8, 8-9, 13-14

℟. (1a) **The Lord is my light and my salvation.**

The LORD is my light and my salvation;
whom should I fear?

(continued)

The LORD is my life's refuge;
of whom should I be afraid? ℟.

Hear, O LORD, the sound of my call;
have pity on me, and answer me.
Of you my heart speaks; you my glance seeks. ℟.

Your presence, O LORD, I seek.
Hide not your face from me;
do not in anger repel your servant.
You are my helper: cast me not off. ℟.

I believe that I shall see the bounty of the LORD
in the land of the living.
Wait for the LORD with courage;
be stouthearted, and wait for the LORD. ℟.

READING II (Philippians 3:17—4:1) *or* Shorter Form [ ] (Philippians 3:20—4:1)

A reading from the Letter of Saint Paul to the Philippians

Christ will change our lowly body to conform with his glorified body.

Join with others in being imitators of me, brothers and sisters,
and observe those who thus conduct themselves
according to the model you have in us.
For many, as I have often told you
and now tell you even in tears,
conduct themselves as enemies of the cross of Christ.
Their end is destruction.
Their god is their stomach;
their glory is in their "shame."
Their minds are occupied with earthly things.
But [our citizenship is in heaven,
and from it we also await a savior, the Lord Jesus Christ.
He will change our lowly body
to conform with his glorified body
by the power that enables him also
to bring all things into subjection to himself.

Therefore, my brothers and sisters,
whom I love and long for, my joy and crown,
in this way stand firm in the Lord.]

The word of the Lord. All: **Thanks be to God.**

GOSPEL (Luke 9:28b-36)

VERSE BEFORE THE GOSPEL (See Matthew 17:5)

℣. Praise and honor to you, Lord Jesus Christ!
℟. **Praise and honor to you, Lord Jesus Christ!**
℣. From the shining cloud the Father's voice is heard:
This is my beloved Son, hear him. ℟.

✠ **A reading from the holy Gospel according to Luke**

All: **Glory to you, O Lord.**

While he was praying his face changed in appearance and his clothing became dazzling white.

Jesus took Peter, John, and James
and went up the mountain to pray.
While he was praying his face changed in appearance
and his clothing became dazzling white.
And behold, two men were conversing with him, Moses and Elijah,
who appeared in glory and spoke of his exodus
that he was going to accomplish in Jerusalem.
Peter and his companions had been overcome by sleep,
but becoming fully awake,
they saw his glory and the two men standing with him.
As they were about to part from him, Peter said to Jesus,
"Master, it is good that we are here;
let us make three tents,
one for you, one for Moses, and one for Elijah."
But he did not know what he was saying.
While he was still speaking,
a cloud came and cast a shadow over them,
and they became frightened when they entered the cloud.

Then from the cloud came a voice that said,
"This is my chosen Son; listen to him."
After the voice had spoken, Jesus was found alone.
They fell silent and did not at that time
tell anyone what they had seen.

The Gospel of the Lord. All: **Praise to you, Lord Jesus Christ.**

Prayer over the Offerings

May this sacrifice, O Lord, we pray,
cleanse us of our faults
and sanctify your faithful in body and mind
for the celebration of the paschal festivities.
Through Christ our Lord. All: **Amen.**

Communion Antiphon (Matthew 17:5)

This is my beloved Son, with whom I am well pleased;
listen to him.

Prayer after Communion

As we receive these glorious mysteries,
we make thanksgiving to you, O Lord,
for allowing us while still on earth
to be partakers even now of the things of heaven.
Through Christ our Lord. All: **Amen.**

Third Sunday of Lent

February 28, 2016

Reflection on the Gospel

Jesus attacks a misconception his hearers held: tragic death—and illness or other misfortunes—are not the result of sinning. Sinning is always our own choice, not a consequence of some impersonal outside force. Jesus issues a clear warning: sinfulness is not to be ignored—we must repent and bear the good fruit of right living. If not, we will perish. The work of Lent is to choose the eternal Life God continuously cultivates within us. God never gives up on us.

- *I choose to repent and change that . . .*

—Living Liturgy™, *Third Sunday of Lent 2016*

Entrance Antiphon (Cf. Psalm 25[24]:15-16)

My eyes are always on the Lord,
for he rescues my feet from the snare.
Turn to me and have mercy on me,
for I am alone and poor.

Or:

(Cf. Ezekiel 36:23-26)
When I prove my holiness among you,
I will gather you from all the foreign lands;
and I will pour clean water upon you
and cleanse you from all your impurities,
and I will give you a new spirit, says the Lord.

Collect

O God, author of every mercy and of all goodness,
who in fasting, prayer and almsgiving
have shown us a remedy for sin,
look graciously on this confession of our lowliness,
that we, who are bowed down by our conscience,
may always be lifted up by your mercy.
Through our Lord Jesus Christ, your Son,

who lives and reigns with you in the unity of the Holy Spirit,
one God, for ever and ever. All: **Amen.**

The readings given for Year A, n. 28, may be used in place of these.

READING I (L 30-C) (Exodus 3:1-8a, 13-15)

A reading from the Book of Exodus

"I AM" sent me to you.

Moses was tending the flock of his father-in-law Jethro,
the priest of Midian.
Leading the flock across the desert, he came to Horeb,
the mountain of God.
There an angel of the LORD appeared to Moses in fire
flaming out of a bush.
As he looked on, he was surprised to see that the bush,
though on fire, was not consumed.
So Moses decided,
"I must go over to look at this remarkable sight,
and see why the bush is not burned."

When the LORD saw him coming over to look at it more closely,
God called out to him from the bush, "Moses! Moses!"
He answered, "Here I am."
God said, "Come no nearer!
Remove the sandals from your feet,
for the place where you stand is holy ground.
I am the God of your fathers," he continued,
"the God of Abraham, the God of Isaac, the God of Jacob."
Moses hid his face, for he was afraid to look at God.
But the LORD said,
"I have witnessed the affliction of my people in Egypt
and have heard their cry of complaint against their slave drivers,
so I know well what they are suffering.
Therefore I have come down to rescue them
from the hands of the Egyptians

and lead them out of that land into a good and spacious land,
a land flowing with milk and honey."

Moses said to God, "But when I go to the Israelites
and say to them, 'The God of your fathers has sent me to you,'
if they ask me, 'What is his name?' what am I to tell them?"
God replied, "I am who am."
Then he added, "This is what you shall tell the Israelites:
I AM sent me to you."

God spoke further to Moses, "Thus shall you say to the Israelites:
The LORD, the God of your fathers,
the God of Abraham, the God of Isaac, the God of Jacob,
has sent me to you.

"This is my name forever;
thus am I to be remembered through all generations."

The word of the Lord. All: Thanks be to God.

RESPONSORIAL PSALM 103

P-492

Psalm 103:1-2, 3-4, 6-7, 8, 11

℟. (8a) **The Lord is kind and merciful.**

Bless the LORD, O my soul;
and all my being, bless his holy name.
Bless the LORD, O my soul,
and forget not all his benefits. ℟.

He pardons all your iniquities,
heals all your ills.

(continued)

He redeems your life from destruction,
crowns you with kindness and compassion. ℟.

The LORD secures justice
and the rights of all the oppressed.
He has made known his ways to Moses,
and his deeds to the children of Israel. ℟.

Merciful and gracious is the LORD,
slow to anger and abounding in kindness.
For as the heavens are high above the earth,
so surpassing is his kindness toward those who fear him. ℟.

READING II (1 Corinthians 10:1-6, 10-12)

A reading from the first Letter of Saint Paul to the Corinthians

The life of the people with Moses in the desert was written down as a warning to us.

I do not want you to be unaware, brothers and sisters,
that our ancestors were all under the cloud
and all passed through the sea,
and all of them were baptized into Moses
in the cloud and in the sea.
All ate the same spiritual food,
and all drank the same spiritual drink,
for they drank from a spiritual rock that followed them,
and the rock was the Christ.
Yet God was not pleased with most of them,
for they were struck down in the desert.

These things happened as examples for us,
so that we might not desire evil things, as they did.
Do not grumble as some of them did,
and suffered death by the destroyer.
These things happened to them as an example,
and they have been written down as a warning to us,
upon whom the end of the ages has come.

Therefore, whoever thinks he is standing secure
should take care not to fall.

The word of the Lord. All: **Thanks be to God.**

GOSPEL (Luke 13:1-9)

VERSE BEFORE THE GOSPEL (Matthew 4:17)

℣. Praise to you, Lord Jesus Christ, king of endless glory!
℟. **Praise to you, Lord Jesus Christ, king of endless glory!**
℣. Repent, says the Lord;
the kingdom of heaven is at hand. ℟.

✠ **A reading from the holy Gospel according to Luke**

All: **Glory to you, O Lord.**

If you do not repent, you will all perish as they did.

Some people told Jesus about the Galileans
whose blood Pilate had mingled with the blood of their sacrifices.
Jesus said to them in reply,
"Do you think that because these Galileans suffered in this way
they were greater sinners than all other Galileans?
By no means!
But I tell you, if you do not repent,
you will all perish as they did!
Or those eighteen people who were killed
when the tower at Siloam fell on them—
do you think they were more guilty
than everyone else who lived in Jerusalem?
By no means!
But I tell you, if you do not repent,
you will all perish as they did!"

And he told them this parable:
"There once was a person who had a fig tree planted in his orchard,
and when he came in search of fruit on it but found none,

he said to the gardener,
'For three years now I have come in search of fruit on this fig tree
but have found none.
So cut it down.
Why should it exhaust the soil?'
He said to him in reply,
'Sir, leave it for this year also,
and I shall cultivate the ground around it and fertilize it;
it may bear fruit in the future.
If not you can cut it down.'"

The Gospel of the Lord. All: **Praise to you, Lord Jesus Christ.**

Prayer over the Offerings

Be pleased, O Lord, with these sacrificial offerings,
and grant that we who beseech pardon for our own sins,
may take care to forgive our neighbor.
Through Christ our Lord. All: **Amen.**

Communion Antiphon (Cf. Psalm 84[83]:4-5)

The sparrow finds a home,
and the swallow a nest for her young:
by your altars, O Lord of hosts, my King and my God.
Blessed are they who dwell in your house,
for ever singing your praise.

Prayer after Communion

As we receive the pledge
of things yet hidden in heaven
and are nourished while still on earth
with the Bread that comes from on high,
we humbly entreat you, O Lord,
that what is being brought about in us in mystery
may come to true completion.
Through Christ our Lord. All: **Amen.**

Fourth Sunday of Lent

March 6, 2016

Reflection on the Gospel

According to "the Pharisees and scribes," Jesus entertained all the wrong people! In the parable, the prodigal son entertained all the wrong desires! The elder son entertained anger and jealousy, pettiness and closed heartedness! On the other hand, the father tendered reconciliation leading to feasting. In our lives, God tenders mercy and forgiveness leading to new Life. What do we entertain in our hearts? What do we tender in our relationships? With whom do we feast?

- *Mercy transforms; forgiveness . . .*

—Living Liturgy™, *Fourth Sunday of Lent 2016*

Entrance Antiphon (Cf. Isaiah 66:10-11)

Rejoice, Jerusalem, and all who love her.
Be joyful, all who were in mourning;
exult and be satisfied at her consoling breast.

Collect

O God, who through your Word
reconcile the human race to yourself in a wonderful way,
grant, we pray,
that with prompt devotion and eager faith
the Christian people may hasten
toward the solemn celebrations to come.
Through our Lord Jesus Christ, your Son,
who lives and reigns with you in the unity of the Holy Spirit,
one God, for ever and ever. All: **Amen.**

The readings given for Year A, n. 31, may be used in place of these.

Reading I (L 33-C) (Joshua 5:9a, 10-12)

A reading from the Book of Joshua

The people of God entered the promised land and there kept the Passover.

The LORD said to Joshua,
"Today I have removed the reproach of Egypt from you."

While the Israelites were encamped at Gilgal on the plains of Jericho,
they celebrated the Passover
on the evening of the fourteenth of the month.
On the day after the Passover,
they ate of the produce of the land
in the form of unleavened cakes and parched grain.
On that same day after the Passover,
on which they ate of the produce of the land, the manna ceased.
No longer was there manna for the Israelites,
who that year ate of the yield of the land of Canaan.

The word of the Lord. All: **Thanks be to God.**

RESPONSORIAL PSALM 34

Psalm 34:2-3, 4-5, 6-7

℟. (9a) **Taste and see the goodness of the Lord.**

I will bless the LORD at all times;
his praise shall be ever in my mouth.
Let my soul glory in the LORD;
the lowly will hear me and be glad. ℟.

Glorify the LORD with me,
let us together extol his name.
I sought the LORD, and he answered me
and delivered me from all my fears. ℟.

Look to him that you may be radiant with joy,
and your faces may not blush with shame.
When the poor one called out, the LORD heard,
and from all his distress he saved him. ℟.

READING II (2 Corinthians 5:17-21)

A reading from the second Letter of Saint Paul to the Corinthians

God reconciled us to himself through Christ.

Brothers and sisters:
Whoever is in Christ is a new creation:
the old things have passed away;
behold, new things have come.
And all this is from God,
who has reconciled us to himself through Christ
and given us the ministry of reconciliation,
namely, God was reconciling the world to himself in Christ,
not counting their trespasses against them
and entrusting to us the message of reconciliation.
So we are ambassadors for Christ,
as if God were appealing through us.
We implore you on behalf of Christ,
be reconciled to God.
For our sake he made him to be sin who did not know sin,
so that we might become the righteousness of God in him.

The word of the Lord. All: **Thanks be to God.**

GOSPEL (Luke 15:1-3, 11-32)

VERSE BEFORE THE GOSPEL (Luke 15:18)

℣. Praise to you, Lord Jesus Christ, king of endless glory!
℟. **Praise to you, Lord Jesus Christ, king of endless glory!**
℣. I will get up and go to my Father and shall say to him:
Father, I have sinned against heaven and against you. ℟.

✠ A reading from the holy Gospel according to Luke

All: **Glory to you, O Lord.**

Your brother was dead and has come to life again.

Tax collectors and sinners were all drawing near to listen to Jesus,
but the Pharisees and scribes began to complain, saying,
"This man welcomes sinners and eats with them."
So to them Jesus addressed this parable:
"A man had two sons, and the younger son said to his father,
'Father give me the share of your estate that should come to me.'
So the father divided the property between them.
After a few days, the younger son collected all his belongings
and set off to a distant country
where he squandered his inheritance on a life of dissipation.
When he had freely spent everything,
a severe famine struck that country,
and he found himself in dire need.
So he hired himself out to one of the local citizens
who sent him to his farm to tend the swine.
And he longed to eat his fill of the pods on which the swine fed,
but nobody gave him any.
Coming to his senses he thought,
'How many of my father's hired workers
have more than enough food to eat,
but here am I, dying from hunger.
I shall get up and go to my father and I shall say to him,
"Father, I have sinned against heaven and against you.
I no longer deserve to be called your son;
treat me as you would treat one of your hired workers."'

So he got up and went back to his father.
While he was still a long way off,
his father caught sight of him, and was filled with compassion.
He ran to his son, embraced him and kissed him.
His son said to him,
'Father, I have sinned against heaven and against you;
I no longer deserve to be called your son.'
But his father ordered his servants,
'Quickly bring the finest robe and put it on him;
put a ring on his finger and sandals on his feet.
Take the fattened calf and slaughter it.
Then let us celebrate with a feast,
because this son of mine was dead, and has come to life again;
he was lost, and has been found.'
Then the celebration began.
Now the older son had been out in the field
and, on his way back, as he neared the house,
he heard the sound of music and dancing.
He called one of the servants and asked what this might mean.
The servant said to him,
'Your brother has returned
and your father has slaughtered the fattened calf
because he has him back safe and sound.'
He became angry,
and when he refused to enter the house,
his father came out and pleaded with him.
He said to his father in reply,
'Look, all these years I served you
and not once did I disobey your orders;
yet you never gave me even a young goat to feast on with my friends.

But when your son returns
who swallowed up your property with prostitutes,
for him you slaughter the fattened calf.'
He said to him,
'My son, you are here with me always;
everything I have is yours.
But now we must celebrate and rejoice,
because your brother was dead and has come to life again;
he was lost and has been found.' "

The Gospel of the Lord. All: **Praise to you, Lord Jesus Christ.**

Prayer over the Offerings

We place before you with joy these offerings,
which bring eternal remedy, O Lord,
praying that we may both faithfully revere them
and present them to you, as is fitting,
for the salvation of all the world.
Through Christ our Lord. All: **Amen.**

Communion Antiphon (Luke 15:32)

You must rejoice, my son,
for your brother was dead and has come to life;
he was lost and is found.

Prayer after Communion

O God, who enlighten everyone who comes into this world,
illuminate our hearts, we pray,
with the splendor of your grace,
that we may always ponder
what is worthy and pleasing to your majesty
and love you in all sincerity.
Through Christ our Lord. All: **Amen.**

Fifth Sunday of Lent

March 13, 2016

Reflection on the Gospel

The "scribes and the Pharisees" use the proscription of the law in an attempt to entrap Jesus. He responds by confronting them with the reality of their own hard-heartedness and sinfulness. They slink away "one by one," leaving the adulterous woman alone to face Jesus. He extends mercy and compassion as well as judgment and a command to change her life. Do we dare to stand alone before Jesus, bare our own sinfulness, and hear him say to us, "Go, and from now on do not sin any more"?

- *I choose to . . . the stone of hard-heartedness.*

—Living Liturgy™, *Fifth Sunday of Lent 2016*

Entrance Antiphon (Cf. Psalm 43[42]:1-2)

Give me justice, O God,
and plead my cause against a nation that is faithless.
From the deceitful and cunning rescue me,
for you, O God, are my strength.

Collect

By your help, we beseech you, Lord our God,
may we walk eagerly in that same charity
with which, out of love for the world,
your Son handed himself over to death.
Through our Lord Jesus Christ, your Son,
who lives and reigns with you in the unity of the Holy Spirit,
one God, for ever and ever. All: **Amen.**

The readings given for Year A, n. 34, may be used in place of these.

Reading I (L 36-C) (Isaiah 43:16-21)

A reading from the Book of the Prophet Isaiah

See, I am doing something new and I give my people drink.

Thus says the Lord,
who opens a way in the sea
and a path in the mighty waters,

who leads out chariots and horsemen,
a powerful army,
till they lie prostrate together, never to rise,
snuffed out and quenched like a wick.
Remember not the events of the past,
the things of long ago consider not;
see, I am doing something new!
Now it springs forth, do you not perceive it?
In the desert I make a way,
in the wasteland, rivers.
Wild beasts honor me,
jackals and ostriches,
for I put water in the desert
and rivers in the wasteland
for my chosen people to drink,
the people whom I formed for myself,
that they might announce my praise.

The word of the Lord. All: **Thanks be to God.**

Responsorial Psalm 126

P-494

Psalm 126:1-2, 2-3, 4-5, 6

℟. (3) **The Lord has done great things for us; we are filled with joy.**

When the Lord brought back the captives of Zion,
we were like men dreaming.
Then our mouth was filled with laughter,
and our tongue with rejoicing. ℟.

Then they said among the nations,
"The Lord has done great things for them."

The LORD has done great things for us;
we are glad indeed. ℟.

Restore our fortunes, O LORD,
like the torrents in the southern desert.
Those that sow in tears
shall reap rejoicing. ℟.

Although they go forth weeping,
carrying the seed to be sown,
they shall come back rejoicing,
carrying their sheaves. ℟.

READING II (Philippians 3:8-14)

A reading from the Letter of Saint Paul to the Philippians

Because of Christ, I consider everything as a loss, being conformed to his death.

Brothers and sisters:
I consider everything as a loss
because of the supreme good of knowing Christ Jesus my Lord.
For his sake I have accepted the loss of all things
and I consider them so much rubbish,
that I may gain Christ and be found in him,
not having any righteousness of my own based on the law
but that which comes through faith in Christ,
the righteousness from God,
depending on faith to know him and the power of his resurrection
and the sharing of his sufferings by being conformed to his death,
if somehow I may attain the resurrection from the dead.

It is not that I have already taken hold of it
or have already attained perfect maturity,
but I continue my pursuit in hope that I may possess it,
since I have indeed been taken possession of by Christ Jesus.

Brothers and sisters, I for my part
do not consider myself to have taken possession.
Just one thing: forgetting what lies behind
but straining forward to what lies ahead,
I continue my pursuit toward the goal,
the prize of God's upward calling, in Christ Jesus.

The word of the Lord. All: **Thanks be to God.**

GOSPEL (John 8:1-11)

VERSE BEFORE THE GOSPEL (Joel 2:12-13)

℣. Glory to you, Word of God, Lord Jesus Christ!
℟. **Glory to you, Word of God, Lord Jesus Christ!**
℣. Even now, says the Lord,
return to me with your whole heart;
for I am gracious and merciful. ℟.

✠ A reading from the holy Gospel according to John

All: **Glory to you, O Lord.**

Let the one among you who is without sin be the first to throw a stone at her.

Jesus went to the Mount of Olives.
But early in the morning he arrived again in the temple area,
and all the people started coming to him,
and he sat down and taught them.
Then the scribes and the Pharisees brought a woman
who had been caught in adultery
and made her stand in the middle.
They said to him,
"Teacher, this woman was caught
in the very act of committing adultery.
Now in the law, Moses commanded us to stone such women.
So what do you say?"
They said this to test him,
so that they could have some charge to bring against him.

Jesus bent down and began to write on the ground with his finger.
But when they continued asking him,
he straightened up and said to them,
"Let the one among you who is without sin
be the first to throw a stone at her."
Again he bent down and wrote on the ground.
And in response, they went away one by one,
beginning with the elders.
So he was left alone with the woman before him.
Then Jesus straightened up and said to her,
"Woman, where are they?
Has no one condemned you?"
She replied, "No one, sir."
Then Jesus said, "Neither do I condemn you.
Go, and from now on do not sin any more."

The Gospel of the Lord. All: **Praise to you, Lord Jesus Christ.**

Prayer over the Offerings

Hear us, almighty God,
and, having instilled in your servants
the teachings of the Christian faith,
graciously purify them
by the working of this sacrifice.
Through Christ our Lord. All: **Amen.**

Communion Antiphon (John 8:10-11)

Has no one condemned you, woman? No one, Lord.
Neither shall I condemn you. From now on, sin no more.

Prayer after Communion

We pray, almighty God,
that we may always be counted among the members of Christ,
in whose Body and Blood we have communion.
Who lives and reigns for ever and ever. All: **Amen.**

Palm Sunday of the Lord's Passion

March 20, 2016

Reflection on the Gospel

Neither the Jewish leadership, the Roman leadership, nor the apostles understand. Throughout Luke's passion account, Jesus is trying to turn his accusers and hearers away from their understanding of kingdom to embracing "the kingdom of God." Even on the cross, he continues to show how different his kingdom is, for he forgives the very ones who cause him suffering and death. The gift of his death? He confers on us his kingdom and invites us to be with him in Paradise.

- *Like Jesus, I hope to be guilty of . . .*

—Living Liturgy™, *Palm Sunday 2016*

The Commemoration of the Lord's Entrance into Jerusalem

FIRST FORM: THE PROCESSION

The congregation assembles in a secondary church or chapel or in some other suitable place distinct from the church to which the procession will move. The faithful carry palm branches.

Antiphon

Hosanna to the Son of David;
blessed is he who comes in the name of the Lord, the King of Israel.
Hosanna in the highest.

Priest: In the name of the Father, and of the Son, and of the Holy Spirit.
All: **Amen.**

Then he greets the people in the usual way. A brief address is given, in which the faithful are invited to participate actively and consciously in the celebration of this day, in these or similar words:

Dear brethren (brothers and sisters),
since the beginning of Lent until now

we have prepared our hearts by penance and charitable works.
Today we gather together to herald with the whole Church
the beginning of the celebration
of our Lord's Paschal Mystery,
that is to say, of his Passion and Resurrection.
For it was to accomplish this mystery
that he entered his own city of Jerusalem.
Therefore, with all faith and devotion,
let us commemorate
the Lord's entry into the city for our salvation,
following in his footsteps,
so that, being made by his grace partakers of the Cross,
we may have a share also in his Resurrection and in his life.

Let us pray.

A Almighty ever-living God,
sanctify ✠ these branches with your blessing,
that we, who follow Christ the King in exultation,
may reach the eternal Jerusalem through him.
Who lives and reigns for ever and ever. All: **Amen.**

B Increase the faith of those who place their hope in you, O God,
and graciously hear the prayers of those who call on you,
that we, who today hold high these branches
to hail Christ in his triumph,
may bear fruit for you by good works accomplished in him.
Who lives and reigns for ever and ever. All: **Amen.**

THE READING OF THE GOSPEL

GOSPEL (L 37-C) (Luke 19:28-40)

✠ A reading from the holy Gospel according to Luke

All: **Glory to you, O Lord.**

Blessed is he who comes in the name of the Lord.

**Jesus proceeded on his journey up to Jerusalem.
As he drew near to Bethphage and Bethany
at the place called the Mount of Olives,
he sent two of his disciples.
He said, "Go into the village opposite you,
and as you enter it you will find a colt tethered
on which no one has ever sat.
Untie it and bring it here.**

And if anyone should ask you,
'Why are you untying it?'
you will answer,
'The Master has need of it.'"
So those who had been sent went off
and found everything just as he had told them.
And as they were untying the colt, its owners said to them,
"Why are you untying this colt?"
They answered,
"The Master has need of it."
So they brought it to Jesus,
threw their cloaks over the colt,
and helped Jesus to mount.
As he rode along,
the people were spreading their cloaks on the road;
and now as he was approaching the slope of the Mount of Olives,
the whole multitude of his disciples
began to praise God aloud with joy
for all the mighty deeds they had seen.
They proclaimed:
"Blessed is the king who comes
in the name of the Lord.
Peace in heaven
and glory in the highest."
Some of the Pharisees in the crowd said to him,
"Teacher, rebuke your disciples."
He said in reply,
"I tell you, if they keep silent,
the stones will cry out!"

The Gospel of the Lord. All: **Praise to you, Lord Jesus Christ.**

PROCESSION WITH THE BLESSED BRANCHES

SECOND FORM: THE SOLEMN ENTRANCE

The commemoration of the Lord's entrance may be celebrated before the principal Mass with the solemn entrance, which takes place within the church.

THIRD FORM: THE SIMPLE ENTRANCE
The Lord's entrance is commemorated with the following simple entrance.

ENTRANCE ANTIPHON (Cf. John 12:1, 12-13; Psalm 24[23]:9-10)
Six days before the Passover,
when the Lord came into the city of Jerusalem,
the children ran to meet him;
in their hands they carried palm branches
and with a loud voice cried out:
*Hosanna in the highest!

Blessed are you, who have come in your abundant mercy!
O gates, lift high your heads;
grow higher, ancient doors.
Let him enter, the king of glory!
Who is this king of glory?
He, the Lord of hosts, he is the king of glory.
*Hosanna in the highest!

Blessed are you, who have come in your abundant mercy!

COLLECT
Almighty ever-living God,
who as an example of humility for the human race to follow
caused our Savior to take flesh and submit to the Cross,
graciously grant that we may heed his lesson of patient suffering
and so merit a share in his Resurrection.
Who lives and reigns with you in the unity of the Holy Spirit,
one God, for ever and ever. All: **Amen.**

READING I (L 38-ABC) (Isaiah 50:4-7)
A reading from the Book of the Prophet Isaiah

My face I did not shield from buffets and spitting, knowing that I shall not be put to shame.

The Lord GOD has given me
a well-trained tongue,
that I might know how to speak to the weary
a word that will rouse them.
Morning after morning
he opens my ear that I may hear;
and I have not rebelled,
have not turned back.

I gave my back to those who beat me,
my cheeks to those who plucked my beard;
my face I did not shield
from buffets and spitting.

The Lord God is my help,
therefore I am not disgraced;
I have set my face like flint,
knowing that I shall not be put to shame.

The word of the Lord. All: **Thanks be to God.**

Responsorial Psalm 22

P-115

Psalm 22:8-9, 17-18, 19-20, 23-24

℟. (2a) **My God, my God, why have you abandoned me?**

All who see me scoff at me;
they mock me with parted lips, they wag their heads:
"He relied on the Lord; let him deliver him,
let him rescue him, if he loves him." ℟.

Indeed, many dogs surround me,
a pack of evildoers closes in upon me;
they have pierced my hands and my feet;
I can count all my bones. ℟.

They divide my garments among them,
and for my vesture they cast lots.
But you, O Lord, be not far from me;
O my help, hasten to aid me. ℟.

I will proclaim your name to my brethren;
in the midst of the assembly I will praise you:
"You who fear the Lord, praise him;
all you descendants of Jacob, give glory to him;
revere him, all you descendants of Israel!" ℟.

Reading II (Philippians 2:6-11)

A reading from the Letter of Saint Paul to the Philippians

Christ humbled himself. Because of this God greatly exalted him.

Christ Jesus, though he was in the form of God,
did not regard equality with God
something to be grasped.
Rather, he emptied himself,
taking the form of a slave,
coming in human likeness;
and found human in appearance,
he humbled himself,
becoming obedient to the point of death,
even death on a cross.
Because of this, God greatly exalted him
and bestowed on him the name
which is above every name,
that at the name of Jesus
every knee should bend,
of those in heaven and on earth and under the earth,
and every tongue confess that
Jesus Christ is Lord,
to the glory of God the Father.

The word of the Lord. All: **Thanks be to God.**

* The message of the liturgy in proclaiming the passion narratives in full is to enable the assembly to see vividly the love of Christ for each person, despite their sins, a love that even death could not vanquish. The crimes during the Passion of Christ cannot be attributed indiscriminately to all Jews of that time, nor to Jews today. The Jewish people should not be referred to as though rejected or cursed, as if this view followed from Scripture. The Church ever keeps in mind that Jesus, his mother Mary, and the Apostles all were Jewish. As the Church has always held, Christ freely suffered his passion and death because of the sins of all, that all might be saved.

Gospel (Luke 22:14—23:56) *or* Shorter Form [ ] (Luke 23:1-49)

Verse before the Gospel (Philippians 2:8-9)

℣. Praise to you, Lord Jesus Christ, King of endless glory!

℟. Praise to you, Lord Jesus Christ, King of endless glory!

℣. Christ became obedient to the point of death,
even death on a cross.
Because of this, God greatly exalted him
and bestowed on him the name which is above every
name. ℟.

The symbols in the following passion narrative represent:

C. Narrator;
✠ Christ;
S. speakers other than Christ;
SS. groups of speakers.

The Passion of our Lord Jesus Christ according to Luke

The Passion of our Lord Jesus Christ.

C. **When the hour came,**
Jesus took his place at table with the apostles.
He said to them,
✠ **"I have eagerly desired to eat this Passover with you before I suffer,**
for, I tell you, I shall not eat it again
until there is fulfillment in the kingdom of God."
C. **Then he took a cup, gave thanks, and said,**
✠ **"Take this and share it among yourselves;**
for I tell you that from this time on
I shall not drink of the fruit of the vine
until the kingdom of God comes."
C. **Then he took the bread, said the blessing,**
broke it, and gave it to them, saying,
✠ **"This is my body, which will be given for you;**
do this in memory of me."
C. **And likewise the cup after they had eaten, saying,**
✠ **"This cup is the new covenant in my blood,**
which will be shed for you.

"And yet behold, the hand of the one who is to betray me
is with me on the table;
for the Son of Man indeed goes as it has been determined;
but woe to that man by whom he is betrayed."

C. And they began to debate among themselves
who among them would do such a deed.

Then an argument broke out among them
about which of them should be regarded as the greatest.
He said to them,

✠ "The kings of the Gentiles lord it over them
and those in authority over them are addressed as 'Benefactors';
but among you it shall not be so.
Rather, let the greatest among you be as the youngest,
and the leader as the servant.
For who is greater:
the one seated at table or the one who serves?
Is it not the one seated at table?
I am among you as the one who serves.
It is you who have stood by me in my trials;
and I confer a kingdom on you,
just as my Father has conferred one on me,
that you may eat and drink at my table in my kingdom;
and you will sit on thrones
judging the twelve tribes of Israel.

"Simon, Simon, behold Satan has demanded
to sift all of you like wheat,
but I have prayed that your own faith may not fail;
and once you have turned back,
you must strengthen your brothers."

C. **He said to him,**

S. **"Lord, I am prepared to go to prison and to die with you."**

C. **But he replied,**

✠ **"I tell you, Peter, before the cock crows this day,**
you will deny three times that you know me."

C. **He said to them,**

✠ **"When I sent you forth without a money bag or a sack or sandals,**
were you in need of anything?"

S. **"No, nothing,"**

C. **they replied.**
He said to them,

✠ **"But now one who has a money bag should take it,**
and likewise a sack,
and one who does not have a sword
should sell his cloak and buy one.
For I tell you that this Scripture must be fulfilled in me,
namely, *He was counted among the wicked*;
and indeed what is written about me is coming to fulfillment."

C. **Then they said,**

SS. **"Lord, look, there are two swords here."**

C. **But he replied,**

✠ **"It is enough!"**

C. **Then going out, he went, as was his custom, to the Mount of Olives,**
and the disciples followed him.
When he arrived at the place he said to them,

✠ **"Pray that you may not undergo the test."**

C. **After withdrawing about a stone's throw from them and kneeling,**
he prayed, saying,

✠ **"Father, if you are willing,**
take this cup away from me;
still, not my will but yours be done."

C. And to strengthen him an angel from heaven appeared to him.
He was in such agony and he prayed so fervently
that his sweat became like drops of blood
falling on the ground.
When he rose from prayer and returned to his disciples,
he found them sleeping from grief.
He said to them,
✠ "Why are you sleeping?
Get up and pray that you may not undergo the test."

C. While he was still speaking, a crowd approached
and in front was one of the Twelve, a man named Judas.
He went up to Jesus to kiss him.
Jesus said to him,
✠ "Judas, are you betraying the Son of Man with a kiss?"
C. His disciples realized what was about to happen, and they asked,
SS. "Lord, shall we strike with a sword?"
C. And one of them struck the high priest's servant
and cut off his right ear.
But Jesus said in reply,
✠ "Stop, no more of this!"
C. Then he touched the servant's ear and healed him.
And Jesus said to the chief priests and temple guards
and elders who had come for him,
✠ "Have you come out as against a robber, with swords and clubs?
Day after day I was with you in the temple area,
and you did not seize me;
but this is your hour, the time for the power of darkness."

C. **After arresting him they led him away**
and took him into the house of the high priest;
Peter was following at a distance.
They lit a fire in the middle of the courtyard and sat around it,
and Peter sat down with them.
When a maid saw him seated in the light,
she looked intently at him and said,
S. **"This man too was with him."**
C. **But he denied it saying,**
S. **"Woman, I do not know him."**
C. **A short while later someone else saw him and said,**
S. **"You too are one of them";**
C. **but Peter answered,**
S. **"My friend, I am not."**
C. **About an hour later, still another insisted,**
S. **"Assuredly, this man too was with him,**
for he also is a Galilean."
C. **But Peter said,**
S. **"My friend, I do not know what you are talking about."**
C. **Just as he was saying this, the cock crowed,**
and the Lord turned and looked at Peter;
and Peter remembered the word of the Lord,
how he had said to him,
"Before the cock crows today, you will deny me three times."
He went out and began to weep bitterly.
The men who held Jesus in custody were ridiculing and beating him.
They blindfolded him and questioned him, saying,
SS. **"Prophesy! Who is it that struck you?"**
C. **And they reviled him in saying many other things against him.**

When day came the council of elders of the people met,
both chief priests and scribes,
and they brought him before their Sanhedrin.
They said,
SS. "If you are the Christ, tell us,"
C. but he replied to them,
✠ "If I tell you, you will not believe,
and if I question, you will not respond.
But from this time on the Son of Man will be seated at the right hand of the power of God."
C. They all asked,
SS. "Are you then the Son of God?"
C. He replied to them,
✠ "You say that I am."
C. Then they said,
SS. "What further need have we for testimony?
We have heard it from his own mouth."

C. Then the whole assembly of them arose and brought him before Pilate.
[(The elders of the people, chief priests and scribes, arose and brought Jesus before Pilate.)
They brought charges against him, saying,
SS. "We found this man misleading our people;
he opposes the payment of taxes to Caesar
and maintains that he is the Christ, a king."
C. Pilate asked him,
S. "Are you the king of the Jews?"
C. He said to him in reply,
✠ "You say so."
C. Pilate then addressed the chief priests and the crowds,
S. "I find this man not guilty."
C. But they were adamant and said,
SS. "He is inciting the people with his teaching throughout all Judea,
from Galilee where he began even to here."

C. **On hearing this Pilate asked if the man was a Galilean;**
and upon learning that he was under Herod's jurisdiction,
he sent him to Herod who was in Jerusalem at that time.
Herod was very glad to see Jesus;
he had been wanting to see him for a long time,
for he had heard about him
and had been hoping to see him perform some sign.
He questioned him at length,
but he gave him no answer.
The chief priests and scribes, meanwhile,
stood by accusing him harshly.
Herod and his soldiers treated him contemptuously and mocked him,
and after clothing him in resplendent garb,
he sent him back to Pilate.
Herod and Pilate became friends that very day,
even though they had been enemies formerly.
Pilate then summoned the chief priests, the rulers, and the people
and said to them,

S. **"You brought this man to me**
and accused him of inciting the people to revolt.
I have conducted my investigation in your presence
and have not found this man guilty
of the charges you have brought against him,
nor did Herod, for he sent him back to us.
So no capital crime has been committed by him.
Therefore I shall have him flogged and then release him."

C. **But all together they shouted out,**

SS. **"Away with this man!**
Release Barabbas to us."

C. —Now Barabbas had been imprisoned for a rebellion
that had taken place in the city and for murder.—
Again Pilate addressed them, still wishing to release
Jesus,
but they continued their shouting,
SS. "Crucify him! Crucify him!"
C. Pilate addressed them a third time,
S. "What evil has this man done?
I found him guilty of no capital crime.
Therefore I shall have him flogged and then release
him."
C. With loud shouts, however,
they persisted in calling for his crucifixion,
and their voices prevailed.
The verdict of Pilate was that their demand should
be granted.
So he released the man who had been imprisoned
for rebellion and murder, for whom they asked,
and he handed Jesus over to them to deal with as
they wished.

As they led him away
they took hold of a certain Simon, a Cyrenian,
who was coming in from the country;
and after laying the cross on him,
they made him carry it behind Jesus.
A large crowd of people followed Jesus,
including many women who mourned and
lamented him.
Jesus turned to them and said,
✠ "Daughters of Jerusalem, do not weep for me;
weep instead for yourselves and for your children
for indeed, the days are coming when people will
say,
'Blessed are the barren,
the wombs that never bore
and the breasts that never nursed.'

At that time people will say to the mountains,
'Fall upon us!'
and to the hills, 'Cover us!'
for if these things are done when the wood is green
what will happen when it is dry?"

C. **Now two others, both criminals,**
were led away with him to be executed.

When they came to the place called the Skull,
they crucified him and the criminals there,
one on his right, the other on his left.
Then Jesus said,

✠ **"Father, forgive them, they know not what they do."**

C. **They divided his garments by casting lots.**
The people stood by and watched;
the rulers, meanwhile, sneered at him and said,

SS. **"He saved others, let him save himself**
if he is the chosen one, the Christ of God."

C. **Even the soldiers jeered at him.**
As they approached to offer him wine they called out,

SS. **"If you are King of the Jews, save yourself."**

C. **Above him there was an inscription that read,**
"This is the King of the Jews."

Now one of the criminals hanging there reviled Jesus, saying,

S. **"Are you not the Christ?**
Save yourself and us."

C. **The other, however, rebuking him, said in reply,**

S. **"Have you no fear of God,**
for you are subject to the same condemnation?
And indeed, we have been condemned justly,
for the sentence we received corresponds to our crimes,
but this man has done nothing criminal."

C. **Then he said,**

S. **"Jesus, remember me when you come into your kingdom."**

C. **He replied to him,**

✠ **"Amen, I say to you,**
today you will be with me in Paradise."

C. **It was now about noon and darkness came over the whole land**
until three in the afternoon
because of an eclipse of the sun.
Then the veil of the temple was torn down the middle.
Jesus cried out in a loud voice,

✠ **"Father, into your hands I commend my spirit";**

C. **and when he had said this he breathed his last.**

Here all kneel and pause for a short time.

C. **The centurion who witnessed what had happened glorified God and said,**

S. **"This man was innocent beyond doubt."**

C. **When all the people who had gathered for this spectacle saw what had happened,**
they returned home beating their breasts;
but all his acquaintances stood at a distance,
including the women who had followed him from Galilee
and saw these events.]

Now there was a virtuous and righteous man named Joseph who,
though he was a member of the council,
had not consented to their plan of action.
He came from the Jewish town of Arimathea
and was awaiting the kingdom of God.
He went to Pilate and asked for the body of Jesus.
After he had taken the body down,
he wrapped it in a linen cloth
and laid him in a rock-hewn tomb
in which no one had yet been buried.
It was the day of preparation,
and the sabbath was about to begin.

The women who had come from Galilee with him followed behind,
and when they had seen the tomb
and the way in which his body was laid in it,
they returned and prepared spices and perfumed oils.
Then they rested on the sabbath according to the commandment.

The Gospel of the Lord. All: **Praise to you, Lord Jesus Christ.**

Prayer over the Offerings

Through the Passion of your Only Begotten Son, O Lord,
may our reconciliation with you be near at hand,
so that, though we do not merit it by our own deeds,
yet by this sacrifice made once for all,
we may feel already the effects of your mercy.
Through Christ our Lord. All: **Amen.**

Communion Antiphon (Matthew 26:42)

Father, if this chalice cannot pass without my drinking it,
your will be done.

Prayer after Communion

Nourished with these sacred gifts,
we humbly beseech you, O Lord,
that, just as through the death of your Son
you have brought us to hope for what we believe,
so by his Resurrection
you may lead us to where you call.
Through Christ our Lord. All: **Amen.**

THE SACRED PASCHAL TRIDUUM

How often do the gospels speak of faith! How often does Jesus recognize the faith of another, extol faith, teach about faith, address the power of faith! How often does Jesus heal because of the faith of the other! During these high holy days of the Easter Triduum, we celebrate the "saving" mystery of Jesus Christ. We might coin a word and phrase here: we celebrate the "faithing" mystery of Jesus Christ.

- *Real faith means . . .*

—Living Liturgy™, *Easter Triduum 2016*

Holy Thursday solemnly inaugurates "the triduum during which the Lord died, was buried and rose again" (St. Augustine). *To these days Jesus referred when he prophesied: "Destroy this temple and in three days I will raise it up again"* (John 2:14).

Thursday of the Lord's Supper

AT THE EVENING MASS

March 24, 2016

Reflection on the Gospel

Jesus sums up in the simple action of washing feet what his whole life and ministry have been about. The profound message Jesus proclaimed by his faith-in-action is the extent of his love—"he loved them to the end." Jesus' self-sacrificing love is not simply a word, but is deeds for the sake of others. Loving is serving; loving is spilling out our very body and blood for others. Pouring forth one's body and blood is indeed an act of Eucharist—it is giving oneself for another's life.

- *Serving is . . .*

—Living Liturgy™, *Holy Thursday 2016*

Entrance Antiphon (Cf. Galatians 6:14)

We should glory in the Cross of our Lord Jesus Christ,
in whom is our salvation, life and resurrection,
through whom we are saved and delivered.

Collect

O God, who have called us to participate
in this most sacred Supper,
in which your Only Begotten Son,
when about to hand himself over to death,
entrusted to the Church a sacrifice new for all eternity,
the banquet of his love,
grant, we pray,
that we may draw from so great a mystery,
the fullness of charity and of life.
Through our Lord Jesus Christ, your Son,
who lives and reigns with you in the unity of the Holy Spirit,
one God, for ever and ever. All: **Amen.**

Reading I (L 39-ABC) (Exodus 12:1-8, 11-14)

A reading from the Book of Exodus

The law regarding the Passover meal.

The Lord said to Moses and Aaron in the land of Egypt,
"This month shall stand at the head of your calendar;
you shall reckon it the first month of the year.
Tell the whole community of Israel:
On the tenth of this month every one of your families
must procure for itself a lamb, one apiece for each household.
If a family is too small for a whole lamb,
it shall join the nearest household in procuring one
and shall share in the lamb
in proportion to the number of persons who partake of it.
The lamb must be a year-old male and without blemish.
You may take it from either the sheep or the goats.
You shall keep it until the fourteenth day of this month,
and then, with the whole assembly of Israel present,
it shall be slaughtered during the evening twilight.

They shall take some of its blood
and apply it to the two doorposts and the lintel
of every house in which they partake of the lamb.
That same night they shall eat its roasted flesh
with unleavened bread and bitter herbs.

"This is how you are to eat it:
with your loins girt, sandals on your feet and your staff in hand,
you shall eat like those who are in flight.
It is the Passover of the LORD.
For on this same night I will go through Egypt,
striking down every firstborn of the land, both man and beast,
and executing judgment on all the gods of Egypt—I, the LORD!
But the blood will mark the houses where you are.
Seeing the blood, I will pass over you;
thus, when I strike the land of Egypt,
no destructive blow will come upon you.

"This day shall be a memorial feast for you,
which all your generations shall celebrate
with pilgrimage to the LORD, as a perpetual institution."

The word of the Lord. All: **Thanks be to God.**

RESPONSORIAL PSALM 116

P-116

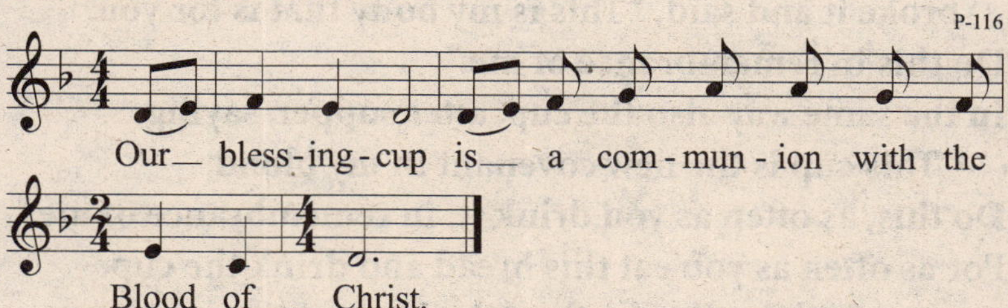

Psalm 116:12-13, 15-16bc, 17-18

℟. (*See* 1 Corinthians 10:16) **Our blessing-cup is a communion with the Blood of Christ.**

How shall I make a return to the LORD
for all the good he has done for me?
The cup of salvation I will take up,
and I will call upon the name of the LORD. ℟.

Precious in the eyes of the LORD
is the death of his faithful ones.
I am your servant, the son of your handmaid;
you have loosed my bonds. ℟.

To you will I offer sacrifice of thanksgiving,
and I will call upon the name of the LORD.
My vows to the LORD I will pay
in the presence of all his people. ℟.

READING II (1 Corinthians 11:23-26)

A reading from the first Letter of Saint Paul to the Corinthians

For as often as you eat this bread and drink the cup, you proclaim the death of the Lord.

Brothers and sisters:
I received from the Lord what I also handed on to you,
that the Lord Jesus, on the night he was handed over,
took bread, and, after he had given thanks,
broke it and said, "This is my body that is for you.
Do this in remembrance of me."
In the same way also the cup, after supper, saying,
"This cup is the new covenant in my blood.
Do this, as often as you drink it, in remembrance of me."
For as often as you eat this bread and drink the cup,
you proclaim the death of the Lord until he comes.

The word of the Lord. All: **Thanks be to God.**

GOSPEL (John 13:1-15)

VERSE BEFORE THE GOSPEL (John 13:34)

℣. Praise to you, Lord Jesus Christ, King of endless glory!
℟. **Praise to you, Lord Jesus Christ, King of endless glory!**
℣. I give you a new commandment, says the Lord:
love one another as I have loved you. ℟.

✠ **A reading from the holy Gospel according to John**

All: **Glory to you, O Lord.**

Jesus loved them to the end.

Before the feast of Passover, Jesus knew that his hour had come
to pass from this world to the Father.
He loved his own in the world and he loved them to the end.
The devil had already induced Judas, son of Simon the Iscariot, to hand him over.
So, during supper,
fully aware that the Father had put everything into his power
and that he had come from God and was returning to God,
he rose from supper and took off his outer garments.
He took a towel and tied it around his waist.
Then he poured water into a basin
and began to wash the disciples' feet
and dry them with the towel around his waist.
He came to Simon Peter, who said to him,
"Master, are you going to wash my feet?"
Jesus answered and said to him,
"What I am doing, you do not understand now,
but you will understand later."
Peter said to him, "You will never wash my feet."
Jesus answered him,
"Unless I wash you, you will have no inheritance with me."

Simon Peter said to him,
"Master, then not only my feet, but my hands and head as well."
Jesus said to him,
"Whoever has bathed has no need except to have his feet washed,
for he is clean all over;
so you are clean, but not all."
For he knew who would betray him;
for this reason, he said, "Not all of you are clean."
So when he had washed their feet
and put his garments back on and reclined at table again,
he said to them, "Do you realize what I have done for you?
You call me 'teacher' and 'master,' and rightly so,
for indeed I am.
If I, therefore, the master and teacher, have washed your feet,
you ought to wash one another's feet.
I have given you a model to follow,
so that as I have done for you, you should also do."

The Gospel of the Lord. All: **Praise to you, Lord Jesus Christ.**

WASHING OF FEET

Antiphons or other appropriate songs are sung.

PRAYER OVER THE OFFERINGS

Grant us, O Lord, we pray,
that we may participate worthily in these mysteries,
for whenever the memorial of this sacrifice is celebrated
the work of our redemption is accomplished.
Through Christ our Lord. All: **Amen.**

COMMUNION ANTIPHON (1 Corinthians 11:24-25)

This is the Body that will be given up for you;
this is the Chalice of the new covenant in my Blood,
says the Lord;
do this, whenever you receive it, in memory of me.

Prayer after Communion
Grant, almighty God,
that, just as we are renewed
by the Supper of your Son in this present age,
so we may enjoy his banquet for all eternity.
Who lives and reigns for ever and ever. All: **Amen.**

TRANSFER OF THE MOST BLESSED SACRAMENT

Friday of the Passion of the Lord (Good Friday)

March 25, 2016

Reflection on the Gospel

Good Friday is more than a step to resurrection; it is a day on which we celebrate Jesus' obedience, his kingship, the everlasting establishment of his reign, his side being opened and himself being poured out so that we can be washed in his very blood and water. The real scandal of the cross isn't suffering and death; the real scandal of the cross is that death is vanquished by Jesus' self-giving, visible love. Death has no power over God.

- *Sorrow is a temptation . . .*

—Living Liturgy™, *Good Friday 2016*

The Celebration of the Passion of the Lord

Prayer (Let us pray is not said)
Remember your mercies, O Lord,
and with your eternal protection sanctify your servants,
for whom Christ your Son,
by the shedding of his Blood,
established the Paschal Mystery.
Who lives and reigns for ever and ever. All: **Amen.**

Or:

O God, who by the Passion of Christ your Son, our Lord,
abolished the death inherited from ancient sin
by every succeeding generation,
grant that just as, being conformed to him,
we have borne by the law of nature
the image of the man of earth,
so by the sanctification of grace
we may bear the image of the Man of heaven.
Through Christ our Lord. All: **Amen.**

FIRST PART: LITURGY OF THE WORD

READING I (L 40-ABC) (Isaiah 52:13—53:12)

A reading from the Book of the Prophet Isaiah

He himself was wounded for our sins.
(Fourth oracle of the Servant of the Lord.)

See, my servant shall prosper,
he shall be raised high and greatly exalted.
Even as many were amazed at him—
so marred was his look beyond human semblance
and his appearance beyond that of the sons of man—
so shall he startle many nations,
because of him kings shall stand speechless;
for those who have not been told shall see,
those who have not heard shall ponder it.

Who would believe what we have heard?
To whom has the arm of the LORD been revealed?
He grew up like a sapling before him,
like a shoot from the parched earth;
there was in him no stately bearing to make us look at him,
nor appearance that would attract us to him.
He was spurned and avoided by people,
a man of suffering, accustomed to infirmity,
one of those from whom people hide their faces,
spurned, and we held him in no esteem.

Yet it was our infirmities that he bore,
our sufferings that he endured,
while we thought of him as stricken,
as one smitten by God and afflicted.
But he was pierced for our offenses,
crushed for our sins;
upon him was the chastisement that makes us whole,
by his stripes we were healed.
We had all gone astray like sheep,
each following his own way;
but the LORD laid upon him
the guilt of us all.

Though he was harshly treated, he submitted
and opened not his mouth;
like a lamb led to the slaughter
or a sheep before the shearers,
he was silent and opened not his mouth.
Oppressed and condemned, he was taken away,
and who would have thought any more of his destiny?
When he was cut off from the land of the living,
and smitten for the sin of his people,
a grave was assigned him among the wicked
and a burial place with evildoers,
though he had done no wrong
nor spoken any falsehood.
But the LORD was pleased
to crush him in infirmity.

If he gives his life as an offering for sin,
he shall see his descendants in a long life,
and the will of the LORD shall be accomplished
through him.

Because of his affliction
he shall see the light in fullness of days;
through his suffering, my servant shall justify many,
and their guilt he shall bear.

Therefore I will give him his portion among the great,
and he shall divide the spoils with the mighty,
because he surrendered himself to death
and was counted among the wicked;
and he shall take away the sins of many,
and win pardon for their offenses.

The word of the Lord. All: **Thanks be to God.**

Responsorial Psalm 31

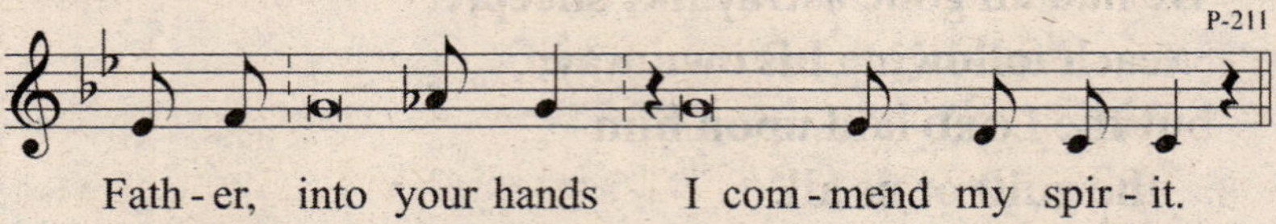

Music: Bartholomew Sayles, O.S.B., and Cecile Gertken, O.S.B., adapt., © 1977, 1989, Order of Saint Benedict.

Psalm 31:2, 6, 12-13, 15-16, 17, 25

℟. (Luke 23:46) **Father, into your hands I commend my spirit.**

In you, O Lord, I take refuge;
let me never be put to shame.
In your justice rescue me.
Into your hands I commend my spirit;
you will redeem me, O Lord, O faithful God. ℟.

For all my foes I am an object of reproach,
a laughingstock to my neighbors, and a dread to my friends;
they who see me abroad flee from me.
I am forgotten like the unremembered dead;
I am like a dish that is broken. ℟.

But my trust is in you, O Lord;
I say, "You are my God.
In your hands is my destiny; rescue me
from the clutches of my enemies and my persecutors." ℟.

Let your face shine upon your servant;
save me in your kindness.
Take courage and be stouthearted,
all you who hope in the Lord. ℟.

READING II (Hebrews 4:14-16; 5:7-9)

A reading from the Letter to the Hebrews

Jesus learned obedience and became the source of salvation for all who obey him.

Brothers and sisters:
Since we have a great high priest who has passed through the heavens,
Jesus, the Son of God,
let us hold fast to our confession.
For we do not have a high priest
who is unable to sympathize with our weaknesses,
but one who has similarly been tested in every way,
yet without sin.
So let us confidently approach the throne of grace
to receive mercy and to find grace for timely help.

In the days when Christ was in the flesh,
he offered prayers and supplications with loud cries and tears
to the one who was able to save him from death,
and he was heard because of his reverence.
Son though he was, he learned obedience from what he suffered;
and when he was made perfect,
he became the source of eternal salvation for all who obey him.

The word of the Lord. All: **Thanks be to God.**

* *See* statement on page 151.

GOSPEL (John 18:1—19:42)

VERSE BEFORE THE GOSPEL (Philippians 2:8-9)

℣. Praise to you, Lord Jesus Christ, King of endless glory!
℟. **Praise to you, Lord Jesus Christ, King of endless glory!**
℣. Christ became obedient to the point of death,
even death on a cross.
Because of this, God greatly exalted him
and bestowed on him the name which is above every other name. ℟.

The symbols in the following passion narrative represent:

C. Narrator;
✠ Christ;
S. speakers other than Christ;
SS. groups of speakers.

The Passion of our Lord Jesus Christ according to John

The Passion of our Lord Jesus Christ.

C. **Jesus went out with his disciples across the Kidron valley**
to where there was a garden,
into which he and his disciples entered.
Judas his betrayer also knew the place,
because Jesus had often met there with his disciples.
So Judas got a band of soldiers and guards
from the chief priests and the Pharisees
and went there with lanterns, torches, and weapons.
Jesus, knowing everything that was going to happen to him,
went out and said to them,
✠ **"Whom are you looking for?"**
C. **They answered him,**
SS. **"Jesus the Nazorean."**
C. **He said to them,**
✠ **"I AM."**
C. **Judas his betrayer was also with them.**
When he said to them, "I AM,"
they turned away and fell to the ground.
So he again asked them,
✠ **"Whom are you looking for?"**
C. **They said,**
SS. **"Jesus the Nazorean."**
C. **Jesus answered,**
✠ **"I told you that I AM.**
So if you are looking for me, let these men go."
C. **This was to fulfill what he had said,**
"I have not lost any of those you gave me."

Then Simon Peter, who had a sword, drew it,
struck the high priest's slave, and cut off his right ear.
The slave's name was Malchus.
Jesus said to Peter,
✠ "Put your sword into its scabbard.
Shall I not drink the cup that the Father gave me?"

C. So the band of soldiers, the tribune, and the Jewish guards seized Jesus,
bound him, and brought him to Annas first.
He was the father-in-law of Caiaphas,
who was high priest that year.
It was Caiaphas who had counseled the Jews
that it was better that one man should die rather than the people.

Simon Peter and another disciple followed Jesus.
Now the other disciple was known to the high priest,
and he entered the courtyard of the high priest with Jesus.
But Peter stood at the gate outside.
So the other disciple, the acquaintance of the high priest,
went out and spoke to the gatekeeper and brought Peter in.
Then the maid who was the gatekeeper said to Peter,
S. "You are not one of this man's disciples, are you?"
C. He said,
S. "I am not."
C. Now the slaves and the guards were standing around a charcoal fire
that they had made, because it was cold,
and were warming themselves.
Peter was also standing there keeping warm.

The high priest questioned Jesus
about his disciples and about his doctrine.
Jesus answered him,

✠ "I have spoken publicly to the world.
I have always taught in a synagogue
or in the temple area where all the Jews gather,
and in secret I have said nothing. Why ask me?
Ask those who heard me what I said to them.
They know what I said."

C. When he had said this,
one of the temple guards standing there struck Jesus and said,

S. "Is this the way you answer the high priest?"

C. Jesus answered him,

✠ "If I have spoken wrongly, testify to the wrong;
but if I have spoken rightly, why do you strike me?"

C. Then Annas sent him bound to Caiaphas the high priest.

Now Simon Peter was standing there keeping warm.
And they said to him,

S. "You are not one of his disciples, are you?"

C. He denied it and said,

S. "I am not."

C. One of the slaves of the high priest,
a relative of the one whose ear Peter had cut off, said,

S. "Didn't I see you in the garden with him?"

C. Again Peter denied it.
And immediately the cock crowed.

Then they brought Jesus from Caiaphas to the praetorium.
It was morning.
And they themselves did not enter the praetorium,
in order not to be defiled so that they could eat the Passover.
So Pilate came out to them and said,

S. "What charge do you bring against this man?"

C. They answered and said to him,

SS. "If he were not a criminal,
we would not have handed him over to you."
C. At this, Pilate said to them,
S. "Take him yourselves, and judge him according to your law."
C. The Jews answered him,
SS. "We do not have the right to execute anyone,"
C. in order that the word of Jesus might be fulfilled
that he said indicating the kind of death he would die.
So Pilate went back into the praetorium
and summoned Jesus and said to him,
S. "Are you the King of the Jews?"
C. Jesus answered,
✠ "Do you say this on your own
or have others told you about me?"
C. Pilate answered,
S. "I am not a Jew, am I?
Your own nation and the chief priests handed you over to me.
What have you done?"
C. Jesus answered,
✠ "My kingdom does not belong to this world.
If my kingdom did belong to this world,
my attendants would be fighting
to keep me from being handed over to the Jews.
But as it is, my kingdom is not here."
C. So Pilate said to him,
S. "Then you are a king?"
C. Jesus answered,
✠ "You say I am a king.
For this I was born and for this I came into the world,
to testify to the truth.
Everyone who belongs to the truth listens to my voice."
C. Pilate said to him,
S. "What is truth?"

C. When he had said this,
he again went out to the Jews and said to them,
S. "I find no guilt in him.
But you have a custom that I release one prisoner to you at Passover.
Do you want me to release to you the King of the Jews?"
C. They cried out again,
SS. "Not this one but Barabbas!"
C. Now Barabbas was a revolutionary.

Then Pilate took Jesus and had him scourged.
And the soldiers wove a crown out of thorns and placed it on his head,
and clothed him in a purple cloak,
and they came to him and said,
SS. "Hail, King of the Jews!"
C. And they struck him repeatedly.
Once more Pilate went out and said to them,
S. "Look, I am bringing him out to you,
so that you may know that I find no guilt in him."
C. So Jesus came out,
wearing the crown of thorns and the purple cloak.
And Pilate said to them,
S. "Behold, the man!"
C. When the chief priests and the guards saw him they cried out,
SS. "Crucify him, crucify him!"
C. Pilate said to them,
S. "Take him yourselves and crucify him.
I find no guilt in him."
C. The Jews answered,
SS. "We have a law, and according to that law he ought to die,
because he made himself the Son of God."
C. Now when Pilate heard this statement,
he became even more afraid,
and went back into the praetorium and said to Jesus,

S. "Where are you from?"
C. Jesus did not answer him.
So Pilate said to him,
S. "Do you not speak to me?
Do you not know that I have power to release you
and I have power to crucify you?"
C. Jesus answered him,
✠ "You would have no power over me
if it had not been given to you from above.
For this reason the one who handed me over to you
has the greater sin."
C. Consequently, Pilate tried to release him; but the
Jews cried out,
SS. "If you release him, you are not a Friend of Caesar.
Everyone who makes himself a king opposes Caesar."

C. When Pilate heard these words he brought Jesus out
and seated him on the judge's bench
in the place called Stone Pavement, in Hebrew,
Gabbatha.
It was preparation day for Passover, and it was
about noon.
And he said to the Jews,
S. "Behold, your king!"
C. They cried out,
SS. "Take him away, take him away! Crucify him!"
C. Pilate said to them,
S. "Shall I crucify your king?"
C. The chief priests answered,
SS. "We have no king but Caesar."
C. Then he handed him over to them to be crucified.

So they took Jesus, and, carrying the cross himself,
he went out to what is called the Place of the Skull,
in Hebrew, Golgotha.
There they crucified him, and with him two others,
one on either side, with Jesus in the middle.

Pilate also had an inscription written and put on the cross.
It read,
"Jesus the Nazorean, the King of the Jews."
Now many of the Jews read this inscription,
because the place where Jesus was crucified was near the city;
and it was written in Hebrew, Latin, and Greek.
So the chief priests of the Jews said to Pilate,
SS. "Do not write 'The King of the Jews,'
but that he said, 'I am the King of the Jews.'"
C. Pilate answered,
S. "What I have written, I have written."
C. When the soldiers had crucified Jesus,
they took his clothes and divided them into four shares,
a share for each soldier.
They also took his tunic, but the tunic was seamless,
woven in one piece from the top down.
So they said to one another,
SS. "Let's not tear it, but cast lots for it to see whose it will be,"
C. in order that the passage of Scripture might be fulfilled that says:
They divided my garments among them,
and for my vesture they cast lots.
This is what the soldiers did.
Standing by the cross of Jesus were his mother
and his mother's sister, Mary the wife of Clopas,
and Mary of Magdala.
When Jesus saw his mother and the disciple there whom he loved he said to his mother,
✠ "Woman, behold, your son."
C. Then he said to the disciple,
✠ "Behold, your mother."
C. And from that hour the disciple took her into his home.

After this, aware that everything was now finished,
in order that the Scripture might be fulfilled,
Jesus said,

✠ "I thirst."

C. There was a vessel filled with common wine.
So they put a sponge soaked in wine on a sprig of hyssop
and put it up to his mouth.
When Jesus had taken the wine, he said,

✠ "It is finished."

C. And bowing his head, he handed over the spirit.

Here all kneel and pause for a short time.

Now since it was preparation day,
in order that the bodies might not remain
on the cross on the sabbath,
for the sabbath day of that week was a solemn one,
the Jews asked Pilate that their legs be broken
and that they be taken down.
So the soldiers came and broke the legs of the first
and then of the other one who was crucified with Jesus.
But when they came to Jesus and saw that he was already dead,
they did not break his legs,
but one soldier thrust his lance into his side,
and immediately blood and water flowed out.
An eyewitness has testified, and his testimony is true;
he knows that he is speaking the truth,
so that you also may come to believe.
For this happened so that the Scripture passage might be fulfilled:
Not a bone of it will be broken.
And again another passage says:
They will look upon him whom they have pierced.

After this, Joseph of Arimathea,
secretly a disciple of Jesus for fear of the Jews,
asked Pilate if he could remove the body of Jesus.
And Pilate permitted it.
So he came and took his body.
Nicodemus, the one who had first come to him at night,
also came bringing a mixture of myrrh and aloes
weighing about one hundred pounds.
They took the body of Jesus
and bound it with burial cloths along with the spices,
according to the Jewish burial custom.
Now in the place where he had been crucified there was a garden,
and in the garden a new tomb, in which no one had yet been buried.
So they laid Jesus there because of the Jewish preparation day;
for the tomb was close by.

The Gospel of the Lord. All: **Praise to you, Lord Jesus Christ.**

THE SOLEMN INTERCESSIONS

I. FOR HOLY CHURCH

Let us pray, dearly beloved, for the holy Church of God,
that our God and Lord be pleased to give her peace,
to guard her and to unite her throughout the whole world
and grant that, leading our life in tranquility and quiet,
we may glorify God the Father almighty.

Prayer in silence. Then the Priest sings or says:

Almighty ever-living God,
who in Christ revealed your glory to all the nations,
watch over the works of your mercy,
that your Church, spread throughout all the world,
may persevere with steadfast faith in confessing your name.
Through Christ our Lord. All: **Amen.**

II. FOR THE POPE

Let us pray also for our most Holy Father Pope N.,
that our God and Lord,
who chose him for the Order of Bishops,

may keep him safe and unharmed for the Lord's holy Church,
to govern the holy People of God.

Prayer in silence. Then the Priest sings or says:

Almighty ever-living God,
by whose decree all things are founded,
look with favor on our prayers
and in your kindness protect the Pope chosen for us,
that, under him, the Christian people,
governed by you their maker,
may grow in merit by reason of their faith.
Through Christ our Lord. All: **Amen.**

III. For All Orders and Degrees of the Faithful

Let us pray also for our Bishop N.,*
for all Bishops, Priests, and Deacons of the Church
and for the whole of the faithful people.

Prayer in silence. Then the Priest sings or says:

Almighty ever-living God,
by whose Spirit the whole body of the Church
is sanctified and governed,
hear our humble prayer for your ministers,
that, by the gift of your grace,
all may serve you faithfully.
Through Christ our Lord. All: **Amen.**

IV. For Catechumens

Let us pray also for (our) catechumens,
that our God and Lord
may open wide the ears of their inmost hearts
and unlock the gates of his mercy,
that, having received forgiveness of all their sins
through the waters of rebirth,
they, too, may be one with Christ Jesus our Lord.

Prayer in silence. Then the Priest sings or says:

Almighty ever-living God,
who make your Church ever fruitful with new offspring,
increase the faith and understanding of (our) catechumens,
that, reborn in the font of Baptism,
they may be added to the number of your adopted children.
Through Christ our Lord. All: **Amen.**

* Mention may be made here of the Coadjutor Bishop, or Auxiliary Bishops, as noted in the *General Instruction of the Roman Missal*, no. 149.

V. For the Unity of Christians

Let us pray also for all our brothers and sisters who believe in Christ,
that our God and Lord may be pleased,
as they live the truth,
to gather them together and keep them in his one Church.

Prayer in silence. Then the Priest sings or says:

Almighty ever-living God,
who gather what is scattered
and keep together what you have gathered,
look kindly on the flock of your Son,
that those whom one Baptism has consecrated
may be joined together by integrity of faith
and united in the bond of charity.
Through Christ our Lord. All: **Amen.**

VI. For the Jewish People

Let us pray also for the Jewish people,
to whom the Lord our God spoke first,
that he may grant them to advance in love of his name
and in faithfulness to his covenant.

Prayer in silence. Then the Priest sings or says:

Almighty ever-living God,
who bestowed your promises on Abraham and his descendants,
graciously hear the prayers of your Church,
that the people you first made your own
may attain the fullness of redemption.
Through Christ our Lord. All: **Amen.**

VII. For Those Who Do Not Believe in Christ

Let us pray also for those who do not believe in Christ,
that, enlightened by the Holy Spirit,
they, too, may enter on the way of salvation.

Prayer in silence. Then the Priest sings or says:

Almighty ever-living God,
grant to those who do not confess Christ
that, by walking before you with a sincere heart,
they may find the truth
and that we ourselves, being constant in mutual love
and striving to understand more fully the mystery of your life,
may be made more perfect witnesses to your love in the world.
Through Christ our Lord. All: **Amen.**

VIII. For Those Who Do Not Believe in God

Let us pray also for those who do not acknowledge God,
that, following what is right in sincerity of heart,
they may find the way to God himself.

Prayer in silence. Then the Priest sings or says:

Almighty ever-living God,
who created all people
to seek you always by desiring you
and, by finding you, come to rest,
grant, we pray,
that, despite every harmful obstacle,
all may recognize the signs of your fatherly love
and the witness of the good works
done by those who believe in you,
and so in gladness confess you,
the one true God and Father of our human race.
Through Christ our Lord. All: **Amen.**

IX. For Those in Public Office

Let us pray also for those in public office,
that our God and Lord
may direct their minds and hearts according to his will
for the true peace and freedom of all.

Prayer in silence. Then the Priest sings or says:

Almighty ever-living God,
in whose hand lies every human heart
and the rights of peoples,
look with favor, we pray,
on those who govern with authority over us,
that throughout the whole world,
the prosperity of peoples,
the assurance of peace,
and freedom of religion
may through your gift be made secure.
Through Christ our Lord. All: **Amen.**

X. For Those in Tribulation

Let us pray, dearly beloved,
to God the Father almighty,
that he may cleanse the world of all errors,
banish disease, drive out hunger,
unlock prisons, loosen fetters,
granting to travelers safety, to pilgrims return,
health to the sick, and salvation to the dying.

Prayer in silence. Then the Priest sings or says:

Almighty ever-living God,
comfort of mourners, strength of all who toil,
may the prayers of those who cry out in any tribulation
come before you,
that all may rejoice,
because in their hour of need
your mercy was at hand.
Through Christ our Lord. All: **Amen.**

SECOND PART: THE ADORATION OF THE HOLY CROSS

The Showing of the Holy Cross

First Form

℣. Ecce lignum Crucis (Behold the wood of the Cross).
All respond: **Venite adoremus (Come, let us adore).**

Second Form

℣. Behold the wood of the Cross,
on which hung the salvation of the world.
All respond: **Come, let us adore.**

The Adoration of the Holy Cross

The Priest, clergy, and faithful approach to venerate the cross in a kind of procession.

THIRD PART: HOLY COMMUNION

At the Savior's command
and formed by divine teaching,
we dare to say:

The Priest, with hands extended says, and all present continue:

Our Father, who art in heaven,
hallowed be thy name;
thy kingdom come,
thy will be done
on earth as it is in heaven.
Give us this day our daily bread,
and forgive us our trespasses,
as we forgive those who trespass against us;
and lead us not into temptation,
but deliver us from evil.

With hands extended, the Priest continues alone:
Deliver us, Lord, we pray, from every evil,
graciously grant peace in our days,
that, by the help of your mercy,
we may be always free from sin
and safe from all distress,
as we await the blessed hope
and the coming of our Savior, Jesus Christ.

He joins his hands. The people conclude the prayer, acclaiming:
For the kingdom, the power and the glory are yours
now and for ever.

Then the Priest, with hands joined, says quietly:
May the receiving of your Body and Blood,
Lord Jesus Christ,
not bring me to judgment and condemnation,
but through your loving mercy
be for me protection in mind and body
and a healing remedy.

The Priest then genuflects, takes a particle, and, holding it slightly raised over the ciborium, while facing the people, says aloud:
Behold the Lamb of God,
behold him who takes away the sins of the world.
Blessed are those called to the supper of the Lamb.

And together with the people he adds once:
Lord, I am not worthy
that you should enter under my roof,
but only say the word
and my soul shall be healed.

Prayer after Communion
Almighty ever-living God,
who have restored us to life
by the blessed Death and Resurrection of your Christ,
preserve in us the work of your mercy,
that, by partaking of this mystery,
we may have a life unceasingly devoted to you.
Through Christ our Lord. All: **Amen.**

Prayer over the People
May abundant blessing, O Lord, we pray,
descend upon your people,
who have honored the Death of your Son
in the hope of their resurrection:
may pardon come,

comfort be given,
holy faith increase,
and everlasting redemption be made secure.
Through Christ our Lord. All: **Amen.**

After genuflecting to the Cross, all depart in silence. The altar is stripped; the cross remains, however, with four candles.

HOLY SATURDAY

The Easter Vigil in the Holy Night

March 26, 2016

Reflection on the Gospel

This is the night when Jesus passes from death to risen Life. This is the night when our own being and doing collapse into a living faith that is full, robust, eager to announce the Good News that death is overcome, that our belief is not in vain, that Jesus lives on in us who are baptized. This is the night—just this one night—when we can ignore the sting of death because life is so abundant.

- *Jesus lives, so I will . . .*

—Living Liturgy™, *Easter Vigil 2016*

FIRST PART: THE SOLEMN BEGINNING OF THE VIGIL OR LUCERNARIUM

The Blessing of the Fire and Preparation of the Candle

Priest: In the name of the Father, and of the Son, and of the Holy Spirit.
All: **Amen.**

Then he greets the assembled people in the usual way and briefly instructs them about the night vigil in these or similar words:

Dear brethren (brothers and sisters),
on this most sacred night,
in which our Lord Jesus Christ

passed over from death to life,
the Church calls upon her sons and daughters,
scattered throughout the world,
to come together to watch and pray.
If we keep the memorial
of the Lord's paschal solemnity in this way,
listening to his word and celebrating his mysteries,
then we shall have the sure hope
of sharing his triumph over death
and living with him in God.

Let us pray.
O God, who through your Son
bestowed upon the faithful the fire of your glory,
sanctify ✠ this new fire, we pray,
and grant that,
by these paschal celebrations,
we may be so inflamed with heavenly desires,
that with minds made pure
we may attain festivities of unending splendor.
Through Christ our Lord. All: **Amen.**

PREPARATION OF THE CANDLE

(1) CHRIST YESTERDAY AND TODAY (he cuts a vertical line);
(2) THE BEGINNING AND THE END (he cuts a horizontal line);
(3) THE ALPHA (he cuts the letter Alpha above the vertical line);
(4) AND THE OMEGA (he cuts the letter Omega below the vertical line).
(5) ALL TIME BELONGS TO HIM (he cuts the first numeral of the current year in the upper left corner of the cross);
(6) AND ALL THE AGES (he cuts the second numeral of the current year in the upper right corner of the cross).
(7) TO HIM BE GLORY AND POWER (he cuts the third numeral of the current year in the lower left corner of the cross);
(8) THROUGH EVERY AGE AND FOR EVER. AMEN. (he cuts the fourth numeral of the current year in the lower right corner of the cross).

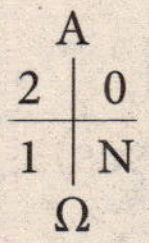

(1) BY HIS HOLY 1
(2) AND GLORIOUS WOUNDS,
(3) MAY CHRIST THE LORD 4 2 5
(4) GUARD US
(5) AND PROTECT US. AMEN. 3

May the light of Christ rising in glory
dispel the darkness of our hearts and minds.

PROCESSION

℣. The Light of Christ.	*or*	℣. Lumen Christi.
℟. **Thanks be to God.**		℟. **Deo Gratias.**
℣. The Light of Christ.	*or*	℣. Lumen Christi.
℟. **Thanks be to God.**		℟. **Deo Gratias.**
℣. The Light of Christ.	*or*	℣. Lumen Christi.
℟. **Thanks be to God.**		℟. **Deo Gratias.**

THE EASTER PROCLAMATION (EXSULTET)
Longer Form of the Easter Proclamation
[Shorter Form]

[Exult, let them exult, the hosts of heaven,
exult, let Angel ministers of God exult,
let the trumpet of salvation
sound aloud our mighty King's triumph!
Be glad, let earth be glad, as glory floods her,
ablaze with light from her eternal King,
let all corners of the earth be glad,
knowing an end to gloom and darkness.
Rejoice, let Mother Church also rejoice,
arrayed with the lightning of his glory,
let this holy building shake with joy,
filled with the mighty voices of the peoples.]

(Therefore, dearest friends,
standing in the awesome glory of this holy light,
invoke with me, I ask you,
the mercy of God almighty,
that he, who has been pleased to number me,
though unworthy, among the Levites,
may pour into me his light unshadowed,
that I may sing this candle's perfect praises).

[(℣. The Lord be with you. *Sung only by an ordained minister.
℟. **And with your spirit.**)

℣. Lift up your hearts. *Sung only by an ordained minister.
℟. **We lift them up to the Lord.**

℣. Let us give thanks to the Lord our God.
℟. **It is right and just.** *Sung only by an ordained minister.

It is truly right and just,
with ardent love of mind and heart
and with devoted service of our voice,
to acclaim our God invisible, the almighty Father,
and Jesus Christ, our Lord, his Son, his Only Begotten.

Who for our sake paid Adam's debt to the eternal Father,
and, pouring out his own dear Blood,
wiped clean the record of our ancient sinfulness.

These then are the feasts of Passover,
in which is slain the Lamb, the one true Lamb,
whose Blood anoints the doorposts of believers.

This is the night,
when once you led our forebears, Israel's children,
from slavery in Egypt
and made them pass dry-shod through the Red Sea.

This is the night
that with a pillar of fire
banished the darkness of sin.

This is the night
that even now, throughout the world,
sets Christian believers apart from worldly vices
and from the gloom of sin,
leading them to grace
and joining them to his holy ones.

This is the night,
when Christ broke the prison-bars of death
and rose victorious from the underworld.]

Our birth would have been no gain,
had we not been redeemed.
[O wonder of your humble care for us!
O love, O charity beyond all telling,
to ransom a slave you gave away your Son!

O truly necessary sin of Adam,
destroyed completely by the Death of Christ!

O happy fault
that earned so great, so glorious a Redeemer!]

O truly blessed night,
worthy alone to know the time and hour
when Christ rose from the underworld!

This is the night
of which it is written:
The night shall be as bright as day,
dazzling is the night for me,
and full of gladness.

[The sanctifying power of this night
dispels wickedness, washes faults away,
restores innocence to the fallen, and joy to mourners,]
drives out hatred, fosters concord, and brings down the
mighty.

[** On this, your night of grace, O holy Father,
accept this candle, a solemn offering,
the work of bees and of your servants' hands,
an evening sacrifice of praise,
this gift from your most holy Church.]

But now we know the praises of this pillar,
which glowing fire ignites for God's honor,
a fire into many flames divided,
yet never dimmed by sharing of its light,
for it is fed by melting wax,
drawn out by mother bees
to build a torch so precious.

[O truly blessed night,
when things of heaven are wed to those of earth,
and divine to the human.] [**]

[Therefore, O Lord,
we pray you that this candle,
hallowed to the honor of your name,
may persevere undimmed,
to overcome the darkness of this night.
Receive it as a pleasing fragrance,
and let it mingle with the lights of heaven.
May this flame be found still burning
by the Morning Star:

the one Morning Star who never sets,
Christ your Son,
who, coming back from death's domain,
has shed his peaceful light on humanity,
and lives and reigns for ever and ever. All: **Amen.**]

SECOND PART: THE LITURGY OF THE WORD

Dear brethren (brothers and sisters),
now that we have begun our solemn Vigil,
let us listen with quiet hearts to the Word of God.
Let us meditate on how God in times past saved his people
and in these, the last days, has sent us his Son as our Redeemer.
Let us pray that our God may complete this paschal work of salvation
by the fullness of redemption.

READING I (L 41-ABC) (Genesis 1:1—2:2) *or* Shorter Form [ ] (Genesis 1:1, 26-31a)

A reading from the Book of Genesis

God looked at everything he had made, and he found it very good.

[In the beginning, when God created the heavens and the earth,]
the earth was a formless wasteland, and darkness covered the abyss,
while a mighty wind swept over the waters.

Then God said,
"Let there be light," and there was light.
God saw how good the light was.
God then separated the light from the darkness.
God called the light "day," and the darkness he called "night."
Thus evening came, and morning followed—the first day.

Then God said,
"Let there be a dome in the middle of the waters,
to separate one body of water from the other."
And so it happened:
God made the dome,

and it separated the water above the dome from the water below it.
God called the dome "the sky."
Evening came, and morning followed—the second day.

Then God said,
"Let the water under the sky be gathered into a single basin,
so that the dry land may appear."
And so it happened:
the water under the sky was gathered into its basin,
and the dry land appeared.
God called the dry land "the earth,"
and the basin of the water he called "the sea."
God saw how good it was.
Then God said,
"Let the earth bring forth vegetation:
every kind of plant that bears seed
and every kind of fruit tree on earth
that bears fruit with its seed in it."
And so it happened:
the earth brought forth every kind of plant that bears seed
and every kind of fruit tree on earth
that bears fruit with its seed in it.
God saw how good it was.
Evening came, and morning followed—the third day.

Then God said:
"Let there be lights in the dome of the sky,
to separate day from night.
Let them mark the fixed times, the days and the years,
and serve as luminaries in the dome of the sky,
to shed light upon the earth."
And so it happened:
God made the two great lights,
the greater one to govern the day,

and the lesser one to govern the night;
and he made the stars.
God set them in the dome of the sky,
to shed light upon the earth,
to govern the day and the night,
and to separate the light from the darkness.
God saw how good it was.
Evening came, and morning followed—the fourth day.

Then God said,
"Let the water teem with an abundance of living creatures,
and on the earth let birds fly beneath the dome of the sky."
And so it happened:
God created the great sea monsters
and all kinds of swimming creatures with which the water teems,
and all kinds of winged birds.
God saw how good it was, and God blessed them, saying,
"Be fertile, multiply, and fill the water of the seas;
and let the birds multiply on the earth."
Evening came, and morning followed—the fifth day.

Then God said,
"Let the earth bring forth all kinds of living creatures:
cattle, creeping things, and wild animals of all kinds."
And so it happened:
God made all kinds of wild animals, all kinds of cattle,
and all kinds of creeping things of the earth.
God saw how good it was.
Then [God said:
"Let us make man in our image, after our likeness.
Let them have dominion over the fish of the sea,
the birds of the air, and the cattle,
and over all the wild animals
and all the creatures that crawl on the ground."

God created man in his image;
in the image of God he created him;
male and female he created them.
God blessed them, saying:
"Be fertile and multiply;
fill the earth and subdue it.
Have dominion over the fish of the sea, the birds of the air,
and all the living things that move on the earth."
God also said:
"See, I give you every seed-bearing plant all over the earth
and every tree that has seed-bearing fruit on it to be your food;
and to all the animals of the land, all the birds of the air,
and all the living creatures that crawl on the ground,
I give all the green plants for food."
And so it happened.
God looked at everything he had made, and he found it very good.]
Evening came, and morning followed—the sixth day.

Thus the heavens and the earth and all their array were completed.
Since on the seventh day God was finished
with the work he had been doing,
he rested on the seventh day from all the work he had undertaken.

The word of the Lord.

RESPONSORIAL PSALM 104 or 33

P-118

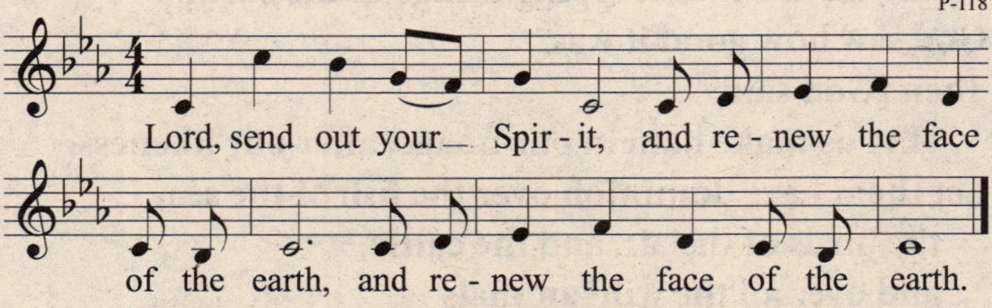

A Psalm 104:1-2, 5-6, 10, 12, 13-14, 24, 35

℟. (30) **Lord, send out your Spirit, and renew the face of the earth.**

Bless the LORD, O my soul!
O LORD, my God, you are great indeed!
You are clothed with majesty and glory,
robed in light as with a cloak. ℟.

You fixed the earth upon its foundation,
not to be moved forever;
with the ocean, as with a garment, you covered it;
above the mountains the waters stood. ℟.

You send forth springs into the watercourses
that wind among the mountains.
Beside them the birds of heaven dwell;
from among the branches they send forth their song. ℟.

You water the mountains from your palace;
the earth is replete with the fruit of your works.
You raise grass for the cattle,
and vegetation for man's use,
producing bread from the earth. ℟.

How manifold are your works, O LORD!
In wisdom you have wrought them all—
the earth is full of your creatures.
Bless the LORD, O my soul! ℟.

Or:

P-119

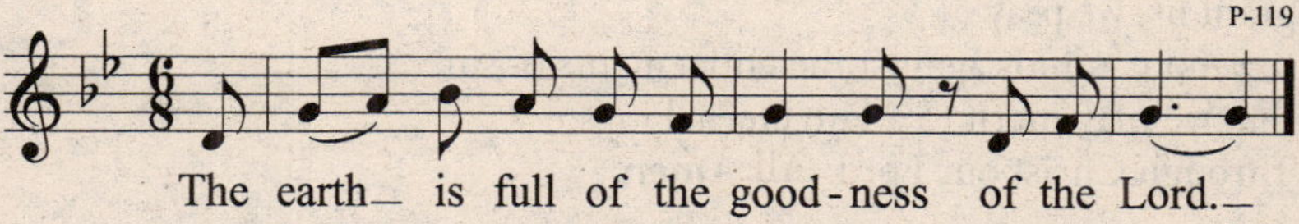

B Psalm 33:4-5, 6-7, 12-13, 20 and 22

℟. (5b) **The earth is full of the goodness of the Lord.**

Upright is the word of the LORD,
and all his works are trustworthy.
He loves justice and right;
of the kindness of the LORD the earth is full. ℟.

(continued)

By the word of the LORD the heavens were made;
by the breath of his mouth all their host.
He gathers the waters of the sea as in a flask;
in cellars he confines the deep. ℟.

Blessed the nation whose God is the LORD,
the people he has chosen for his own inheritance.
From heaven the LORD looks down;
he sees all mankind. ℟.

Our soul waits for the LORD,
who is our help and our shield.
May your kindness, O LORD, be upon us
who have put our hope in you. ℟.

PRAYER

Let us pray.

Almighty ever-living God,
who are wonderful in the ordering of all your works,
may those you have redeemed understand
that there exists nothing more marvelous
than the world's creation in the beginning
except that, at the end of the ages,
Christ our Passover has been sacrificed.
Who lives and reigns for ever and ever. All: **Amen.**

Or:

On the creation of man:

O God, who wonderfully created human nature
and still more wonderfully redeemed it,
grant us, we pray,
to set our minds against the enticements of sin,
that we may merit to attain eternal joys.
Through Christ our Lord. All: **Amen.**

READING II (Genesis 22:1-18) *or* Shorter Form [ ]
(Genesis 22:1-2, 9a, 10-13, 15-18)

A reading from the Book of Genesis

The sacrifice of Abraham, our father in faith.

[God put Abraham to the test.
He called to him, "Abraham!"
"Here I am," he replied.

Then God said:
"Take your son Isaac, your only one, whom you love,
and go to the land of Moriah.
There you shall offer him up as a holocaust
on a height that I will point out to you."]
Early the next morning Abraham saddled his donkey,
took with him his son Isaac and two of his servants
as well,
and with the wood that he had cut for the holocaust,
set out for the place of which God had told him.

On the third day Abraham got sight of the place from afar.
Then he said to his servants:
"Both of you stay here with the donkey,
while the boy and I go on over yonder.
We will worship and then come back to you."
Thereupon Abraham took the wood for the holocaust
and laid it on his son Isaac's shoulders,
while he himself carried the fire and the knife.
As the two walked on together, Isaac spoke to his father
Abraham:
"Father!" Isaac said.
"Yes, son," he replied.
Isaac continued, "Here are the fire and the wood,
but where is the sheep for the holocaust?"
"Son," Abraham answered,
"God himself will provide the sheep for the holocaust."
Then the two continued going forward.

[When they came to the place of which God had told him,
Abraham built an altar there and arranged the wood
on it.]
Next he tied up his son Isaac,
and put him on top of the wood on the altar.
[Then he reached out and took the knife to slaughter
his son.

But the LORD's messenger called to him from heaven,
"Abraham, Abraham!"
"Here I am!" he answered.
"Do not lay your hand on the boy," said the messenger.
"Do not do the least thing to him.
I know now how devoted you are to God,
since you did not withhold from me your own beloved son."
As Abraham looked about,
he spied a ram caught by its horns in the thicket.
So he went and took the ram
and offered it up as a holocaust in place of his son.]
Abraham named the site Yahweh-yireh;
hence people now say, "On the mountain the LORD will see."

[Again the LORD's messenger called to Abraham from heaven and said:
"I swear by myself, declares the LORD,
that because you acted as you did
in not withholding from me your beloved son,
I will bless you abundantly
and make your descendants as countless
as the stars of the sky and the sands of the seashore;
your descendants shall take possession
of the gates of their enemies,
and in your descendants all the nations of the earth shall find blessing—
all this because you obeyed my command."]

The word of the Lord.

RESPONSORIAL PSALM 16

P-120

Psalm 16:5, 8, 9-10, 11

℟. (1) **You are my inheritance, O Lord.**

O Lord, my allotted portion and my cup,
you it is who hold fast my lot.
I set the Lord ever before me;
with him at my right hand I shall not be disturbed. ℟.

Therefore my heart is glad and my soul rejoices,
my body, too, abides in confidence;
because you will not abandon my soul to the netherworld,
nor will you suffer your faithful one to undergo
corruption. ℟.

You will show me the path to life,
fullness of joys in your presence,
the delights at your right hand forever. ℟.

Prayer

Let us pray.

O God, supreme Father of the faithful,
who increase the children of your promise
by pouring out the grace of adoption
throughout the whole world
and who through the Paschal Mystery
make your servant Abraham father of nations,
as once you swore,
grant, we pray,
that your peoples may enter worthily
into the grace to which you call them.
Through Christ our Lord. All: **Amen.**

Reading III (Exodus 14:15—15:1)

A reading from the Book of Exodus

The Israelites marched on dry land through the midst of the sea.

The Lord said to Moses, "Why are you crying out to me?
Tell the Israelites to go forward.
And you, lift up your staff and, with hand outstretched
over the sea,
split the sea in two,
that the Israelites may pass through it on dry land.

But I will make the Egyptians so obstinate
that they will go in after them.
Then I will receive glory through Pharaoh and all his army,
his chariots and charioteers.
The Egyptians shall know that I am the Lord,
when I receive glory through Pharaoh
and his chariots and charioteers."

The angel of God, who had been leading Israel's camp,
now moved and went around behind them.
The column of cloud also, leaving the front,
took up its place behind them,
so that it came between the camp of the Egyptians
and that of Israel.
But the cloud now became dark, and thus the night passed
without the rival camps coming any closer together
all night long.
Then Moses stretched out his hand over the sea,
and the Lord swept the sea
with a strong east wind throughout the night
and so turned it into dry land.
When the water was thus divided,
the Israelites marched into the midst of the sea on dry land,
with the water like a wall to their right and to their left.

The Egyptians followed in pursuit;
all Pharaoh's horses and chariots and charioteers went after them
right into the midst of the sea.
In the night watch just before dawn
the Lord cast through the column of the fiery cloud
upon the Egyptian force a glance that threw it into a panic;
and he so clogged their chariot wheels
that they could hardly drive.

With that the Egyptians sounded the retreat before Israel,
because the LORD was fighting for them against the Egyptians.

Then the LORD told Moses, "Stretch out your hand over the sea,
that the water may flow back upon the Egyptians,
upon their chariots and their charioteers."
So Moses stretched out his hand over the sea,
and at dawn the sea flowed back to its normal depth.
The Egyptians were fleeing head on toward the sea,
when the LORD hurled them into its midst.
As the water flowed back,
it covered the chariots and the charioteers of Pharaoh's whole army
which had followed the Israelites into the sea.
Not a single one of them escaped.
But the Israelites had marched on dry land
through the midst of the sea,
with the water like a wall to their right and to their left.
Thus the LORD saved Israel on that day
from the power of the Egyptians.
When Israel saw the Egyptians lying dead on the seashore
and beheld the great power that the LORD
had shown against the Egyptians,
they feared the LORD and believed in him and in his servant Moses.

Then Moses and the Israelites sang this song to the LORD:
I will sing to the LORD, for he is gloriously triumphant;
horse and chariot he has cast into the sea.

The word of the Lord.

Responsorial Psalm (Exodus 15)

P-121

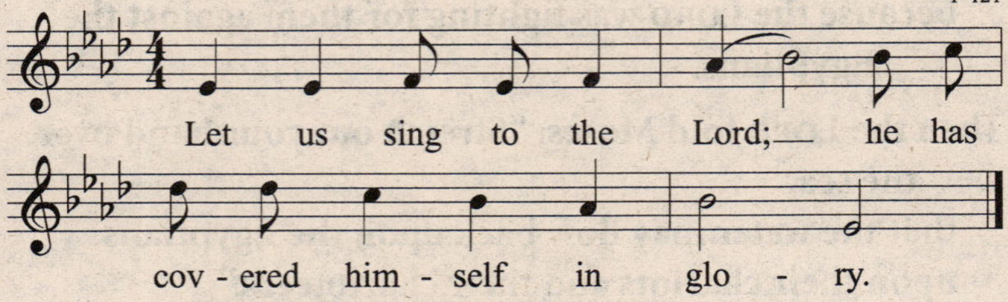

Exodus 15:1-2, 3-4, 5-6, 17-18

℟. (1b) **Let us sing to the Lord; he has covered himself in glory.**

I will sing to the Lord, for he is gloriously triumphant;
horse and chariot he has cast into the sea.
My strength and my courage is the Lord,
and he has been my savior.
He is my God, I praise him;
the God of my father, I extol him. ℟.

The Lord is a warrior,
Lord is his name!
Pharaoh's chariots and army he hurled into the sea;
the elite of his officers were submerged in the
Red Sea. ℟.

The flood waters covered them,
they sank into the depths like a stone.
Your right hand, O Lord, magnificent in power,
your right hand, O Lord, has shattered the enemy. ℟.

You brought in the people you redeemed
and planted them on the mountain of your inheritance—
the place where you made your seat, O Lord,
the sanctuary, Lord, which your hands established.
The Lord shall reign forever and ever. ℟.

Prayer

Let us pray.

O God, whose ancient wonders
remain undimmed in splendor even in our day,
for what you once bestowed on a single people,

freeing them from Pharaoh's persecution
by the power of your right hand,
now you bring about as the salvation of the nations
through the waters of rebirth,
grant, we pray, that the whole world
may become children of Abraham
and inherit the dignity of Israel's birthright.
Through Christ our Lord. All: **Amen.**

Or:

O God, who by the light of the New Testament
have unlocked the meaning
of wonders worked in former times,
so that the Red Sea prefigures the sacred font
and the nation delivered from slavery
foreshadows the Christian people,
grant, we pray, that all nations,
obtaining the privilege of Israel by merit of faith,
may be reborn by partaking of your Spirit.
Through Christ our Lord. All: **Amen.**

Reading IV (Isaiah 54:5-14)

A reading from the Book of the Prophet Isaiah

With enduring love, the Lord your redeemer takes pity on you.

The One who has become your husband is your Maker;
his name is the Lord of hosts;
your redeemer is the Holy One of Israel,
called God of all the earth.
The Lord calls you back,
like a wife forsaken and grieved in spirit,
a wife married in youth and then cast off,
says your God.
For a brief moment I abandoned you,
but with great tenderness I will take you back.
In an outburst of wrath, for a moment
I hid my face from you;
but with enduring love I take pity on you,
says the Lord, your redeemer.
This is for me like the days of Noah,
when I swore that the waters of Noah

should never again deluge the earth;
so I have sworn not to be angry with you,
or to rebuke you.
Though the mountains leave their place
and the hills be shaken,
my love shall never leave you
nor my covenant of peace be shaken,
says the LORD, who has mercy on you.
O afflicted one, storm-battered and unconsoled,
I lay your pavements in carnelians,
and your foundations in sapphires;
I will make your battlements of rubies,
your gates of carbuncles,
and all your walls of precious stones.
All your children shall be taught by the LORD,
and great shall be the peace of your children.
In justice shall you be established,
far from the fear of oppression,
where destruction cannot come near you.

The word of the Lord.

RESPONSORIAL PSALM 30

P-122

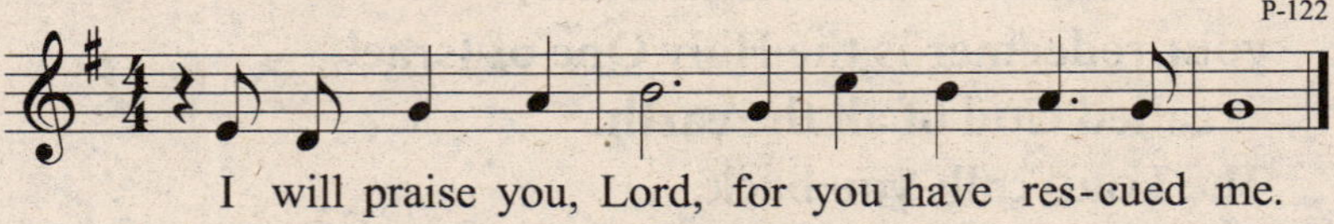

Psalm 30:2, 4, 5-6, 11-12, 13

℟. (2a) **I will praise you, Lord, for you have rescued me.**

I will extol you, O LORD, for you drew me clear
and did not let my enemies rejoice over me.
O LORD, you brought me up from the netherworld;
you preserved me from among those going down into
the pit. ℟.

Sing praise to the LORD, you his faithful ones,
and give thanks to his holy name.

For his anger lasts but a moment;
  a lifetime, his good will.
At nightfall, weeping enters in,
  but with the dawn, rejoicing. ℟.

Hear, O LORD, and have pity on me;
  O LORD, be my helper.
You changed my mourning into dancing;
  O LORD, my God, forever will I give you thanks. ℟.

PRAYER

Let us pray.

Almighty ever-living God,
surpass, for the honor of your name,
what you pledged to the Patriarchs by reason of their faith,
and through sacred adoption increase the children of your promise,
so that what the Saints of old never doubted would come to pass
your Church may now see in great part fulfilled.
Through Christ our Lord. All: **Amen.**

READING V (Isaiah 55:1-11)

A reading from the Book of the Prophet Isaiah

Come to me that you may have life. I will renew with you an everlasting covenant.

Thus says the LORD:
All you who are thirsty,
  come to the water!
You who have no money,
  come, receive grain and eat;
come, without paying and without cost,
  drink wine and milk!
Why spend your money for what is not bread,
  your wages for what fails to satisfy?
Heed me, and you shall eat well,
  you shall delight in rich fare.
Come to me heedfully,
  listen, that you may have life.
I will renew with you the everlasting covenant,
  the benefits assured to David.

As I made him a witness to the peoples,
a leader and commander of nations,
so shall you summon a nation you knew not,
and nations that knew you not shall run to you,
because of the LORD, your God,
the Holy One of Israel, who has glorified you.

Seek the LORD while he may be found,
call him while he is near.
Let the scoundrel forsake his way,
and the wicked man his thoughts;
let him turn to the LORD for mercy;
to our God, who is generous in forgiving.
For my thoughts are not your thoughts,
nor are your ways my ways, says the LORD.
As high as the heavens are above the earth,
so high are my ways above your ways
and my thoughts above your thoughts.

For just as from the heavens
the rain and snow come down
and do not return there
till they have watered the earth,
making it fertile and fruitful,
giving seed to the one who sows
and bread to the one who eats,
so shall my word be
that goes forth from my mouth;
my word shall not return to me void,
but shall do my will,
achieving the end for which I sent it.

The word of the Lord.

RESPONSORIAL PSALM (Isaiah 12)

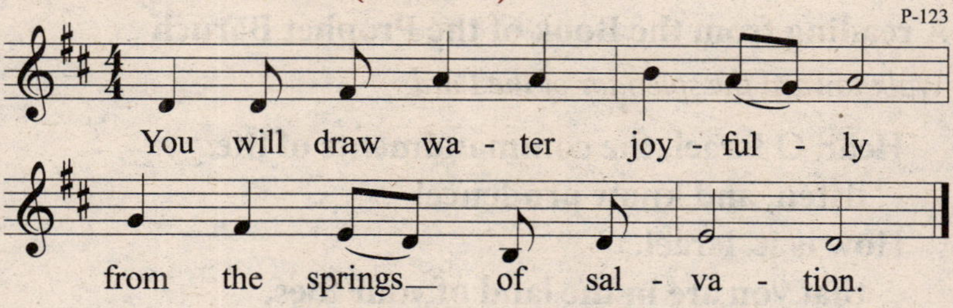

Music: Jay F. Hunstiger, © 1990, administered by Liturgical Press.

Isaiah 12:2-3, 4, 5-6

℟. (3) **You will draw water joyfully from the springs of salvation.**

God indeed is my savior;
  I am confident and unafraid.
My strength and my courage is the LORD,
  and he has been my savior.
With joy you will draw water
  at the fountain of salvation. ℟.

Give thanks to the LORD, acclaim his name;
  among the nations make known his deeds,
  proclaim how exalted is his name. ℟.

Sing praise to the LORD for his glorious achievement;
  let this be known throughout all the earth.
Shout with exultation, O city of Zion,
  for great in your midst
  is the Holy One of Israel! ℟.

PRAYER

Let us pray.

Almighty ever-living God,
sole hope of the world,
who by the preaching of your Prophets
unveiled the mysteries of this present age,
graciously increase the longing of your people,
for only at the prompting of your grace
do the faithful progress in any kind of virtue.
Through Christ our Lord. All: **Amen.**

READING VI (Baruch 3:9-15, 32—4:4).

A reading from the Book of the Prophet Baruch

Walk toward the splendor of the Lord.

Hear, O Israel, the commandments of life:
listen, and know prudence!
How is it, Israel,
that you are in the land of your foes,
grown old in a foreign land,
defiled with the dead,
accounted with those destined for the netherworld?
You have forsaken the fountain of wisdom!
Had you walked in the way of God,
you would have dwelt in enduring peace.
Learn where prudence is,
where strength, where understanding;
that you may know also
where are length of days, and life,
where light of the eyes, and peace.
Who has found the place of wisdom,
who has entered into her treasuries?

The One who knows all things knows her;
he has probed her by his knowledge—
the One who established the earth for all time,
and filled it with four-footed beasts;
he who dismisses the light, and it departs,
calls it, and it obeys him trembling;
before whom the stars at their posts
shine and rejoice;
when he calls them, they answer, "Here we are!"
shining with joy for their Maker.
Such is our God;
no other is to be compared to him:
he has traced out the whole way of understanding,
and has given her to Jacob, his servant,
to Israel, his beloved son.

Since then she has appeared on earth,
and moved among people.
She is the book of the precepts of God,
the law that endures forever;
all who cling to her will live,
but those will die who forsake her.
Turn, O Jacob, and receive her:
walk by her light toward splendor.
Give not your glory to another,
your privileges to an alien race.
Blessed are we, O Israel;
for what pleases God is known to us!

The word of the Lord.

Responsorial Psalm 19

P-124

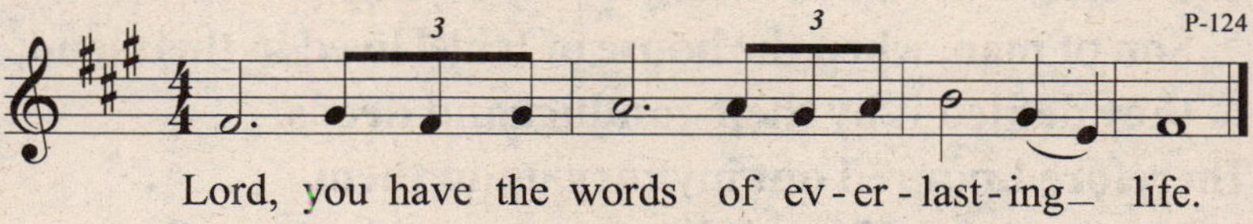

Psalm 19:8, 9, 10, 11

℟. (John 6:68c) **Lord, you have the words of everlasting life.**

The law of the LORD is perfect,
refreshing the soul;
the decree of the LORD is trustworthy,
giving wisdom to the simple. ℟.

The precepts of the LORD are right,
rejoicing the heart;
the command of the LORD is clear,
enlightening the eye. ℟.

The fear of the LORD is pure,
enduring forever;
the ordinances of the LORD are true,
all of them just. ℟.

They are more precious than gold,
than a heap of purest gold;

(continued)

sweeter also than syrup
or honey from the comb. ℟.

PRAYER

Let us pray.

O God, who constantly increase your Church
by your call to the nations,
graciously grant
to those you wash clean in the waters of Baptism
the assurance of your unfailing protection.
Through Christ our Lord. All: **Amen.**

READING VII (Ezekiel 36:16-17a, 18-28)

A reading from the Book of the Prophet Ezekiel

I shall sprinkle clean water upon you and I shall give you a new heart.

The word of the LORD came to me, saying:
Son of man, when the house of Israel lived in their land,
they defiled it by their conduct and deeds.
Therefore I poured out my fury upon them
because of the blood that they poured out on the ground,
and because they defiled it with idols.
I scattered them among the nations,
dispersing them over foreign lands;
according to their conduct and deeds I judged them.
But when they came among the nations wherever they came,
they served to profane my holy name,
because it was said of them: "These are the people of the LORD,
yet they had to leave their land."
So I have relented because of my holy name
which the house of Israel profaned
among the nations where they came.
Therefore say to the house of Israel: Thus says the Lord GOD:
Not for your sakes do I act, house of Israel,

but for the sake of my holy name,
which you profaned among the nations to which you came.
I will prove the holiness of my great name, profaned among the nations,
in whose midst you have profaned it.
Thus the nations shall know that I am the LORD, says the Lord GOD,
when in their sight I prove my holiness through you.
For I will take you away from among the nations,
gather you from all the foreign lands,
and bring you back to your own land.
I will sprinkle clean water upon you
to cleanse you from all your impurities,
and from all your idols I will cleanse you.
I will give you a new heart and place a new spirit within you,
taking from your bodies your stony hearts
and giving you natural hearts.
I will put my spirit within you and make you live by my statutes,
careful to observe my decrees.
You shall live in the land I gave your fathers;
you shall be my people, and I will be your God.

The word of the Lord.

RESPONSORIAL PSALM

A *When baptism is celebrated*

H-291

Psalms 42:3, 5; 43:3, 4

℟. (42:2) **Like a deer that longs for running streams, my soul longs for you, my God.**

Athirst is my soul for God, the living God.
When shall I go and behold the face of God? ℟.

I went with the throng
and led them in procession to the house of God,
amid loud cries of joy and thanksgiving,
with the multitude keeping festival. ℟.

Send forth your light and your fidelity;
they shall lead me on
and bring me to your holy mountain,
to your dwelling-place. ℟.

Then will I go in to the altar of God,
the God of my gladness and joy;
then will I give you thanks upon the harp,
O God, my God! ℟.

B *When baptism is not celebrated*

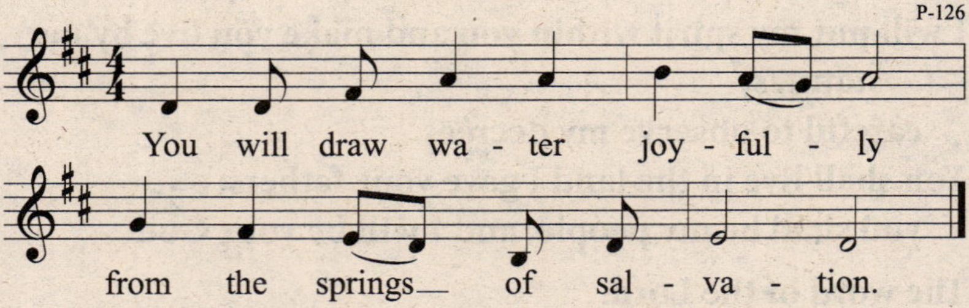

Isaiah 12:2-3, 4bcd, 5-6

℟. (3) **You will draw water joyfully from the springs of salvation.**

God indeed is my savior;
I am confident and unafraid.
My strength and my courage is the LORD,
and he has been my savior.
With joy you will draw water
at the fountain of salvation. ℟.

Give thanks to the LORD, acclaim his name;
 among the nations make known his deeds,
 proclaim how exalted is his name. ℟.

Sing praise to the LORD for his glorious achievement;
 let this be known throughout all the earth.
Shout with exultation, O city of Zion,
 for great in your midst
 is the Holy One of Israel! ℟.

C *When baptism is not celebrated*

P-127

Psalm 51:12-13, 14-15, 18-19

℟. (12a) **Create a clean heart in me, O God.**

A clean heart create for me, O God,
 and a steadfast spirit renew within me.
Cast me not out from your presence,
 and your Holy Spirit take not from me. ℟.

Give me back the joy of your salvation,
 and a willing spirit sustain in me.
I will teach transgressors your ways,
 and sinners shall return to you. ℟.

For you are not pleased with sacrifices;
 should I offer a holocaust, you would not accept it.
My sacrifice, O God, is a contrite spirit;
 a heart contrite and humbled, O God, you will not
  spurn. ℟.

PRAYER

Let us pray.

O God of unchanging power and eternal light,
look with favor on the wondrous mystery of the whole Church
and serenely accomplish the work of human salvation,
which you planned from all eternity;
may the whole world know and see

that what was cast down is raised up,
what had become old is made new,
and all things are restored to integrity through Christ,
just as by him they came into being.
Who lives and reigns for ever and ever. All: **Amen.**

Or:

O God, who by the pages of both Testaments
instruct and prepare us to celebrate the Paschal Mystery,
grant that we may comprehend your mercy,
so that the gifts we receive from you this night
may confirm our hope of the gifts to come.
Through Christ our Lord. All: **Amen.**

Gloria (*See* page 3).

Collect

O God, who make this most sacred night radiant
with the glory of the Lord's Resurrection,
stir up in your Church a spirit of adoption,
so that, renewed in body and mind,
we may render you undivided service.
Through our Lord Jesus Christ, your Son,
who lives and reigns with you in the unity of the Holy Spirit,
one God, for ever and ever. All: **Amen.**

Epistle (Romans 6:3-11)

A reading from the Letter of Saint Paul to the Romans

Christ, raised from the dead, dies no more.

Brothers and sisters:
Are you unaware that we who were baptized into Christ Jesus
were baptized into his death?
We were indeed buried with him through baptism into death,
so that, just as Christ was raised from the dead
by the glory of the Father,
we too might live in newness of life.
For if we have grown into union with him through a death like his,
we shall also be united with him in the resurrection.

We know that our old self was crucified with him,
so that our sinful body might be done away with,
that we might no longer be in slavery to sin.
For a dead person has been absolved from sin.
If, then, we have died with Christ,
we believe that we shall also live with him.
We know that Christ, raised from the dead, dies no more;
death no longer has power over him.
As to his death, he died to sin once and for all;
as to his life, he lives for God.
Consequently, you too must think of yourselves as being dead to sin
and living for God in Christ Jesus.

The word of the Lord.

The Priest solemnly intones the Alleluia three times, raising his voice by a step each time, with all repeating it.

RESPONSORIAL PSALM 118

P-128

Psalm 118:1-2, 16-17, 22-23

℟. **Alleluia, alleluia, alleluia.**

Give thanks to the LORD, for he is good,
for his mercy endures forever.
Let the house of Israel say,
"His mercy endures forever." ℟.

"The right hand of the LORD has struck with power;
the right hand of the LORD is exalted.

(continued)

I shall not die, but live,
and declare the works of the LORD." ℟.

The stone which the builders rejected
has become the cornerstone.
By the LORD has this been done;
it is wonderful in our eyes. ℟.

GOSPEL C (Luke 24:1-12)

✠ **A reading from the holy Gospel according to Luke**

All: **Glory to you, O Lord.**

Why do you seek the Living One among the dead?

At daybreak on the first day of the week
the women who had come from Galilee with Jesus
took the spices they had prepared
and went to the tomb.
They found the stone rolled away from the tomb;
but when they entered,
they did not find the body of the Lord Jesus.
While they were puzzling over this, behold,
two men in dazzling garments appeared to them.
They were terrified and bowed their faces to the ground.
They said to them,
"Why do you seek the living one among the dead?
He is not here, but he has been raised.
Remember what he said to you while he was still in Galilee,
that the Son of Man must be handed over to sinners
and be crucified, and rise on the third day."
And they remembered his words.
Then they returned from the tomb
and announced all these things to the eleven
and to all the others.
The women were Mary Magdalene, Joanna, and Mary the mother of James;
the others who accompanied them also told this to the apostles,

but their story seemed like nonsense
and they did not believe them.
But Peter got up and ran to the tomb,
bent down, and saw the burial cloths alone;
then he went home amazed at what had happened.

The Gospel of the Lord. All: **Praise to you, Lord Jesus Christ.**

THIRD PART: BAPTISMAL LITURGY

If there are candidates to be baptized:

Dearly beloved,
with one heart and one soul, let us by our prayers
come to the aid of these our brothers and sisters in their blessed hope,
so that, as they approach the font of rebirth,
the almighty Father may bestow on them
all his merciful help.

If the font is to be blessed, but there is no one to be baptized:

Dearly beloved,
let us humbly invoke upon this font
the grace of God the almighty Father,
that those who from it are born anew
may be numbered among the children of adoption in Christ.

The Litany is sung by two cantors, with all standing (because it is Easter Time) and responding.

The Litany of the Saints

If there are candidates to be baptized, the Priest says the following prayer:

Almighty ever-living God,
be present by the mysteries of your great love
and send forth the spirit of adoption
to create the new peoples
brought to birth for you in the font of Baptism,
so that what is to be carried out by our humble service
may be brought to fulfillment by your mighty power.
Through Christ our Lord. All: **Amen.**

Blessing of Baptismal Water

O God, who by invisible power
accomplish a wondrous effect
through sacramental signs
and who in many ways have prepared water, your creation,
to show forth the grace of Baptism;

O God, whose Spirit
in the first moments of the world's creation
hovered over the waters,
so that the very substance of water
would even then take to itself the power to sanctify;

O God, who by the outpouring of the flood
foreshadowed regeneration,
so that from the mystery of one and the same element of water
would come an end to vice and a beginning of virtue;

O God, who caused the children of Abraham
to pass dry-shod through the Red Sea,
so that the chosen people,
set free from slavery to Pharaoh,
would prefigure the people of the baptized;

O God, whose Son,
baptized by John in the waters of the Jordan,
was anointed with the Holy Spirit,
and, as he hung upon the Cross,
gave forth water from his side along with blood,
and after his Resurrection, commanded his disciples:
"Go forth, teach all nations, baptizing them
in the name of the Father and of the Son and of the Holy Spirit,"
look now, we pray, upon the face of your Church
and graciously unseal for her the fountain of Baptism.

May this water receive by the Holy Spirit
the grace of your Only Begotten Son,
so that human nature, created in your image
and washed clean through the Sacrament of Baptism
from all the squalor of the life of old,
may be found worthy to rise to the life of newborn children
through water and the Holy Spirit.

May the power of the Holy Spirit,
O Lord, we pray,
come down through your Son
into the fullness of this font,
so that all who have been buried with Christ
by Baptism into death
may rise again to life with him.
Who lives and reigns with you in the unity of the Holy Spirit,
one God, for ever and ever. All: **Amen.**

Celebration of Baptism

Renunciation of Sin and Profession of Faith

The celebrant in a series of questions to which the candidates and the parents and godparents reply **I DO**, asks the candidates and parents and godparents to renounce sin and profess their faith.

Baptism of Adults

Celebrant: Is it your will to be baptized in the faith of the Church, which we have all professed with you?

Candidate: **It is.**

He baptizes the candidate, saying:

N., I baptize you in the name of the Father,

He immerses the candidate or pours water upon him.

and of the Son,

He immerses the candidate or pours water upon him a second time.

and of the Holy Spirit.

He immerses the candidate or pours water upon him a third time. He asks the same question and performs the same action for each candidate.

After each baptism it is appropriate for the people to sing a short acclamation:

This is the fountain of life,
water made holy by the suffering of Christ, washing all the world.
You who are washed in this water have hope of heaven's kingdom.

Baptism of Children

Celebrant: Is it your will that N. should be baptized in the faith of the Church, which we have all professed with you?

Parents and godparents: **It is.**

He baptizes the child, saying:

N., I baptize you in the name of the Father,

He immerses the child or pours water upon it.

and of the Son,

He immerses the child or pours water upon it a second time.

and of the Holy Spirit.

He immerses the child or pours water upon it a third time. He asks the same question and performs the same action for each child.

After each baptism it is appropriate for the people to sing a short acclamation:

This is the fountain of life,
water made holy by the suffering of Christ, washing all the world.
You who are washed in this water have hope of heaven's kingdom.

Anointing with Chrism

God the Father of our Lord Jesus Christ has freed you from sin, given you a new birth by water and the Holy Spirit, and welcomed you into his holy people. He now anoints you with the chrism of salvation. As Christ was anointed Priest, Prophet, and King, so may you live always as members of his body, sharing everlasting life. All: **Amen.**

Clothing with the White Garment

(N., N.,) you have become a new creation, and have clothed yourselves in Christ. See in this white garment the outward sign of your Christian dignity. With your family and friends to help you by word and example, bring that dignity unstained into the everlasting life of heaven.
All: **Amen.**

Celebration of Confirmation *

If the bishop has conferred baptism, he should now also confer confirmation. If the bishop is not present, the priest who conferred baptism and received the candidates into full communion is authorized to confirm. The infants who were baptized during this celebration are not confirmed. However, the newly baptized children who have gone through the RCIA process are confirmed.

Invitation

My dear friends, let us pray to God our Father, that he will pour out the Holy Spirit on these candidates for confirmation to strengthen them with his gifts and anoint them to be more like Christ, the Son of God.

Laying on of Hands

All-powerful God, Father of our Lord Jesus Christ,
by water and the Holy Spirit
you freed your sons
and daughters from sin and gave them new life.
Send your Holy Spirit upon them to be their helper and guide.
Give them the spirit of wisdom and understanding,
the spirit of right judgment and courage,
the spirit of knowledge and reverence.
Fill them with the spirit of wonder and awe in your presence.
We ask this through Christ our Lord. All: **Amen.**

Anointing with Chrism

N., be sealed with the Gift of the Holy Spirit.
Newly confirmed: **Amen.**

The minister of the sacrament adds: Peace be with you.
Newly confirmed: **And with your Spirit.**

*From the RCIA, nos. 232–235.

The Blessing of Water

If no one is to be baptized and the font is not to be blessed, the priest blesses the water with the following prayer:

Dear brothers and sisters,
let us humbly beseech the Lord our God
to bless this water he has created,
which will be sprinkled upon us
as a memorial of our Baptism.
May he graciously renew us,
that we may remain faithful to the Spirit
whom we have received.

And after a brief pause in silence, he proclaims the following prayer, with hands extended:

Lord our God,
in your mercy be present to your people
who keep vigil on this most sacred night,
and, for us who recall the wondrous work of our creation
and the still greater work of our redemption,
graciously bless this water.
For you created water to make the fields fruitful
and to refresh and cleanse our bodies.
You also made water the instrument of your mercy:
for through water you freed your people from slavery
and quenched their thirst in the desert;
through water the Prophets proclaimed the new covenant
you were to enter upon with the human race;
and last of all,
through water, which Christ made holy in the Jordan,
you have renewed our corrupted nature
in the bath of regeneration.
Therefore, may this water be for us
a memorial of the Baptism we have received,
and grant that we may share
in the gladness of our brothers and sisters,
who at Easter have received their Baptism.
Through Christ our Lord. All: **Amen.**

The Renewal of Baptismal Promises

Dear brethren (brothers and sisters), through the Paschal Mystery
we have been buried with Christ in Baptism,
so that we may walk with him in newness of life.
And so, now that our Lenten observance is concluded,
let us renew the promises of Holy Baptism,

by which we once renounced Satan and his works
and promised to serve God in the holy Catholic Church.

And so I ask you:

A

Priest: Do you renounce Satan? All: **I do.**
Priest: And all his works? All: **I do.**
Priest: And all his empty show? All: **I do.**

Or:

B

Priest: Do you renounce sin,
so as to live in the freedom of the children of God?
All: **I do.**

Priest: Do you renounce the lure of evil,
so that sin may have no mastery over you?
All: **I do.**

Priest: Do you renounce Satan,
the author and prince of sin?
All: **I do.**

Then the priest continues:

Priest: Do you believe in God,
the Father almighty,
Creator of heaven and earth?
All: **I do.**

Priest: Do you believe in Jesus Christ, his only Son, our Lord,
who was born of the Virgin Mary,
suffered death and was buried,
rose again from the dead,
and is seated at the right hand of the Father?
All: **I do.**

Priest: Do you believe in the Holy Spirit,
the holy Catholic Church,
the communion of saints,
the forgiveness of sins,
the resurrection of the body,
and life everlasting?
All: **I do.**

And may almighty God, the Father of our Lord Jesus Christ,
who has given us new birth by water and the Holy Spirit
and bestowed on us forgiveness of our sins,
keep us by his grace,
in Christ Jesus our Lord,
for eternal life. All: **Amen.**

The Priest sprinkles the people with the blessed water, while all sing:

Ant. I saw water flowing from the Temple,
from its right-hand side, alleluia;
and all to whom this water came were saved
and shall say: Alleluia, alleluia.

Prayer of the Faithful

FOURTH PART: THE LITURGY OF THE EUCHARIST

Prayer over the Offerings

Accept, we ask, O Lord,
the prayers of your people
with the sacrificial offerings,
that what has begun in the paschal mysteries
may, by the working of your power,
bring us to the healing of eternity.
Through Christ our Lord. All: **Amen.**

Communion Antiphon (1 Corinthians 5:7-8)

Christ our Passover has been sacrificed;
therefore let us keep the feast
with the unleavened bread of purity and truth, alleluia.

Prayer after Communion

Pour out on us, O Lord, the Spirit of your love,
and in your kindness make those you have nourished
by this paschal Sacrament
one in mind and heart.
Through Christ our Lord. All: **Amen.**

Dismissal

To dismiss the people the Deacon or, if there is no Deacon, the Priest himself sings or says:

Go forth, the Mass is ended, alleluia, alleluia.

Or:

Go in peace, alleluia, alleluia.

All reply: **Thanks be to God, alleluia, alleluia.**

This practice is observed throughout the Octave of Easter.

Easter Sunday

THE RESURRECTION OF THE LORD

MASS DURING THE DAY

March 27, 2016

Reflection on the Gospel

It was "early in the morning, / while it was still dark" that Mary Magdalene went to the tomb. How did she see? How did she know? She ran to Peter and John and they ran to the tomb. They, too, saw. More than saw. Their seeing could penetrate the darkness of not understanding. Their seeing was a response of the heart that led to their believing. The mystery of the resurrection is able to be seen because God gives us eyes of faith.

- *Jesus lives, so Mary Magdalene, Peter, John, and I . . .*

—Living Liturgy™, *Easter Sunday 2016*

ENTRANCE ANTIPHON (Cf. Psalm 139[138]:18, 5-6)

I have risen, and I am with you still, alleluia.
You have laid your hand upon me, alleluia.
Too wonderful for me, this knowledge, alleluia, alleluia.

Or:

(Luke 24:34; cf. Revelation 1:6)

The Lord is truly risen, alleluia.
To him be glory and power
for all the ages of eternity, alleluia, alleluia.

COLLECT

O God, who on this day,
through your Only Begotten Son,
have conquered death
and unlocked for us the path to eternity,
grant, we pray, that we who keep
the solemnity of the Lord's Resurrection
may, through the renewal brought by your Spirit,
rise up in the light of life.

Through our Lord Jesus Christ, your Son,
who lives and reigns with you in the unity of the Holy Spirit,
one God, for ever and ever. All: **Amen.**

Reading I (L 42) (Acts of the Apostles 10:34a, 37-43)

A reading from the Acts of the Apostles

We ate and drank with him after he rose from the dead.

Peter proceeded to speak and said:
"You know what has happened all over Judea,
beginning in Galilee after the baptism
that John preached,
how God anointed Jesus of Nazareth
with the Holy Spirit and power.
He went about doing good
and healing all those oppressed by the devil,
for God was with him.
We are witnesses of all that he did
both in the country of the Jews and in Jerusalem.
They put him to death by hanging him on a tree.
This man God raised on the third day and granted that he be visible,
not to all the people, but to us,
the witnesses chosen by God in advance,
who ate and drank with him after he rose from the dead.
He commissioned us to preach to the people
and testify that he is the one appointed by God
as judge of the living and the dead.
To him all the prophets bear witness,
that everyone who believes in him
will receive forgiveness of sins through his name."

The word of the Lord. All: **Thanks be to God.**

Responsorial Psalm 118

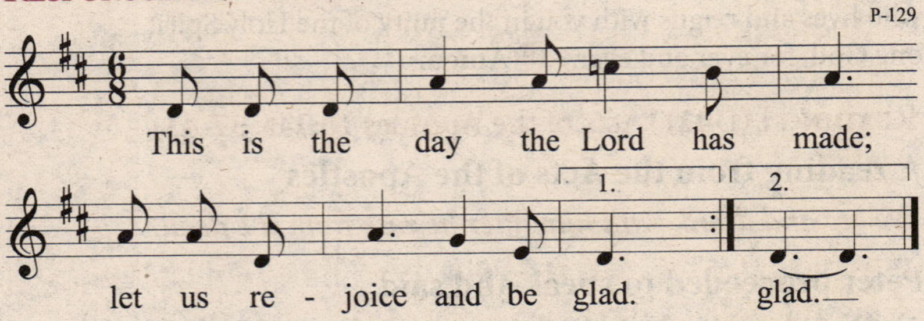

Music: Jay F. Hunstiger, © 1990, administered by Liturgical Press.

Psalm 118:1-2, 16-17, 22-23

℟. (24) **This is the day the Lord has made; let us rejoice and be glad.** *or:* ℟. **Alleluia.**

Give thanks to the LORD, for he is good,
for his mercy endures forever.
Let the house of Israel say,
"His mercy endures forever." ℟.

"The right hand of the LORD has struck with power;
the right hand of the LORD is exalted.
I shall not die, but live,
and declare the works of the LORD." ℟.

The stone which the builders rejected
has become the cornerstone.
By the LORD has this been done;
it is wonderful in our eyes. ℟.

Reading II

A (Colossians 3:1-4)

A reading from the Letter of Saint Paul to the Colossians

Seek what is above, where Christ is.

Brothers and sisters:
If then you were raised with Christ, seek what is above,
where Christ is seated at the right hand of God.
Think of what is above, not of what is on earth.
For you have died, and your life is hidden with Christ
in God.

When Christ your life appears,
then you too will appear with him in glory.

The word of the Lord. All: **Thanks be to God.**

Or:

B (1 Corinthians 5:6b-8)

A reading from the first Letter of Saint Paul to the Corinthians

Clear out the old yeast, so that you may become a fresh batch of dough.

Brothers and sisters:
Do you not know that a little yeast leavens all the dough?
Clear out the old yeast,
so that you may become a fresh batch of dough,
inasmuch as you are unleavened.
For our paschal lamb, Christ, has been sacrificed.
Therefore, let us celebrate the feast,
not with the old yeast, the yeast of malice and wickedness,
but with the unleavened bread of sincerity and truth.

The word of the Lord. All: **Thanks be to God.**

SEQUENCE
Victimae paschali laudes

Christians, to the Paschal Victim
Offer your thankful praises!
A Lamb the sheep redeems;
Christ, who only is sinless,
Reconciles sinners to the Father.
Death and life have contended in that combat stupendous:
The Prince of life, who died, reigns immortal.
Speak, Mary, declaring
What you saw, wayfaring.
"The tomb of Christ, who is living,
The glory of Jesus' resurrection;

Bright angels attesting,
The shroud and napkin resting.
Yes, Christ my hope is arisen;
To Galilee he goes before you."
Christ indeed from death is risen, our new life obtaining.
Have mercy, victor King, ever reigning!
Amen. Alleluia.

GOSPEL
(John 20:1-9) *or* (Luke 24:1-12) *or* afternoon (Luke 24:13-35)
ALLELUIA (*See* 1 Corinthians 5:7b-8a)

℣. Alleluia, alleluia. ℟. **Alleluia, alleluia.**
℣. Christ, our paschal lamb, has been sacrificed;
let us then feast with joy in the Lord. ℟.

✠ **A reading from the holy Gospel according to John**

All: **Glory to you, O Lord.**

He had to rise from the dead.

On the first day of the week,
Mary of Magdala came to the tomb early in the morning,
while it was still dark,
and saw the stone removed from the tomb.
So she ran and went to Simon Peter
and to the other disciple whom Jesus loved, and told them,
"They have taken the Lord from the tomb,
and we don't know where they put him."
So Peter and the other disciple went out and came to the tomb.
They both ran, but the other disciple ran faster than Peter
and arrived at the tomb first;
he bent down and saw the burial cloths there, but did not go in.
When Simon Peter arrived after him,
he went into the tomb and saw the burial cloths there,
and the cloth that had covered his head,

not with the burial cloths but rolled up in a separate place.
Then the other disciple also went in,
the one who had arrived at the tomb first,
and he saw and believed.
For they did not yet understand the Scripture
that he had to rise from the dead.

The Gospel of the Lord. All: **Praise to you, Lord Jesus Christ.**

Renewal of Baptismal Promises

The renewal of baptismal promises may take place at all Masses today. The form followed is the same as at the Easter Vigil, page 223.

Prayer over the Offerings

Exultant with paschal gladness, O Lord,
we offer the sacrifice
by which your Church
is wondrously reborn and nourished.
Through Christ our Lord. All: **Amen.**

Communion Antiphon (1 Corinthians 5:7-8)

Christ our Passover has been sacrificed, alleluia;
therefore let us keep the feast with the unleavened bread
of purity and truth, alleluia, alleluia.

Prayer after Communion

Look upon your Church, O God,
with unfailing love and favor,
so that, renewed by the paschal mysteries,
she may come to the glory of the resurrection.
Through Christ our Lord. All: **Amen.**

Dismissal (*See* p. 225)

Second Sunday of Easter

(or OF DIVINE MERCY)

April 3, 2016

Reflection on the Gospel

When the risen Lord appears to the disciples locked away behind closed doors, fear is allayed by peace, sin is allayed by forgiveness, doubt is allayed by Presence, unbelieving is allayed by seeing-believing. We know to whom and what *our belief is directed: to Jesus and the gift of risen Life. We know* how *we receive risen Life: through Jesus' gift of the breath of the Holy Spirit dwelling within us. Risen Life is God's divine Life transforming who and how we are.*

- *Jesus lives, so I know . . .*

—Living Liturgy™, *Second Sunday of Easter 2016*

Entrance Antiphon (1 Peter 2:2)

Like newborn infants, you must long for the pure,
  spiritual milk,
that in him you may grow to salvation, alleluia.

Or:

(4 Esdras 2:36-37)

Receive the joy of your glory, giving thanks to God,
who has called you into the heavenly kingdom, alleluia.

Collect

God of everlasting mercy,
who in the very recurrence of the paschal feast
kindle the faith of the people you have made your own,
increase, we pray, the grace you have bestowed,
that all may grasp and rightly understand
in what font they have been washed,
by whose Spirit they have been reborn,
by whose Blood they have been redeemed.
Through our Lord Jesus Christ, your Son,
who lives and reigns with you in the unity of the Holy Spirit,
one God, for ever and ever. All: **Amen.**

Reading I (L 45-C) (Acts of the Apostles 5:12-16)

A reading from the Acts of the Apostles

More than ever, believers in the Lord, great numbers of men and women, were added to them.

**Many signs and wonders were done among the people
at the hands of the apostles.
They were all together in Solomon's portico.
None of the others dared to join them, but the people esteemed them.
Yet more than ever, believers in the Lord,
great numbers of men and women, were added to them.
Thus they even carried the sick out into the streets
and laid them on cots and mats
so that when Peter came by,
at least his shadow might fall on one or another of them.
A large number of people from the towns
in the vicinity of Jerusalem also gathered,
bringing the sick and those disturbed by unclean spirits,
and they were all cured.**

The word of the Lord. All: **Thanks be to God.**

Responsorial Psalm 118

P-495

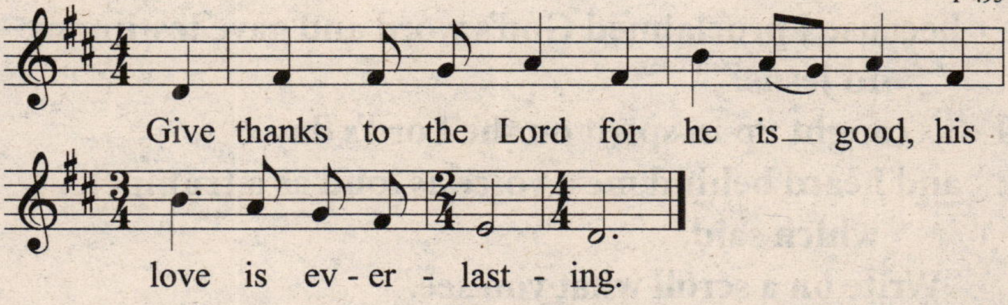

Psalm 118:2-4, 13-15, 22-24

℟. (1) **Give thanks to the Lord for he is good, his love is everlasting.** *or:* ℟. **Alleluia.**

Let the house of Israel say,
"His mercy endures forever."

(continued)

Let the house of Aaron say,
"His mercy endures forever."
Let those who fear the LORD say,
"His mercy endures forever." ℟.

I was hard pressed and was falling,
but the LORD helped me.
My strength and my courage is the LORD,
and he has been my savior.
The joyful shout of victory
in the tents of the just. ℟.

The stone which the builders rejected
has become the cornerstone.
By the LORD has this been done;
it is wonderful in our eyes.
This is the day the LORD has made;
let us be glad and rejoice in it. ℟.

READING II (Revelation 1:9-11a, 12-13, 17-19)

A reading from the Book of Revelation

I was dead, but now I am alive forever and ever.

I, John, your brother, who share with you
the distress, the kingdom, and the endurance we have in Jesus,
found myself on the island called Patmos
because I proclaimed God's word and gave testimony to Jesus.
I was caught up in spirit on the Lord's day
and heard behind me a voice as loud as a trumpet, which said,
"Write on a scroll what you see."
Then I turned to see whose voice it was that spoke to me,
and when I turned, I saw seven gold lampstands
and in the midst of the lampstands one like a son of man,
wearing an ankle-length robe, with a gold sash around his chest.

When I caught sight of him, I fell down at his feet as though dead.
He touched me with his right hand and said, "Do not be afraid.
I am the first and the last, the one who lives.
Once I was dead, but now I am alive forever and ever.
I hold the keys to death and the netherworld.
Write down, therefore, what you have seen,
and what is happening, and what will happen afterwards."

The word of the Lord. All: **Thanks be to God.**

GOSPEL (John 20:19-31)

ALLELUIA (John 20:29)

℣. Alleluia, alleluia. ℟. **Alleluia, alleluia.**
℣. You believe in me, Thomas, because you have seen me, says the Lord;
blessed are they who have not seen me, but still believe! ℟.

✠ **A reading from the holy Gospel according to John**

All: **Glory to you, O Lord.**

Eight days later Jesus came and stood in their midst.

On the evening of that first day of the week,
when the doors were locked, where the disciples were,
for fear of the Jews,
Jesus came and stood in their midst
and said to them, "Peace be with you."
When he had said this, he showed them his hands and his side.
The disciples rejoiced when they saw the Lord.
Jesus said to them again, "Peace be with you.
As the Father has sent me, so I send you."
And when he had said this, he breathed on them and said to them,
"Receive the Holy Spirit.

**Whose sins you forgive are forgiven them,
and whose sins you retain are retained."**

**Thomas, called Didymus, one of the Twelve,
was not with them when Jesus came.
So the other disciples said to him, "We have seen the Lord."
But he said to them,
"Unless I see the mark of the nails in his hands
and put my finger into the nailmarks
and put my hand into his side, I will not believe."**

**Now a week later his disciples were again inside
and Thomas was with them.
Jesus came, although the doors were locked,
and stood in their midst and said, "Peace be with you."
Then he said to Thomas, "Put your finger here and see my hands,
and bring your hand and put it into my side,
and do not be unbelieving, but believe."
Thomas answered and said to him, "My Lord and my God!"
Jesus said to him, "Have you come to believe because you have seen me?
Blessed are those who have not seen and have believed."**

**Now Jesus did many other signs in the presence of his disciples
that are not written in this book.
But these are written that you may come to believe
that Jesus is the Christ, the Son of God,
and that through this belief you may have life in his name.**

The Gospel of the Lord. All: **Praise to you, Lord Jesus Christ.**

PRAYER OVER THE OFFERINGS

Accept, O Lord, we pray,
the oblations of your people
(and of those you have brought to new birth),

that, renewed by confession of your name and by Baptism,
they may attain unending happiness.
Through Christ our Lord. All: **Amen.**

Communion Antiphon (Cf. John 20:27)

Bring your hand and feel the place of the nails,
and do not be unbelieving but believing, alleluia.

Prayer after Communion

Grant, we pray, almighty God,
that our reception of this paschal Sacrament
may have a continuing effect
in our minds and hearts.
Through Christ our Lord. All: **Amen.**

Third Sunday of Easter

April 10, 2016

Reflection on the Gospel

The risen Christ transforms the way we are, enabling us to obey his ongoing invitation, "Follow me." We are fortified by Jesus' risen Presence, by his invitation to follow, by his own love for us that transforms our love into faithfulness and fruitfulness. Risen Life fortifies us for the transformation needed on our discipleship journey of seeing-believing. Risen Life is given to us by Christ, but we must also seek it. Risen Life is a gift, but we must also grasp it.

- *Jesus lives, so I will now . . .*

—Living Liturgy™, *Third Sunday of Easter 2016*

Entrance Antiphon (Cf. Psalm 66[65]:1-2)

Cry out with joy to God, all the earth;
O sing to the glory of his name.
O render him glorious praise, alleluia.

COLLECT

May your people exult for ever, O God,
in renewed youthfulness of spirit,
so that, rejoicing now in the restored glory of our adoption,
we may look forward in confident hope
to the rejoicing of the day of resurrection.
Through our Lord Jesus Christ, your Son,
who lives and reigns with you in the unity of the Holy Spirit,
one God, for ever and ever. All: **Amen.**

READING I (L 48-C) (Acts of the Apostles 5:27-32, 40b-41)

A reading from the Acts of the Apostles

We are witnesses of these words as is the Holy Spirit.

When the captain and the court officers had brought the apostles in
and made them stand before the Sanhedrin,
the high priest questioned them,
"We gave you strict orders, did we not,
to stop teaching in that name?
Yet you have filled Jerusalem with your teaching
and want to bring this man's blood upon us."
But Peter and the apostles said in reply,
"We must obey God rather than men.
The God of our ancestors raised Jesus,
though you had him killed by hanging him on a tree.
God exalted him at his right hand as leader and savior
to grant Israel repentance and forgiveness of sins.
We are witnesses of these things,
as is the Holy Spirit whom God has given to those who obey him."

The Sanhedrin ordered the apostles
to stop speaking in the name of Jesus, and dismissed them.
So they left the presence of the Sanhedrin,
rejoicing that they had been found worthy
to suffer dishonor for the sake of the name.

The word of the Lord. All: **Thanks be to God.**

Responsorial Psalm 30

P-496

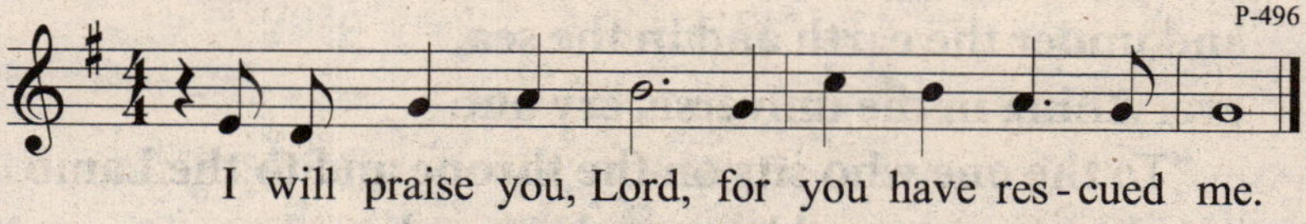

Psalm 30:2, 4, 5-6, 11-12, 13

℟. (2a) **I will praise you, Lord, for you have rescued me.**
or: ℟. **Alleluia.**

I will extol you, O LORD, for you drew me clear
and did not let my enemies rejoice over me.
O LORD, you brought me up from the netherworld;
you preserved me from among those going down into the pit. ℟.

Sing praise to the LORD, you his faithful ones,
and give thanks to his holy name.
For his anger lasts but a moment;
a lifetime, his good will.
At nightfall, weeping enters in,
but with the dawn, rejoicing. ℟.

Hear, O LORD, and have pity on me;
O LORD, be my helper.
You changed my mourning into dancing;
O LORD, my God, forever will I give you thanks. ℟.

Reading II (Revelation 5:11-14)

A reading from the Book of Revelation

Worthy is the Lamb that was slain to receive power and riches.

I, John, looked and heard the voices of many angels
who surrounded the throne
and the living creatures and the elders.
They were countless in number, and they cried out in a loud voice:
"Worthy is the Lamb that was slain
to receive power and riches, wisdom and strength,
honor and glory and blessing."

Then I heard every creature in heaven and on earth
and under the earth and in the sea,
everything in the universe, cry out:
"To the one who sits on the throne and to the Lamb
be blessing and honor, glory and might,
forever and ever."
The four living creatures answered, "Amen,"
and the elders fell down and worshiped.

The word of the Lord. All: **Thanks be to God.**

GOSPEL (John 21:1-19) *or* Shorter Form [ ] (John 21:1-14)

ALLELUIA

℣. Alleluia, alleluia. ℟. **Alleluia, alleluia.**
℣. Christ is risen, creator of all;
he has shown pity on all people. ℟.

✠ **A reading from the holy Gospel according to John**

All: **Glory to you, O Lord.**

Jesus came and took the bread and gave it to them and in like manner the fish.

[At that time, Jesus revealed himself again to his
disciples at the Sea of Tiberias.
He revealed himself in this way.
Together were Simon Peter, Thomas called Didymus,
Nathanael from Cana in Galilee,
Zebedee's sons, and two others of his disciples.
Simon Peter said to them, "I am going fishing."
They said to him, "We also will come with you."
So they went out and got into the boat,
but that night they caught nothing.
When it was already dawn, Jesus was standing on the shore;
but the disciples did not realize that it was Jesus.
Jesus said to them, "Children, have you caught anything to eat?"
They answered him, "No."

So he said to them, "Cast the net over the right side of the boat
and you will find something."
So they cast it, and were not able to pull it in
because of the number of fish.
So the disciple whom Jesus loved said to Peter, "It is the Lord."
When Simon Peter heard that it was the Lord,
he tucked in his garment, for he was lightly clad,
and jumped into the sea.
The other disciples came in the boat,
for they were not far from shore, only about a hundred yards,
dragging the net with the fish.
When they climbed out on shore,
they saw a charcoal fire with fish on it and bread.
Jesus said to them, "Bring some of the fish you just caught."
So Simon Peter went over and dragged the net ashore
full of one hundred fifty-three large fish.
Even though there were so many, the net was not torn.
Jesus said to them, "Come, have breakfast."
And none of the disciples dared to ask him, "Who are you?"
because they realized it was the Lord.
Jesus came over and took the bread and gave it to them,
and in like manner the fish.
This was now the third time Jesus was revealed to his disciples
after being raised from the dead.]

When they had finished breakfast, Jesus said to Simon Peter,
"Simon, son of John, do you love me more than these?
Simon Peter answered him, "Yes, Lord, you know that I love you."

Jesus said to him, "Feed my lambs."
He then said to Simon Peter a second time,
"Simon, son of John, do you love me?"
Simon Peter answered him, "Yes, Lord, you know that I love you."
Jesus said to him, "Tend my sheep."
Jesus said to him the third time,
"Simon, son of John, do you love me?"
Peter was distressed that Jesus had said to him a third time,
"Do you love me?" and he said to him,
"Lord, you know everything; you know that I love you."
Jesus said to him, "Feed my sheep.
Amen, amen, I say to you, when you were younger,
you used to dress yourself and go where you wanted;
but when you grow old, you will stretch out your hands,
and someone else will dress you
and lead you where you do not want to go."
He said this signifying by what kind of death he would glorify God.
And when he had said this, he said to him, "Follow me."

The Gospel of the Lord. All: **Praise to you, Lord Jesus Christ.**

Prayer over the Offerings

Receive, O Lord, we pray,
these offerings of your exultant Church,
and, as you have given her cause for such great gladness,
grant also that the gifts we bring
may bear fruit in perpetual happiness.
Through Christ our Lord. All: **Amen.**

Communion Antiphon Year C (Cf. John 21:12-13)

Jesus said to his disciples: Come and eat.
And he took bread and gave it to them, alleluia.

Prayer after Communion

Look with kindness upon your people, O Lord,
and grant, we pray,
that those you were pleased to renew by eternal mysteries

may attain in their flesh
the incorruptible glory of the resurrection.
Through Christ our Lord. All: **Amen.**

Fourth Sunday of Easter

April 17, 2016

Reflection on the Gospel

Gift-giving creates memories of goodness, establishes a habit of self-giving, assures the gift-giver of sharing in the dignity of the receiver. The focus of this gospel is giving, giving, giving. The Father gives us to Jesus as his flock. We give Jesus our attentive listening and faithful following. Jesus gives us eternal Life. There are no qualifying words in this gospel at all, no "ifs" about the giving. This is simply the way living risen Life is.

- *Jesus lives, so I will give . . .*

—Living Liturgy™, *Fourth Sunday of Easter 2016*

Entrance Antiphon (Cf. Psalm 33[32]:5-6)

The merciful love of the Lord fills the earth;
by the word of the Lord the heavens were made, alleluia.

Collect

Almighty ever-living God,
lead us to a share in the joys of heaven,
so that the humble flock may reach
where the brave Shepherd has gone before.
Who lives and reigns with you in the unity of the Holy Spirit,
one God, for ever and ever. All: **Amen.**

Reading I (L 51-C) (Acts of the Apostles 13:14, 43-52)

A reading from the Acts of the Apostles

We now turn to the Gentiles.

Paul and Barnabas continued on from Perga
and reached Antioch in Pisidia.

On the sabbath they entered the synagogue and took
their seats.
Many Jews and worshipers who were converts to Judaism
followed Paul and Barnabas, who spoke to them
and urged them to remain faithful to the grace of God.

On the following sabbath almost the whole city gathered
to hear the word of the Lord.
When the Jews saw the crowds, they were filled with
jealousy
and with violent abuse contradicted what Paul said.
Both Paul and Barnabas spoke out boldly and said,
"It was necessary that the word of God be spoken to
you first,
but since you reject it
and condemn yourselves as unworthy of eternal life,
we now turn to the Gentiles.
For so the Lord has commanded us,
I have made you a light to the Gentiles,
that you may be an instrument of salvation
***to the ends of the earth.*"**

The Gentiles were delighted when they heard this
and glorified the word of the Lord.
All who were destined for eternal life came to believe,
and the word of the Lord continued to spread
through the whole region.
The Jews, however, incited the women of prominence
who were worshipers
and the leading men of the city,
stirred up a persecution against Paul and Barnabas,
and expelled them from their territory.
So they shook the dust from their feet in protest against
them,
and went to Iconium.
The disciples were filled with joy and the Holy Spirit.

The word of the Lord. All: **Thanks be to God.**

Responsorial Psalm 100

P-497

Music: Jay F. Hunstiger, © 1991, administered by Liturgical Press.

Psalm 100:1-2, 3, 5

℟. (3c) We are his people, the sheep of his flock.
or: **℟. Alleluia.**

Sing joyfully to the Lord, all you lands;
serve the Lord with gladness;
come before him with joyful song. ℟.

Know that the Lord is God;
he made us, his we are;
his people, the flock he tends. ℟.

The Lord is good:
his kindness endures forever,
and his faithfulness, to all generations. ℟.

Reading II (Revelation 7:9, 14b-17)

A reading from the Book of Revelation

The Lamb will shepherd them and lead them to springs of life-giving water.

I, John, had a vision of a great multitude,
which no one could count,
from every nation, race, people, and tongue.
They stood before the throne and before the Lamb,
wearing white robes and holding palm branches in their hands.

Then one of the elders said to me,
"These are the ones who have survived the time of great distress;
they have washed their robes
and made them white in the blood of the Lamb.

"For this reason they stand before God's throne
and worship him day and night in his temple.

The one who sits on the throne will shelter them.
They will not hunger or thirst anymore,
nor will the sun or any heat strike them.
For the Lamb who is in the center of the throne
will shepherd them
and lead them to springs of life-giving water,
and God will wipe away every tear from their eyes."

The word of the Lord. All: **Thanks be to God.**

Gospel (John 10:27-30)

Alleluia (John 10:14)

℣. Alleluia, alleluia. ℟. **Alleluia, alleluia.**
℣. I am the good shepherd, says the Lord;
I know my sheep, and mine know me. ℟.

✠ **A reading from the holy Gospel according to John**

All: **Glory to you, O Lord.**

I give my sheep eternal life.

Jesus said:
"My sheep hear my voice;
I know them, and they follow me.
I give them eternal life, and they shall never perish.
No one can take them out of my hand.
My Father, who has given them to me, is greater than all,
and no one can take them out of the Father's hand.
The Father and I are one."

The Gospel of the Lord. All: **Praise to you, Lord Jesus Christ.**

Prayer over the Offerings

Grant, we pray, O Lord,
that we may always find delight in these paschal mysteries,
so that the renewal constantly at work within us
may be the cause of our unending joy.
Through Christ our Lord. All: **Amen.**

Communion Antiphon

The Good Shepherd has risen,
who laid down his life for his sheep
and willingly died for his flock, alleluia.

Prayer after Communion

Look upon your flock, kind Shepherd,
and be pleased to settle in eternal pastures
the sheep you have redeemed
by the Precious Blood of your Son.
Who lives and reigns for ever and ever. All: **Amen.**

Fifth Sunday of Easter

April 24, 2016

Reflection on the Gospel

Judas's departure initiates the events of Jesus' passion, death, and resurrection. Jesus' imminent departure initiates his giving the disciples the commandment to love as he has loved. Jesus' passion and death is the full revelation to us of what it means to love as Jesus loved. His resurrection is the full revelation of God's glory. Love means giving one's life for others. This is God's glory. This is Jesus' glory. This is our glory.

- *Jesus lives, so I must . . .*

—Living Liturgy™, *Fifth Sunday of Easter 2016*

Entrance Antiphon (Cf. Psalm 98[97]:1-2)

O sing a new song to the Lord,
for he has worked wonders;
in the sight of the nations
he has shown his deliverance, alleluia.

Collect

Almighty ever-living God,
constantly accomplish the Paschal Mystery within us,
that those you were pleased to make new in Holy Baptism
may, under your protective care, bear much fruit
and come to the joys of life eternal.
Through our Lord Jesus Christ, your Son,
who lives and reigns with you in the unity of the Holy Spirit,
one God, for ever and ever. All: **Amen.**

READING I (L 54-C) (Acts of the Apostles 14:21-27)

A reading from the Acts of the Apostles

They called the Church together and reported what God had done with them.

After Paul and Barnabas had proclaimed the good news
to that city
and made a considerable number of disciples,
they returned to Lystra and to Iconium and to Antioch.
They strengthened the spirits of the disciples
and exhorted them to persevere in the faith, saying,
"It is necessary for us to undergo many hardships
to enter the kingdom of God."
They appointed elders for them in each church and,
with prayer and fasting, commended them to the Lord
in whom they had put their faith.
Then they traveled through Pisidia and reached
Pamphylia.
After proclaiming the word at Perga they went down to
Attalia.
From there they sailed to Antioch,
where they had been commended to the grace of God
for the work they had now accomplished.
And when they arrived, they called the church together
and reported what God had done with them
and how he had opened the door of faith to the
Gentiles.

The word of the Lord. All: **Thanks be to God.**

RESPONSORIAL PSALM 145

P-498

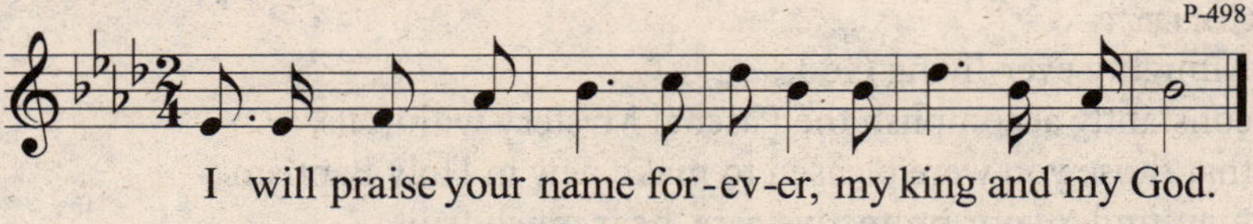

Psalm 145:8-9, 10-11, 12-13

℟. (*See* 1) **I will praise your name for ever, my king and my God.** *or:* ℟. **Alleluia.**

The LORD is gracious and merciful,
slow to anger and of great kindness.
The LORD is good to all
and compassionate toward all his works. ℟.

Let all your works give you thanks, O LORD,
and let your faithful ones bless you.
Let them discourse of the glory of your kingdom
and speak of your might. ℟.

Let them make known your might to the children of Adam,
and the glorious splendor of your kingdom.
Your kingdom is a kingdom for all ages,
and your dominion endures through all generations. ℟.

READING II (Revelation 21:1-5a)

A reading from the Book of Revelation

God will wipe every tear from their eyes.

Then I, John, saw a new heaven and a new earth.
The former heaven and the former earth had passed away,
and the sea was no more.
I also saw the holy city, a new Jerusalem,
coming down out of heaven from God,
prepared as a bride adorned for her husband.
I heard a loud voice from the throne saying,
"Behold, God's dwelling is with the human race.
He will dwell with them and they will be his people
and God himself will always be with them as their God.
He will wipe every tear from their eyes,
and there shall be no more death or mourning,
wailing or pain,
for the old order has passed away."

The One who sat on the throne said,
"Behold, I make all things new."

The word of the Lord. All: **Thanks be to God.**

Gospel (John 13:31-33a, 34-35)

Alleluia (John 13:34)

℣. Alleluia, alleluia. ℟. **Alleluia, alleluia.**
℣. I give you a new commandment, says the Lord:
love one another as I have loved you. ℟.

✠ **A reading from the holy Gospel according to John**

All: **Glory to you, O Lord.**

I give you a new commandment: love one another.

When Judas had left them, Jesus said,
"Now is the Son of Man glorified, and God is glorified in him.
If God is glorified in him,
God will also glorify him in himself,
and God will glorify him at once.
My children, I will be with you only a little while longer.
I give you a new commandment: love one another.
As I have loved you, so you also should love one another.
This is how all will know that you are my disciples,
if you have love for one another."

The Gospel of the Lord. All: **Praise to you, Lord Jesus Christ.**

Prayer over the Offerings

O God, who by the wonderful exchange effected in this sacrifice
have made us partakers of the one supreme Godhead,
grant, we pray,
that, as we have come to know your truth,
we may make it ours by a worthy way of life.
Through Christ our Lord. All: **Amen.**

Communion Antiphon (Cf. John 15:1, 5)

I am the true vine and you are the branches, says the Lord.
Whoever remains in me, and I in him, bears fruit in plenty, alleluia.

Prayer after Communion

Graciously be present to your people, we pray, O Lord,
and lead those you have imbued with heavenly mysteries
to pass from former ways to newness of life.
Through Christ our Lord. All: **Amen.**

Sixth Sunday of Easter

May 1, 2016

Reflection on the Gospel

The word of Jesus we are to keep is his command to love as he loves us. Jesus' word, however, is not simply spoken, but is love-in-action. His love-in-action is the gift of the Spirit of peace, of untroubled hearts, of rejoicing, of believing. His love-in-action is ultimately the gift of the resurrection. Our love-in-action flows from the gift of the Holy Spirit dwelling in us and teaching us to keep Jesus' word-command to love. Our love-in-action is risen Life-made-visible.

- *Jesus lives and gives the Holy Spirit to those who . . .*

—Living Liturgy™, *Sixth Sunday of Easter 2016*

Entrance Antiphon (Cf. Isaiah 48:20)

Proclaim a joyful sound and let it be heard;
proclaim to the ends of the earth:
The Lord has freed his people, alleluia.

Collect

Grant, almighty God,
that we may celebrate with heartfelt devotion these days of joy,
which we keep in honor of the risen Lord,
and that what we relive in remembrance
we may always hold to in what we do.
Through our Lord Jesus Christ, your Son,
who lives and reigns with you in the unity of the Holy Spirit,
one God, for ever and ever. All: **Amen.**

When the Ascension of the Lord is celebrated the following Sunday, the second reading and Gospel from the Seventh Sunday of Easter (*see* nos. 59–61) may be read on the Sixth Sunday of Easter.

Reading I (L 57-C) (Acts of the Apostles 15:1-2, 22-29)

A reading from the Acts of the Apostles

It is the decision of the Holy Spirit and of us not to place on you any burden beyond these necessities.

Some who had come down from Judea were instructing the brothers,
"Unless you are circumcised according to the Mosaic practice,
you cannot be saved."
Because there arose no little dissension and debate
by Paul and Barnabas with them,
it was decided that Paul, Barnabas, and some of the others
should go up to Jerusalem to the apostles and elders
about this question.

The apostles and elders, in agreement with the whole church,
decided to choose representatives
and to send them to Antioch with Paul and Barnabas.
The ones chosen were Judas, who was called Barsabbas,
and Silas, leaders among the brothers.
This is the letter delivered by them:

"The apostles and the elders, your brothers,
to the brothers in Antioch, Syria, and Cilicia
of Gentile origin: greetings.
Since we have heard that some of our number
who went out without any mandate from us
have upset you with their teachings
and disturbed your peace of mind,
we have with one accord decided to choose representatives
and to send them to you along with our beloved Barnabas and Paul,
who have dedicated their lives to the name of our Lord Jesus Christ.

So we are sending Judas and Silas
who will also convey this same message by word of mouth:
'It is the decision of the Holy Spirit and of us
not to place on you any burden beyond these necessities,
namely, to abstain from meat sacrificed to idols,
from blood, from meats of strangled animals,
and from unlawful marriage.
If you keep free of these,
you will be doing what is right. Farewell.' "

The word of the Lord. All: **Thanks be to God.**

RESPONSORIAL PSALM 67

P-499

Psalm 67:2-3, 5, 6, 8

℟. (4) **O God, let all the nations praise you!**
or: ℟. **Alleluia.**

May God have pity on us and bless us;
may he let his face shine upon us.
So may your way be known upon earth;
among all nations, your salvation. ℟.

May the nations be glad and exult
because you rule the peoples in equity;
the nations on the earth you guide. ℟.

May the peoples praise you, O God;
may all the peoples praise you!
May God bless us,
and may all the ends of the earth fear him! ℟.

Reading II (Revelation 21:10-14, 22-23)

A reading from the Book of Revelation

The angel showed me the holy city coming down out of heaven.

The angel took me in spirit to a great, high mountain
and showed me the holy city Jerusalem
coming down out of heaven from God.
It gleamed with the splendor of God.
Its radiance was like that of a precious stone,
like jasper, clear as crystal.
It had a massive, high wall,
with twelve gates where twelve angels were stationed
and on which names were inscribed,
the names of the twelve tribes of the Israelites.
There were three gates facing east,
three north, three south, and three west.
The wall of the city had twelve courses of stones as its foundation,
on which were inscribed the twelve names
of the twelve apostles of the Lamb.

I saw no temple in the city
for its temple is the Lord God almighty and the Lamb.
The city had no need of sun or moon to shine on it,
for the glory of God gave it light,
and its lamp was the Lamb.

The word of the Lord. All: **Thanks be to God.**

Gospel (John 14:23-29)

Alleluia (John 14:23)

℣. Alleluia, alleluia. ℟. **Alleluia, alleluia.**
℣. Whoever loves me will keep my word, says the Lord,
and my Father will love him and we will come to him. ℟.

✠ **A reading from the holy Gospel according to John**

All: **Glory to you, O Lord.**

The Holy Spirit will teach you everything and remind you of all that I told you.

Jesus said to his disciples:
"Whoever loves me will keep my word,
and my Father will love him,
and we will come to him and make our dwelling with him.
Whoever does not love me does not keep my words;
yet the word you hear is not mine
but that of the Father who sent me.

"I have told you this while I am with you.
The Advocate, the Holy Spirit,
whom the Father will send in my name,
will teach you everything
and remind you of all that I told you.
Peace I leave with you; my peace I give to you.
Not as the world gives do I give it to you.
Do not let your hearts be troubled or afraid.
You heard me tell you,
'I am going away and I will come back to you.'
If you loved me,
you would rejoice that I am going to the Father;
for the Father is greater than I.
And now I have told you this before it happens,
so that when it happens you may believe."

The Gospel of the Lord. All: **Praise to you, Lord Jesus Christ.**

Prayer over the Offerings

May our prayers rise up to you, O Lord,
together with the sacrificial offerings,
so that, purified by your graciousness,
we may be conformed to the mysteries of your mighty love.
Through Christ our Lord. All: **Amen.**

Communion Antiphon (John 14:15-16)

If you love me, keep my commandments, says the Lord,
and I will ask the Father and he will send you another Paraclete,
to abide with you for ever, alleluia.

Prayer after Communion

Almighty ever-living God,
who restore us to eternal life in the Resurrection of Christ,
increase in us, we pray, the fruits of this paschal Sacrament
and pour into our hearts the strength of this saving food.
Through Christ our Lord. All: **Amen.**

The Ascension of the Lord

AT THE VIGIL MASS

May 4 or 7, 2016

This Mass is used on the evening of the day before the Solemnity, either before or after First Vespers (Evening Prayer I) of the Ascension.

Reflection on the Gospel

Jesus' ascension, for us, is a gift and commissioning. We receive the gift of the Holy Spirit. We preach and teach in his name. We don't do this on our own, as Jesus promised. We can't set out to take up Jesus' mission to preach the Good News until we open ourselves to the Holy Spirit's Presence with and among us. This ensures us that our work isn't ours but Christ's. Ultimately our mission is to preach not simply events but a Person—Jesus Christ, the risen One.

- *With Jesus taken up to heaven, I . . .*

—Living Liturgy™, *Ascension 2016*

Entrance Antiphon (Psalm 68[67]:33, 35)

You kingdoms of the earth, sing to God;
praise the Lord, who ascends above the highest heavens;
his majesty and might are in the skies, alleluia.

Collect

O God, whose Son today ascended to the heavens
as the Apostles looked on,
grant, we pray, that, in accordance with his promise,

we may be worthy for him to live with us always on earth,
and we with him in heaven.
Who lives and reigns with you in the unity of the Holy Spirit,
one God, for ever and ever. All: **Amen.**

(Readings are those of the day.)

Prayer over the Offerings

O God, whose Only Begotten Son, our High Priest,
is seated ever-living at your right hand to intercede for us,
grant that we may approach with confidence the throne of grace
and there obtain your mercy.
Through Christ our Lord. All: **Amen.**

Communion Antiphon (Cf. Hebrews 10:12)

Christ, offering a single sacrifice for sins,
is seated for ever at God's right hand, alleluia.

Prayer after Communion

May the gifts we have received from your altar, Lord,
kindle in our hearts a longing for the heavenly homeland
and cause us to press forward, following in the Savior's footsteps,
to the place where for our sake he entered before us.
Who lives and reigns for ever and ever. All: **Amen.**

May 5 or 8

AT THE MASS DURING THE DAY

If the feast of the Ascension is celebrated on the Seventh Sunday of Easter in your diocese, please turn to page 263 for the texts for today.

Entrance Antiphon (Acts of the Apostles 1:11)

Men of Galilee, why gaze in wonder at the heavens?
This Jesus whom you saw ascending into heaven
will return as you saw him go, alleluia.

Collect

Gladden us with holy joys, almighty God,
and make us rejoice with devout thanksgiving,
for the Ascension of Christ your Son
is our exaltation,
and, where the Head has gone before in glory,
the Body is called to follow in hope.

Through our Lord Jesus Christ, your Son,
who lives and reigns with you in the unity of the Holy Spirit,
one God, for ever and ever. All: **Amen.**

Or:

Grant, we pray, almighty God,
that we, who believe that your Only Begotten Son, our Redeemer,
ascended this day to the heavens,
may in spirit dwell already in heavenly realms.
Who lives and reigns with you in the unity of the Holy Spirit,
one God, for ever and ever. All: **Amen.**

Reading I (L 58-C) (Acts of the Apostles 1:1-11)

A reading from the beginning of the Acts of the Apostles

As the Apostles were looking on, Jesus was lifted up.

In the first book, Theophilus,
I dealt with all that Jesus did and taught
until the day he was taken up,
after giving instructions through the Holy Spirit
to the apostles whom he had chosen.
He presented himself alive to them
by many proofs after he had suffered,
appearing to them during forty days
and speaking about the kingdom of God.
While meeting with them,
he enjoined them not to depart from Jerusalem,
but to wait for "the promise of the Father
about which you have heard me speak;
for John baptized with water,
but in a few days you will be baptized with the Holy Spirit."

When they had gathered together they asked him,
"Lord, are you at this time going to restore the kingdom to Israel?"
He answered them, "It is not for you to know the times or seasons
that the Father has established by his own authority.

But you will receive power when the Holy Spirit comes
upon you,
and you will be my witnesses in Jerusalem,
throughout Judea and Samaria,
and to the ends of the earth."
When he had said this, as they were looking on,
he was lifted up, and a cloud took him from their sight.
While they were looking intently at the sky as he was going,
suddenly two men dressed in white garments stood
beside them.
They said, "Men of Galilee,
why are you standing there looking at the sky?
This Jesus who has been taken up from you into heaven
will return in the same way as you have seen him
going into heaven."

The word of the Lord. All: **Thanks be to God.**

Responsorial Psalm 47

Psalm 47:2-3, 6-7, 8-9

℟. (6) **God mounts his throne to shouts of joy: a blare of trumpets for the Lord.** *or:* ℟. **Alleluia.**

All you peoples, clap your hands,
shout to God with cries of gladness,
for the LORD, the Most High, the awesome,
is the great king over all the earth. ℟.

God mounts his throne amid shouts of joy;
the LORD, amid trumpet blasts.
Sing praise to God, sing praise;
sing praise to our king, sing praise. ℟.

For king of all the earth is God;
sing hymns of praise.

(continued)

God reigns over the nations,
God sits upon his holy throne. ℟.

Reading II

A (Ephesians 1:17-23)

A reading from the Letter of Saint Paul to the Ephesians

God seated Jesus at his right hand in the heavens.

Brothers and sisters:
May the God of our Lord Jesus Christ, the Father of glory,
give you a Spirit of wisdom and revelation
resulting in knowledge of him.
May the eyes of your hearts be enlightened,
that you may know what is the hope that belongs to his call,
what are the riches of glory
in his inheritance among the holy ones,
and what is the surpassing greatness of his power
for us who believe,
in accord with the exercise of his great might,
which he worked in Christ,
raising him from the dead
and seating him at his right hand in the heavens,
far above every principality, authority, power, and dominion,
and every name that is named
not only in this age but also in the one to come.
And he put all things beneath his feet
and gave him as head over all things to the church,
which is his body,
the fullness of the one who fills all things in every way.

The word of the Lord. All: **Thanks be to God.**

Or:

B (Hebrews 9:24-28; 10:19-23)

A reading from the Letter to the Hebrews

Christ has entered into heaven itself.

**Christ did not enter into a sanctuary made by hands,
a copy of the true one, but heaven itself,
that he might now appear before God on our behalf.
Not that he might offer himself repeatedly,
as the high priest enters each year into the sanctuary
with blood that is not his own;
if that were so, he would have had to suffer repeatedly
from the foundation of the world.
But now once for all he has appeared at the end of the ages
to take away sin by his sacrifice.
Just as it is appointed that men and women die once,
and after this the judgment, so also Christ,
offered once to take away the sins of many,
will appear a second time, not to take away sin
but to bring salvation to those who eagerly await him.**

**Therefore, brothers and sisters, since through the blood of Jesus
we have confidence of entrance into the sanctuary
by the new and living way he opened for us through the veil,
that is, his flesh,
and since we have "a great priest over the house of God,"
let us approach with a sincere heart and in absolute trust,
with our hearts sprinkled clean from an evil conscience
and our bodies washed in pure water.
Let us hold unwaveringly to our confession that gives us hope,
for he who made the promise is trustworthy.**

The word of the Lord. All: **Thanks be to God.**

Gospel (Luke 24:46-53)

Alleluia (Matthew 28:19a, 20b)

℣. Alleluia, alleluia. ℟. **Alleluia, alleluia.**
℣. Go and teach all nations, says the Lord;
I am with you always, until the end of the world. ℟.

✠ **A reading from the conclusion of the holy Gospel according to Luke**

All: **Glory to you, O Lord.**

As he blessed them, he was taken up to heaven.

Jesus said to his disciples:
"Thus it is written that the Christ would suffer
and rise from the dead on the third day
and that repentance, for the forgiveness of sins,
would be preached in his name
to all the nations, beginning from Jerusalem.
You are witnesses of these things.
And behold I am sending the promise of my Father upon you;
but stay in the city
until you are clothed with power from on high."

Then he led them out as far as Bethany,
raised his hands, and blessed them.
As he blessed them he parted from them
and was taken up to heaven.
They did him homage
and then returned to Jerusalem with great joy,
and they were continually in the temple praising God.

The Gospel of the Lord. All: **Praise to you, Lord Jesus Christ.**

Prayer over the Offerings

We offer sacrifice now in supplication, O Lord,
to honor the wondrous Ascension of your Son:
grant, we pray,
that through this most holy exchange
we, too, may rise up to the heavenly realms.
Through Christ our Lord. All: **Amen.**

Communion Antiphon (Matthew 28:20)
Behold, I am with you always,
even to the end of the age, alleluia.

Prayer after Communion
Almighty ever-living God,
who allow those on earth to celebrate divine mysteries,
grant, we pray,
that Christian hope may draw us onward
to where our nature is united with you.
Through Christ our Lord. All: **Amen.**

Seventh Sunday of Easter

May 8, 2016

Reflection on the Gospel

Jesus' prayer for his disciples at the Last Supper is not only for them, "but also for those who will believe in" him because they have heard the disciples' word. This includes each one of us, here and now. His prayer for us? That we "be one" in him, that we share in Jesus' risen glory, that we "be brought to perfection," that we be loved, that we know Jesus was sent by the Father. Our work: to transform the world.

- *Those who believe in Jesus transform the world by . . .*

—Living Liturgy™, *Seventh Sunday of Easter 2016*

Entrance Antiphon (Cf. Psalm 27[26]:7-9)
O Lord, hear my voice, for I have called to you;
of you my heart has spoken: Seek his face;
hide not your face from me, alleluia.

Collect
Graciously hear our supplications, O Lord,
so that we, who believe that the Savior of the human race
is with you in your glory,
may experience, as he promised,

until the end of the world,
his abiding presence among us.
Who lives and reigns with you in the unity of the Holy Spirit,
one God, for ever and ever. All: **Amen.**

In those places where the Solemnity of the Ascension of the Lord has been transferred to the Seventh Sunday of Easter, the Mass and readings of the Ascension are used. See page 257.

Reading I (L 61-C) (Acts of the Apostles 7:55-60)

A reading from the Acts of the Apostles

I see the Son of Man standing at the right hand of God.

Stephen, filled with the Holy Spirit,
looked up intently to heaven and saw the glory of God
and Jesus standing at the right hand of God,
and Stephen said, "Behold, I see the heavens opened
and the Son of Man standing at the right hand of God."
But they cried out in a loud voice,
covered their ears, and rushed upon him together.
They threw him out of the city, and began to stone him.
The witnesses laid down their cloaks
at the feet of a young man named Saul.
As they were stoning Stephen, he called out,
"Lord Jesus, receive my spirit."
Then he fell to his knees and cried out in a loud voice,
"Lord, do not hold this sin against them";
and when he said this, he fell asleep.

The word of the Lord. All: **Thanks be to God.**

Responsorial Psalm 97

P-500

Psalm 97:1-2, 6-7, 9

℟. (1a and 9a) **The Lord is king, the most high over all the earth.** *or:* ℟. **Alleluia.**

The LORD is king; let the earth rejoice;
  let the many islands be glad.
Justice and judgment are the foundation of his throne. ℟.

The heavens proclaim his justice,
  and all peoples see his glory.
All gods are prostrate before him. ℟.

You, O LORD, are the Most High over all the earth,
  exalted far above all gods. ℟.

READING II (Revelation 22:12-14, 16-17, 20)

A reading from the Book of Revelation

Come, Lord Jesus!

I, John, heard a voice saying to me:
"Behold, I am coming soon.
I bring with me the recompense I will give to each according to his deeds.
I am the Alpha and the Omega, the first and the last, the beginning and the end."

Blessed are they who wash their robes
so as to have the right to the tree of life
and enter the city through its gates.

"I, Jesus, sent my angel to give you this testimony for the churches.
I am the root and offspring of David,
the bright morning star."

The Spirit and the bride say, "Come."
Let the hearer say, "Come."
Let the one who thirsts come forward,
and the one who wants it receive the gift of life-giving water.

The one who gives this testimony says, "Yes, I am coming soon."
Amen! Come, Lord Jesus!

The word of the Lord. All: **Thanks be to God.**

Gospel (John 17:20-26)

Alleluia (*See* John 14:18)

℣. Alleluia, alleluia. ℟. **Alleluia, alleluia.**
℣. I will not leave you orphans, says the Lord.
I will come back to you, and your hearts will rejoice. ℟.

✠ A reading from the holy Gospel according to John

All: **Glory to you, O Lord.**

That they may be brought to perfection as one!

Lifting up his eyes to heaven, Jesus prayed, saying:
"Holy Father, I pray not only for them,
but also for those who will believe in me through their word,
so that they may all be one,
as you, Father, are in me and I in you,
that they also may be in us,
that the world may believe that you sent me.
And I have given them the glory you gave me,
so that they may be one, as we are one,
I in them and you in me,
that they may be brought to perfection as one,
that the world may know that you sent me,
and that you loved them even as you loved me.
Father, they are your gift to me.
I wish that where I am they also may be with me,
that they may see my glory that you gave me,
because you loved me before the foundation of the world.
Righteous Father, the world also does not know you,
but I know you, and they know that you sent me.
I made known to them your name and I will make it known,
that the love with which you loved me
may be in them and I in them."

The Gospel of the Lord. All: **Praise to you, Lord Jesus Christ.**

Prayer over the Offerings
Accept, O Lord, the prayers of your faithful
with the sacrificial offerings,
that through these acts of devotedness
we may pass over to the glory of heaven.
Through Christ our Lord. All: **Amen.**

Communion Antiphon (John 17:22)
Father, I pray that they may be one
as we also are one, alleluia.

Prayer after Communion
Hear us, O God our Savior,
and grant us confidence,
that through these sacred mysteries
there will be accomplished in the body of the whole Church
what has already come to pass in Christ her Head.
Who lives and reigns for ever and ever. All: **Amen.**

Pentecost Sunday

VIGIL MASS Simple Form

May 14, 2016

The Mass of the Vigil of Pentecost is used on Saturday evening in those places where the Sunday obligation may be fulfilled on Saturday evening.

Entrance Antiphon (Romans 5:5; cf. 8:11)
The love of God has been poured into our hearts
through the Spirit of God dwelling within us, alleluia.

Collect
Almighty ever-living God,
who willed the Paschal Mystery
to be encompassed as a sign in fifty days,

grant that from out of the scattered nations
the confusion of many tongues
may be gathered by heavenly grace
into one great confession of your name.
Through our Lord Jesus Christ, your Son,
who lives and reigns with you in the unity of the Holy Spirit,
one God, for ever and ever. All: **Amen.**

Or:

Grant, we pray, almighty God,
that the splendor of your glory
may shine forth upon us
and that, by the bright rays of the Holy Spirit,
the light of your light may confirm the hearts
of those born again by your grace.
Through our Lord Jesus Christ, your Son,
who lives and reigns with you in the unity of the Holy Spirit,
one God, for ever and ever. All: **Amen.**

These readings are used at Saturday Evening Mass celebrated either before or after Evening Prayer I of Pentecost Sunday. The first of four options for the First Reading for this Mass is given here. Please see the others in the lectionary: Exodus 19:3-8a, 16-20b; Ezekiel 37:1-14; or Joel 3:1-5.

READING I (L 62) *A* (Genesis 11:1-9)

A reading from the Book of Genesis

It was called Babel because there the Lord confused the speech of all the world.

The whole world spoke the same language, using the same words.
While the people were migrating in the east,
they came upon a valley in the land of Shinar and settled there.
They said to one another,
"Come, let us mold bricks and harden them with fire."
They used bricks for stone, and bitumen for mortar.
Then they said, "Come, let us build ourselves a city
and a tower with its top in the sky,
and so make a name for ourselves;
otherwise we shall be scattered all over the earth."

The LORD came down to see the city and the tower
that the people had built.
Then the LORD said: "If now, while they are one people,
all speaking the same language,
they have started to do this,
nothing will later stop them from doing whatever they presume to do.
Let us then go down there and confuse their language,
so that one will not understand what another says."
Thus the LORD scattered them from there all over the earth,
and they stopped building the city.
That is why it was called Babel,
because there the LORD confused the speech of all the world.
It was from that place that he scattered them all over the earth.

The word of the Lord. All: **Thanks be to God.**

RESPONSORIAL PSALM 104

P-137

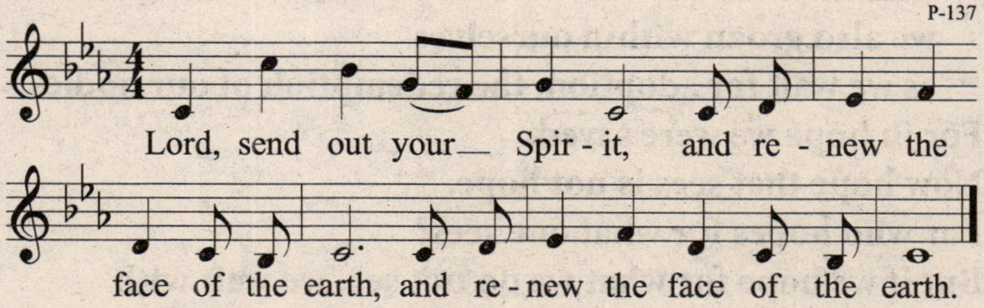

Psalm 104:1-2, 24, 35, 27-28, 29, 30

℟. (*See* 30) **Lord, send out your Spirit, and renew the face of the earth.** *or:* ℟. **Alleluia.**

Bless the LORD, O my soul!
O LORD, my God, you are great indeed!
You are clothed with majesty and glory,
robed in light as with a cloak. ℟.

How manifold are your works, O LORD!
In wisdom you have wrought them all—

(continued)

the earth is full of your creatures;
bless the LORD, O my soul! Alleluia. ℟.

Creatures all look to you
to give them food in due time.
When you give it to them, they gather it;
when you open your hand, they are filled with good things. ℟.

If you take away their breath, they perish
and return to their dust.
When you send forth your spirit, they are created,
and you renew the face of the earth. ℟.

READING II (Romans 8:22-27)

A reading from the Letter of Saint Paul to the Romans

The Spirit intercedes with inexpressible groanings.

Brothers and sisters:
We know that all creation is groaning in labor pains even until now;
and not only that, but we ourselves,
who have the firstfruits of the Spirit,
we also groan within ourselves
as we wait for adoption, the redemption of our bodies.
For in hope we were saved.
Now hope that sees is not hope.
For who hopes for what one sees?
But if we hope for what we do not see, we wait with endurance.

In the same way, the Spirit too comes to the aid of our weakness;
for we do not know how to pray as we ought,
but the Spirit himself intercedes with inexpressible groanings.
And the one who searches hearts
knows what is the intention of the Spirit,
because he intercedes for the holy ones
according to God's will.

The word of the Lord. All: **Thanks be to God.**

GOSPEL (John 7:37-39)

ALLELUIA

℣. Alleluia, alleluia. ℟. **Alleluia, alleluia.**
℣. Come, Holy Spirit, fill the hearts of the faithful
and kindle in them the fire of your love. ℟.

✠ A reading from the holy Gospel according to John

All: **Glory to you, O Lord.**

Rivers of living water will flow.

On the last and greatest day of the feast,
Jesus stood up and exclaimed,
"Let anyone who thirsts come to me and drink.
As Scripture says:
***Rivers of living water will flow from within him* who believes in me."**

He said this in reference to the Spirit
that those who came to believe in him were to receive.
There was, of course, no Spirit yet,
because Jesus had not yet been glorified.

The Gospel of the Lord. All: **Praise to you, Lord Jesus Christ.**

PRAYER OVER THE OFFERINGS

Pour out upon these gifts the blessing of your Spirit,
we pray, O Lord,
so that through them your Church may be imbued with such love
that the truth of your saving mystery
may shine forth for the whole world.
Through Christ our Lord. All: **Amen.**

COMMUNION ANTIPHON (John 7:37)

On the last day of the festival, Jesus stood and cried out:
If anyone is thirsty, let him come to me and drink, alleluia.

PRAYER AFTER COMMUNION

May these gifts we have consumed
benefit us, O Lord,
that we may always be aflame with the same Spirit,
whom you wondrously poured out on your Apostles.
Through Christ our Lord. All: **Amen.**

Dismissal

To dismiss the people the Deacon or, if there is no Deacon, the Priest himself sings or says:

Go forth, the Mass is ended, alleluia, alleluia.

Or:

Go in peace, alleluia, alleluia.

All reply: **Thanks be to God, alleluia, alleluia.**

May 15

MASS DURING THE DAY

Reflection on the Gospel

The Father sent the "Advocate, the Holy Spirit" to teach us "everything." What is this "everything" we need the Spirit to teach us? Why and how keeping Jesus' commandments and word is the unconditional condition of loving him. Why and how this love is the wellspring of our relationship to Jesus and his Father in their Spirit. What the Spirit teaches us, in the end, is why we do anything and how we do everything. Oh, how we need Pentecost!

- *Sent by Jesus the Holy Spirit . . .*

—Living Liturgy™, *Pentecost 2016*

Entrance Antiphon (Wisdom 1:7)

The Spirit of the Lord has filled the whole world
and that which contains all things
understands what is said, alleluia.

Or:

(Romans 5:5; cf. 8:11)

The love of God has been poured into our hearts
through the Spirit of God dwelling within us, alleluia.

Collect

O God, who by the mystery of today's great feast
sanctify your whole Church in every people and nation,
pour out, we pray, the gifts of the Holy Spirit
across the face of the earth
and, with the divine grace that was at work
when the Gospel was first proclaimed,
fill now once more the hearts of believers.

Through our Lord Jesus Christ, your Son,
who lives and reigns with you in the unity of the Holy Spirit,
one God, for ever and ever. All: **Amen.**

Reading I (L 63) (Acts of the Apostles 2:1-11)

A reading from the Acts of the Apostles

They were all filled with the Holy Spirit and began to speak.

**When the time for Pentecost was fulfilled,
they were all in one place together.
And suddenly there came from the sky
a noise like a strong driving wind,
and it filled the entire house in which they were.
Then there appeared to them tongues as of fire,
which parted and came to rest on each one of them.
And they were all filled with the Holy Spirit
and began to speak in different tongues,
as the Spirit enabled them to proclaim.**

**Now there were devout Jews from every nation under heaven staying in Jerusalem.
At this sound, they gathered in a large crowd,
but they were confused
because each one heard them speaking in his own language.
They were astounded, and in amazement they asked,
"Are not all these people who are speaking Galileans?
Then how does each of us hear them in his native language?
We are Parthians, Medes, and Elamites,
inhabitants of Mesopotamia, Judea and Cappadocia,
Pontus and Asia, Phrygia and Pamphylia,
Egypt and the districts of Libya near Cyrene,
as well as travelers from Rome,
both Jews and converts to Judaism, Cretans and Arabs,
yet we hear them speaking in our own tongues
of the mighty acts of God."**

The word of the Lord. All: **Thanks be to God.**

Responsorial Psalm 104

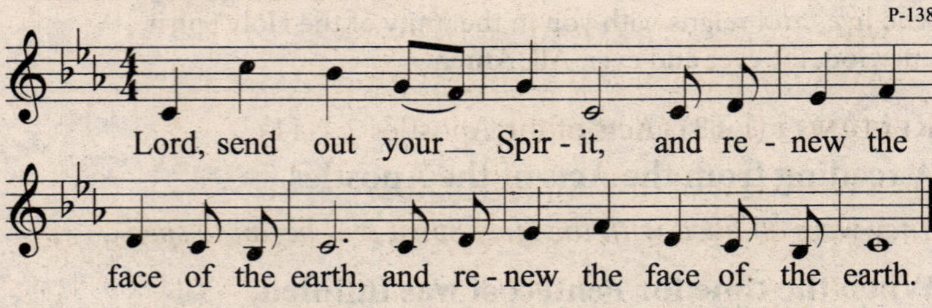

Psalm 104:1, 24, 29-30, 31, 34

℟. (*See* 30) **Lord, send out your Spirit, and renew the face of the earth.** *or:* ℟. **Alleluia.**

Bless the LORD, O my soul!
O LORD, my God, you are great indeed!
How manifold are your works, O LORD!
The earth is full of your creatures. ℟.

If you take away their breath, they perish
and return to their dust.
When you send forth your spirit, they are created,
and you renew the face of the earth. ℟.

May the glory of the LORD endure forever;
may the LORD be glad in his works!
Pleasing to him be my theme;
I will be glad in the LORD. ℟.

Reading II

A (1 Corinthians 12:3b-7, 12-13)

A reading from the first Letter of Saint Paul to the Corinthians

In one Spirit we were all baptized into one body.

Brothers and sisters:
No one can say, "Jesus is Lord," except by the Holy Spirit.

There are different kinds of spiritual gifts but the same Spirit;
there are different forms of service but the same Lord;

there are different workings but the same God
who produces all of them in everyone.
To each individual the manifestation of the Spirit
is given for some benefit.

As a body is one though it has many parts,
and all the parts of the body, though many, are one body,
so also Christ.
For in one Spirit we were all baptized into one body,
whether Jews or Greeks, slaves or free persons,
and we were all given to drink of one Spirit.

The word of the Lord. All: **Thanks be to God.**

Or:

B (Romans 8:8-17)

A reading from the Letter of Saint Paul to the Romans

Those who are led by the Spirit of God are children of God.

Brothers and sisters:
Those who are in the flesh cannot please God.
But you are not in the flesh;
on the contrary, you are in the spirit,
if only the Spirit of God dwells in you.
Whoever does not have the Spirit of Christ does not belong to him.
But if Christ is in you,
although the body is dead because of sin,
the spirit is alive because of righteousness.
If the Spirit of the one who raised Jesus from the dead dwells in you,
the one who raised Christ from the dead
will give life to your mortal bodies also,
through his Spirit that dwells in you.
Consequently, brothers and sisters,
we are not debtors to the flesh,
to live according to the flesh.

For if you live according to the flesh, you will die,
but if by the Spirit you put to death the deeds of the body,
you will live.

For those who are led by the Spirit of God are sons of God.
For you did not receive a spirit of slavery to fall back into fear,
but you received a Spirit of adoption,
through whom we cry, "Abba, Father!"
The Spirit himself bears witness with our spirit
that we are children of God,
and if children, then heirs,
heirs of God and joint heirs with Christ,
if only we suffer with him
so that we may also be glorified with him.

The word of the Lord. All: **Thanks be to God.**

Sequence

Veni, Sancte Spiritus

Come, Holy Spirit, come!
And from your celestial home
Shed a ray of light divine!
Come, Father of the poor!
Come, source of all our store!
Come, within our bosoms shine.
You, of comforters the best;
You, the soul's most welcome guest;
Sweet refreshment here below;
In our labor, rest most sweet;
Grateful coolness in the heat;
Solace in the midst of woe.
O most blessed Light divine,
Shine within these hearts of yours,
And our inmost being fill!
Where you are not, we have naught,
Nothing good in deed or thought,
Nothing free from taint of ill.

Heal our wounds, our strength renew;
On our dryness pour your dew;
Wash the stains of guilt away:
Bend the stubborn heart and will;
Melt the frozen, warm the chill;
Guide the steps that go astray.
On the faithful, who adore
And confess you, evermore
In your sevenfold gift descend;
Give them virtue's sure reward;
Give them your salvation, Lord;
Give them joys that never end. Amen.
Alleluia.

Gospel

Alleluia

℣. Alleluia, alleluia. ℟. **Alleluia, alleluia.**
℣. Come, Holy Spirit, fill the hearts of your faithful and kindle in them the fire of your love. ℟.

A (John 20:19-23)

✠ **A reading from the holy Gospel according to John**

All: **Glory to you, O Lord.**

As the Father sent me, so I send you. Receive the Holy Spirit.

On the evening of that first day of the week,
when the doors were locked, where the disciples were,
for fear of the Jews,
Jesus came and stood in their midst
and said to them, "Peace be with you."
When he had said this, he showed them his hands and his side.
The disciples rejoiced when they saw the Lord.
Jesus said to them again, "Peace be with you.
As the Father has sent me, so I send you."
And when he had said this, he breathed on them and said to them,
"Receive the Holy Spirit.

Whose sins you forgive are forgiven them,
and whose sins you retain are retained."

The Gospel of the Lord. All: **Praise to you, Lord Jesus Christ.**

Or:

B (John 14:15-16, 23b-26)

✠ **A reading from the holy Gospel according to John**

All: **Glory to you, O Lord.**

The Holy Spirit will teach you everything.

Jesus said to his disciples:
"If you love me, you will keep my commandments.
And I will ask the Father,
and he will give you another Advocate to be with you always.

"Whoever loves me will keep my word,
and my Father will love him,
and we will come to him and make our dwelling with him.
Those who do not love me do not keep my words;
yet the word you hear is not mine
but that of the Father who sent me.

"I have told you this while I am with you.
The Advocate, the Holy Spirit whom the Father will send in my name,
will teach you everything
and remind you of all that I told you."

The Gospel of the Lord. All: **Praise to you, Lord Jesus Christ.**

If it is customary or obligatory for the faithful to attend Mass on the Monday or even the Tuesday after Pentecost, the readings from the Mass of Pentecost Sunday may be repeated or the readings of the Ritual Mass for Confirmation, nos. 764–768, may be used in its place.

Prayer over the Offerings

Grant, we pray, O Lord,
that, as promised by your Son,

the Holy Spirit may reveal to us more abundantly
the hidden mystery of this sacrifice
and graciously lead us into all truth.
Through Christ our Lord. All: **Amen.**

Communion Antiphon (Acts of the Apostles 2:4, 11)

They were all filled with the Holy Spirit
and spoke of the marvels of God, alleluia.

Prayer after Communion

O God, who bestow heavenly gifts upon your Church,
safeguard, we pray, the grace you have given,
that the gift of the Holy Spirit poured out upon her
may retain all its force
and that this spiritual food
may gain her abundance of eternal redemption.
Through Christ our Lord. All: **Amen.**

Dismissal

To dismiss the people the Deacon or, if there is no Deacon, the Priest himself sings or says:

Go forth, the Mass is ended, alleluia, alleluia.

Or:

Go in peace, alleluia, alleluia.

All reply: **Thanks be to God, alleluia, alleluia.**

The Most Holy Trinity

May 22, 2016

Reflection on the Gospel

The Father gives everything to Jesus; the Spirit takes from Jesus to "declare to [us] the things that are coming." Give and take. Such is the dynamic of the inner Life of the Trinity. Such is the dynamic of how the Father, Jesus, and the Spirit engage us in their Life. Give and take. We can "bear" the "much more" the Spirit has to tell us when we surrender more fully to the trinitarian Life within us. Give and take.

- *Three in one, the Trinity is . . .*

—Living Liturgy™, *Trinity Sunday 2016*

Entrance Antiphon

Blest be God the Father,
and the Only Begotten Son of God,
and also the Holy Spirit,
for he has shown us his merciful love.

Collect

God our Father, who by sending into the world
the Word of truth and the Spirit of sanctification
made known to the human race your wondrous mystery,
grant us, we pray, that in professing the true faith,
we may acknowledge the Trinity of eternal glory
and adore your Unity, powerful in majesty.
Through our Lord Jesus Christ, your Son,
who lives and reigns with you in the unity of the Holy Spirit,
one God, for ever and ever. All: **Amen.**

Reading I (L 166-C) (Proverbs 8:22-31)

A reading from the Book of Proverbs

Before the earth was made, Wisdom was conceived.

Thus says the wisdom of God:
"The Lord possessed me, the beginning of his ways,
the forerunner of his prodigies of long ago;

from of old I was poured forth,
at the first, before the earth.
When there were no depths I was brought forth,
when there were no fountains or springs of water;
before the mountains were settled into place,
before the hills, I was brought forth;
while as yet the earth and fields were not made,
nor the first clods of the world.

"When the Lord established the heavens I was there,
when he marked out the vault over the face of the deep;
when he made firm the skies above,
when he fixed fast the foundations of the earth;
when he set for the sea its limit,
so that the waters should not transgress his command;
then was I beside him as his craftsman,
and I was his delight day by day,
playing before him all the while,
playing on the surface of his earth;
and I found delight in the human race."

The word of the Lord. All: **Thanks be to God.**

Responsorial Psalm 8

P-535

Psalm 8:4-5, 6-7, 8-9

℟. (2a) **O Lord, our God, how wonderful your name in all the earth!**

When I behold your heavens, the work of your fingers,
the moon and the stars which you set in place—
what is man that you should be mindful of him,
or the son of man that you should care for him? ℟.

(continued)

You have made him little less than the angels,
and crowned him with glory and honor.
You have given him rule over the works of your hands,
putting all things under his feet. ℟.

All sheep and oxen,
yes, and the beasts of the field,
the birds of the air, the fishes of the sea,
and whatever swims the paths of the seas. ℟.

READING II (Romans 5:1-5)

A reading from the Letter of Saint Paul to the Romans

To God, through Christ, in love poured out through the Holy Spirit.

Brothers and sisters:
Therefore, since we have been justified by faith,
we have peace with God through our Lord Jesus Christ,
through whom we have gained access by faith
to this grace in which we stand,
and we boast in hope of the glory of God.
Not only that, but we even boast of our afflictions,
knowing that affliction produces endurance,
and endurance, proven character,
and proven character, hope,
and hope does not disappoint,
because the love of God has been poured out into our hearts
through the Holy Spirit that has been given to us.

The word of the Lord. All: **Thanks be to God.**

GOSPEL (John 16:12-15)

ALLELUIA (*See* Revelation 1:8)

℣. Alleluia, alleluia. ℟. **Alleluia, alleluia.**
℣. Glory to the Father, the Son, and the Holy Spirit;
to God who is, who was, and who is to come. ℟.

✠ **A reading from the holy Gospel according to John**

All: **Glory to you, O Lord.**

Everything that the Father has is mine; the Spirit will take from what is mine and declare it to you.

Jesus said to his disciples:
"I have much more to tell you, but you cannot bear it now.
But when he comes, the Spirit of truth,
he will guide you to all truth.
He will not speak on his own,
but he will speak what he hears,
and will declare to you the things that are coming.
He will glorify me,
because he will take from what is mine and declare it to you.
Everything that the Father has is mine;
for this reason I told you that he will take from what is mine
and declare it to you."

The Gospel of the Lord. All: **Praise to you, Lord Jesus Christ.**

Prayer over the Offerings

Sanctify by the invocation of your name,
we pray, O Lord our God,
this oblation of our service,
and by it make of us an eternal offering to you.
Through Christ our Lord. All: **Amen.**

Communion Antiphon (Galatians 4:6)

Since you are children of God,
God has sent into your hearts the Spirit of his Son,
the Spirit who cries out: Abba, Father.

Prayer after Communion

May receiving this Sacrament, O Lord our God,
bring us health of body and soul,
as we confess your eternal holy Trinity and undivided Unity.
Through Christ our Lord. All: **Amen.**

The Most Holy Body and Blood of Christ

May 29, 2016

Reflection on the Gospel

Jesus does far more than satisfy physical hunger; he foreshadows the gift of his very self as the Bread of Life. Jesus taught the crowds and "healed those who needed to be cured." Our need for Jesus and what he gives us, however, goes beyond teaching and healing. Even more, we need the food Jesus gives in unfathomable abundance. This food transforms us into being the "leftover fragments"—the Body of Christ—continuing Jesus' ministry of giving self over for others.

- *I am transformed by the Body of Christ and it . . .*

—Living Liturgy™, *Body and Blood of Christ 2016*

ENTRANCE ANTIPHON (Cf. Psalm 81[80]:17)

He fed them with the finest wheat
and satisfied them with honey from the rock.

COLLECT

O God, who in this wonderful Sacrament
have left us a memorial of your Passion,
grant us, we pray,
so to revere the sacred mysteries of your Body and Blood
that we may always experience in ourselves
the fruits of your redemption.
Who live and reign with God the Father
in the unity of the Holy Spirit,
one God, for ever and ever. All: **Amen.**

READING I (L 169-C) (Genesis 14:18-20)

A reading from the Book of Genesis

Melchizedek brought out bread and wine.

In those days, Melchizedek, king of Salem, brought out bread and wine,
and being a priest of God Most High,

he blessed Abram with these words:
"Blessed be Abram by God Most High,
the creator of heaven and earth;
and blessed be God Most High,
who delivered your foes into your hand."
Then Abram gave him a tenth of everything.

The word of the Lord. All: **Thanks be to God.**

RESPONSORIAL PSALM 110

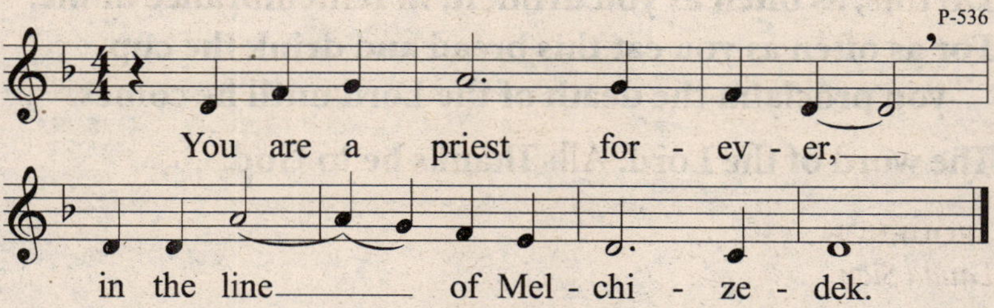

Psalm 110:1, 2, 3, 4

℟. (4b) **You are a priest forever, in the line of Melchizedek.**

The LORD said to my Lord: "Sit at my right hand
till I make your enemies your footstool." ℟.

The scepter of your power the LORD will stretch forth from Zion:
"Rule in the midst of your enemies." ℟.

"Yours is princely power in the day of your birth, in holy splendor;
before the daystar, like the dew, I have begotten you." ℟.

The LORD has sworn, and he will not repent:
"You are a priest forever, according to the order of Melchizedek." ℟.

READING II (1 Corinthians 11:23-26)

A reading from the first Letter of Saint Paul to the Corinthians

For as often as you eat and drink, you proclaim the death of the Lord.

Brothers and sisters:
I received from the Lord what I also handed on to you,
that the Lord Jesus, on the night he was handed over,
took bread, and, after he had given thanks,
broke it and said, "This is my body that is for you.
Do this in remembrance of me."
In the same way also the cup, after supper, saying,
"This cup is the new covenant in my blood.
Do this, as often as you drink it, in remembrance of me."
For as often as you eat this bread and drink the cup,
you proclaim the death of the Lord until he comes.

The word of the Lord. All: **Thanks be to God.**

Sequence
Lauda Sion

The sequence *Laud, O Zion (Lauda Sion)*, or the shorter form beginning with the verse *Lo! the angel's food is given*, may be sung optionally before the Alleluia.

Laud, O Zion, your salvation,
Laud with hymns of exultation,
Christ, your king and shepherd true:

Bring him all the praise you know,
He is more than you bestow.
Never can you reach his due.

Special theme for glad thanksgiving
Is the quick'ning and the living
Bread today before you set:

From his hands of old partaken,
As we know, by faith unshaken,
Where the Twelve at supper met.

Full and clear ring out your chanting,
Joy nor sweetest grace be wanting,
From your heart let praises burst:

For today the feast is holden,
When the institution olden
Of that supper was rehearsed.

Here the new law's new oblation,
By the new king's revelation,
Ends the form of ancient rite:

Now the new the old effaces,
Truth away the shadow chases,
Light dispels the gloom of night.

What he did at supper seated,
Christ ordained to be repeated,
His memorial ne'er to cease:

And his rule for guidance taking,
Bread and wine we hallow, making
Thus our sacrifice of peace.

This the truth each Christian learns,
Bread into his flesh he turns,
To his precious blood the wine:

Sight has fail'd, nor thought conceives,
But a dauntless faith believes,
Resting on a pow'r divine.

Here beneath these signs are hidden
Priceless things to sense forbidden;
Signs, not things are all we see:

Blood is poured and flesh is broken,
Yet in either wondrous token
Christ entire we know to be.

Whoso of this food partakes,
Does not rend the Lord nor breaks;
Christ is whole to all that taste:

Thousands are, as one, receivers,
One, as thousands of believers,
Eats of him who cannot waste.

Bad and good the feast are sharing,
Of what divers dooms preparing,
Endless death, or endless life.

Life to these, to those damnation,
See how like participation
Is with unlike issues rife.

When the sacrament is broken,
Doubt not, but believe 'tis spoken,
That each sever'd outward token
doth the very whole contain.

Nought the precious gift divides,
Breaking but the sign betides
Jesus still the same abides,
still unbroken does remain.

The shorter form of the sequence begins here.

Lo! the angel's food is given
To the pilgrim who has striven;
See the children's bread from heaven,
which on dogs may not be spent.

Truth the ancient types fulfilling,
Isaac bound, a victim willing,
Paschal lamb, its lifeblood spilling,
manna to the fathers sent.

Very bread, good shepherd, tend us,
Jesu, of your love befriend us,
You refresh us, you defend us,
Your eternal goodness send us
In the land of life to see.

You who all things can and know,
Who on earth such food bestow,
Grant us with your saints, though lowest,
Where the heav'nly feast you show,
Fellow heirs and guests to be. Amen. Alleluia.

Gospel (Luke 9:11b-17)

Alleluia (John 6:51)

℣. Alleluia, alleluia. ℟. **Alleluia, alleluia.**
℣. I am the living bread that came down from heaven,
says the Lord;
whoever eats this bread will live forever. ℟.

✠ **A reading from the holy Gospel according to Luke**

All: **Glory to you, O Lord.**

They all ate and were satisfied.

Jesus spoke to the crowds about the kingdom of God,
and he healed those who needed to be cured.
As the day was drawing to a close,
the Twelve approached him and said,
"Dismiss the crowd
so that they can go to the surrounding villages and farms
and find lodging and provisions;
for we are in a deserted place here."
He said to them, "Give them some food yourselves."
They replied, "Five loaves and two fish are all we have,
unless we ourselves go and buy food for all these people."
Now the men there numbered about five thousand.
Then he said to his disciples,
"Have them sit down in groups of about fifty."
They did so and made them all sit down.
Then taking the five loaves and the two fish,
and looking up to heaven,
he said the blessing over them, broke them,
and gave them to the disciples to set before the crowd.
They all ate and were satisfied.
And when the leftover fragments were picked up,
they filled twelve wicker baskets.

The Gospel of the Lord. All: **Praise to you, Lord Jesus Christ.**

Prayer over the Offerings

Grant your Church, O Lord, we pray,
the gifts of unity and peace,
whose signs are to be seen in mystery
in the offerings we here present.
Through Christ our Lord. All: **Amen.**

Communion Antiphon (John 6:57)

Whoever eats my flesh and drinks my blood
remains in me and I in him, says the Lord.

Prayer after Communion

Grant, O Lord, we pray,
that we may delight for all eternity
in that share in your divine life,
which is foreshadowed in the present age
by our reception of your precious Body and Blood.
Who live and reign for ever and ever. All: **Amen.**

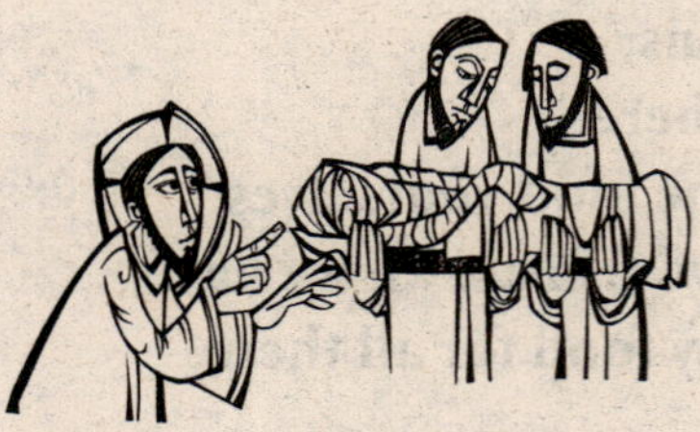

Tenth Sunday in Ordinary Time

June 5, 2016

Reflection on the Gospel

The widow of Nain had lost everything dear to her: her husband and her only son. In them she had lost her life support and any hope of posterity. Without even being asked, Jesus with great compassion raises her son from the dead and gives him back to her. By word and deed Jesus restores the widow's life and hope. In Jesus "God has visited his people." In Jesus God continues to visit us, offering hope and life, even without our asking. Do we accept?

- *Without my asking Jesus . . .*

—Living Liturgy™, *Tenth Sunday in Ordinary Time 2016*

Entrance Antiphon (Cf. Psalm 27[26]:1-2)

The Lord is my light and my salvation; whom shall I fear?
The Lord is the stronghold of my life; whom should I dread?
When those who do evil draw near, they stumble and fall.

Collect

O God, from whom all good things come,
grant that we, who call on you in our need,
may at your prompting discern what is right,
and by your guidance do it.
Through our Lord Jesus Christ, your Son,
who lives and reigns with you in the unity of the Holy Spirit,
one God, for ever and ever. All: **Amen.**

Reading I (L 90-C) (1 Kings 17:17-24)

A reading from the first Book of Kings

See! Your son is alive.

Elijah went to Zarephath of Sidon to the house of a widow.
The son of the mistress of the house fell sick,
and his sickness grew more severe until he stopped breathing.
So she said to Elijah,
"Why have you done this to me, O man of God?
Have you come to me to call attention to my guilt
and to kill my son?"
Elijah said to her, "Give me your son."
Taking him from her lap, he carried the son to the upper room
where he was staying, and put him on his bed.
Elijah called out to the LORD:
"O LORD, my God,
will you afflict even the widow with whom I am staying
by killing her son?"
Then he stretched himself out upon the child three times
and called out to the LORD:
"O LORD, my God,
let the life breath return to the body of this child."
The Lord heard the prayer of Elijah;
the life breath returned to the child's body and he revived.
Taking the child, Elijah brought him down into the house
from the upper room and gave him to his mother.
Elijah said to her, "See! Your son is alive."

The woman replied to Elijah,
"Now indeed I know that you are a man of God.
The word of the LORD comes truly from your mouth."

The word of the Lord. All: **Thanks be to God.**

RESPONSORIAL PSALM 30

P-509

Psalm 30:2, 4, 5-6, 11, 12, 13

℟. (2a) **I will praise you, Lord, for you have rescued me.**

I will extol you, O LORD, for you drew me clear
and did not let my enemies rejoice over me.
O LORD, you brought me up from the nether world;
you preserved me from among those going down into the pit. ℟.

Sing praise to the LORD, you his faithful ones,
and give thanks to his holy name.
For his anger lasts but a moment;
a lifetime, his good will.
At nightfall, weeping enters in,
but with the dawn, rejoicing. ℟.

Hear, O LORD, and have pity on me;
O LORD, be my helper.
You changed my mourning into dancing;
O LORD, my God, forever will I give you thanks. ℟.

READING II (Galatians 1:11-19)

A reading from the Letter of Saint Paul to the Galatians

God revealed his Son to me, so that I might proclaim him to the Gentiles.

I want you to know, brothers and sisters,
that the gospel preached by me is not of human origin.
For I did not receive it from a human being, nor was I taught it,
but it came through a revelation of Jesus Christ.

For you heard of my former way of life in Judaism,
how I persecuted the church of God beyond measure
and tried to destroy it, and progressed in Judaism
beyond many of my contemporaries among my race,
since I was even more a zealot for my ancestral traditions.
But when God, who from my mother's womb had set me apart
and called me through his grace,
was pleased to reveal his Son to me,
so that I might proclaim him to the Gentiles,
I did not immediately consult flesh and blood,
nor did I go up to Jerusalem
to those who were apostles before me;
rather, I went into Arabia and then returned to Damascus.

Then after three years I went up to Jerusalem
to confer with Cephas and remained with him for fifteen days.
But I did not see any other of the apostles,
only James the brother of the Lord.

The word of the Lord. All: **Thanks be to God.**

GOSPEL (Luke 7:11-17)

ALLELUIA (Luke 7:16)

℣. Alleluia, alleluia. ℟. **Alleluia, alleluia.**
℣. A great prophet has risen in our midst,
God has visited his people. ℟.

✠ **A reading from the holy Gospel according to Luke**

All: **Glory to you, O Lord.**

Young man, I tell you, arise!

Jesus journeyed to a city called Nain,
and his disciples and a large crowd accompanied him.
As he drew near to the gate of the city,
a man who had died was being carried out,
the only son of his mother, and she was a widow.

A large crowd from the city was with her.
When the Lord saw her,
he was moved with pity for her and said to her,
"Do not weep."
He stepped forward and touched the coffin;
at this the bearers halted,
and he said, "Young man, I tell you, arise!"
The dead man sat up and began to speak,
and Jesus gave him to his mother.
Fear seized them all, and they glorified God, exclaiming,
"A great prophet has arisen in our midst,"
and "God has visited his people."
This report about him spread through the whole of Judea
and in all the surrounding region.

The Gospel of the Lord. All: **Praise to you, Lord Jesus Christ.**

Prayer over the Offerings

Look kindly upon our service, O Lord, we pray,
that what we offer
may be an acceptable oblation to you
and lead us to grow in charity.
Through Christ our Lord. All: **Amen.**

Communion Antiphon (Psalm 18[17]:3)

The Lord is my rock, my fortress, and my deliverer;
my God is my saving strength.

Or:

(1 John 4:16)
God is love, and whoever abides in love
abides in God, and God in him.

Prayer after Communion

May your healing work, O Lord,
free us, we pray, from doing evil
and lead us to what is right.
Through Christ our Lord. All: **Amen.**

Eleventh Sunday in Ordinary Time

June 12, 2016

Reflection on the Gospel

This gospel depicts two very different ways of relating to Jesus. Simon the Pharisee related to Jesus as a one-time visitor, maintaining only a surface relationship having no power to transform him. The "sinful woman," on the other hand, related to Jesus as an intimate, avowing an underlying relationship that transformed her. How do we relate to Jesus? Do we wish to be intimate and close to Jesus, or do we keep a protective distance?

- *How close do I let Jesus come to me? . . .*

—Living Liturgy™, *Eleventh Sunday in Ordinary Time 2016*

ENTRANCE ANTIPHON (Cf. Psalm 27[26]:7, 9)

O Lord, hear my voice, for I have called to you; be my help. Do not abandon or forsake me, O God, my Savior!

COLLECT

O God, strength of those who hope in you,
graciously hear our pleas,
and, since without you mortal frailty can do nothing,
grant us always the help of your grace,
that in following your commands
we may please you by our resolve and our deeds.
Through our Lord Jesus Christ, your Son,
who lives and reigns with you in the unity of the Holy Spirit,
one God, for ever and ever. All: **Amen.**

READING I (L 93-C) (2 Samuel 12:7-10, 13)

A reading from the second Book of Samuel

The Lord has forgiven your sin; you shall not die.

Nathan said to David:
"Thus says the LORD God of Israel:
'I anointed you king of Israel.

I rescued you from the hand of Saul.
I gave you your lord's house and your lord's wives for
your own.
I gave you the house of Israel and of Judah.
And if this were not enough, I could count up for you
still more.
Why have you spurned the LORD and done evil in his sight?
You have cut down Uriah the Hittite with the sword;
you took his wife as your own,
and him you killed with the sword of the Ammonites.
Now, therefore, the sword shall never depart from your
house,
because you have despised me
and have taken the wife of Uriah to be your wife.' "
Then David said to Nathan,
"I have sinned against the LORD."
Nathan answered David:
"The LORD on his part has forgiven your sin:
you shall not die."

The word of the Lord. All: **Thanks be to God.**

RESPONSORIAL PSALM 32

P-510

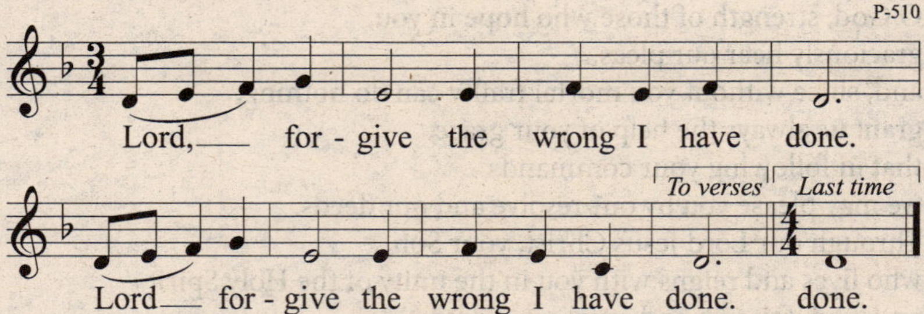

Psalm 32:1-2, 5, 7, 11

℟. (*See* 5c) **Lord, forgive the wrong I have done.**

Blessed is the one whose fault is taken away,
whose sin is covered.
Blessed the man to whom the LORD imputes not guilt,
in whose spirit there is no guile. ℟.

I acknowledged my sin to you,
my guilt I covered not.
I said, "I confess my faults to the LORD,"
and you took away the guilt of my sin. ℟.

You are my shelter; from distress you will preserve me;
with glad cries of freedom you will ring me round. ℟.

Be glad in the LORD and rejoice, you just;
exult, all you upright of heart. ℟.

READING II (Galatians 2:16, 19-21)

A reading from the Letter of Saint Paul to the Galatians

I live, no longer I, but Christ lives in me.

Brothers and sisters:
We who know that a person is not justified by works of the law
but through faith in Jesus Christ,
even we have believed in Christ Jesus
that we may be justified by faith in Christ
and not by works of the law,
because by works of the law no one will be justified.
For through the law I died to the law,
that I might live for God.
I have been crucified with Christ;
yet I live, no longer I, but Christ lives in me;
insofar as I now live in the flesh,
I live by faith in the Son of God
who has loved me and given himself up for me.
I do not nullify the grace of God;
for if justification comes through the law,
then Christ died for nothing.

The word of the Lord. All: **Thanks be to God.**

GOSPEL (Luke 7:36—8:3) *or* Shorter Form [ ] (Luke 7:36-50)
ALLELUIA (1 John 4:10b)

℣. Alleluia, alleluia. ℟. **Alleluia, alleluia.**
℣. God loved us and sent his Son
as expiation for our sins. ℟.

✠ **A reading from the holy Gospel according to Luke**

All: **Glory to you, O Lord.**

Her many sins have been forgiven, because she has shown great love.

[A Pharisee invited Jesus to dine with him,
and he entered the Pharisee's house and reclined at table.
Now there was a sinful woman in the city
who learned that he was at table in the house of the Pharisee.
Bringing an alabaster flask of ointment,
she stood behind him at his feet weeping
and began to bathe his feet with her tears.
Then she wiped them with her hair,
kissed them, and anointed them with the ointment.
When the Pharisee who had invited him saw this he said to himself,
"If this man were a prophet,
he would know who and what sort of woman this is who is touching him,
that she is a sinner."
Jesus said to him in reply,
"Simon, I have something to say to you."
"Tell me, teacher," he said.
"Two people were in debt to a certain creditor;
one owed five hundred days' wages and the other owed fifty.
Since they were unable to repay the debt, he forgave it for both.
Which of them will love him more?"
Simon said in reply,
"The one, I suppose, whose larger debt was forgiven."
He said to him, "You have judged rightly."

Then he turned to the woman and said to Simon,
"Do you see this woman?

When I entered your house, you did not give me water for my feet,
but she has bathed them with her tears
and wiped them with her hair.
You did not give me a kiss,
but she has not ceased kissing my feet since the time I entered.
You did not anoint my head with oil,
but she anointed my feet with ointment.
So I tell you, her many sins have been forgiven
because she has shown great love.
But the one to whom little is forgiven, loves little."
He said to her, "Your sins are forgiven."
The others at table said to themselves,
"Who is this who even forgives sins?"
But he said to the woman,
"Your faith has saved you; go in peace."]

Afterward he journeyed from one town and village to another,
preaching and proclaiming the good news of the kingdom of God.
Accompanying him were the Twelve
and some women who had been cured of evil spirits and infirmities,
Mary, called Magdalene, from whom seven demons had gone out,
Joanna, the wife of Herod's steward Chuza,
Susanna, and many others who provided for them out of their resources.

The Gospel of the Lord. All: **Praise to you, Lord Jesus Christ.**

PRAYER OVER THE OFFERINGS

O God, who in the offerings presented here
provide for the twofold needs of human nature,
nourishing us with food
and renewing us with your Sacrament,
grant, we pray,

that the sustenance they provide
may not fail us in body or in spirit.
Through Christ our Lord. All: **Amen.**

Communion Antiphon (Psalm 27[26]:4)

There is one thing I ask of the Lord, only this do I seek:
to live in the house of the Lord all the days of my life.

Or:

(John 17:11)
Holy Father, keep in your name those you have given me,
that they may be one as we are one, says the Lord.

Prayer after Communion

As this reception of your Holy Communion, O Lord,
foreshadows the union of the faithful in you,
so may it bring about unity in your Church.
Through Christ our Lord. All: **Amen.**

Twelfth Sunday in Ordinary Time

June 19, 2016

Reflection on the Gospel

It was out of his prayer that Jesus asked his disciples, "who do you say that I am?" and revealed that his very identity entailed suffering, rejection, death, and resurrection. Our own prayer is to lead us to clearer understanding of who we are, and to the revelation that our very identity as disciples entails denying self, taking up our daily cross, and losing our life for the sake of others. Dare we pray? Dare we ask Jesus, "who do you say that I am?"

- *Who do I say Jesus is? . . .*

—Living Liturgy™, *Twelfth Sunday in Ordinary Time 2016*

ENTRANCE ANTIPHON (Cf. Psalm 28[27]:8-9)

The Lord is the strength of his people,
a saving refuge for the one he has anointed.
Save your people, Lord, and bless your heritage,
and govern them for ever.

COLLECT

Grant, O Lord,
that we may always revere and love your holy name,
for you never deprive of your guidance
those you set firm on the foundation of your love.
Through our Lord Jesus Christ, your Son,
who lives and reigns with you in the unity of the Holy Spirit,
one God, for ever and ever. All: **Amen.**

READING I (L 96-C) (Zechariah 12:10-11; 13:1)

A reading from the Book of the Prophet Zechariah

They shall look on him whom they have pierced.

Thus says the LORD:
I will pour out on the house of David
and on the inhabitants of Jerusalem
a spirit of grace and petition;
and they shall look on him whom they have pierced,
and they shall mourn for him as one mourns for an only son,
and they shall grieve over him as one grieves over a firstborn.

On that day the mourning in Jerusalem shall be as great as the mourning of Hadadrimmon in the plain of Megiddo.

On that day there shall be open to the house of David
and to the inhabitants of Jerusalem,
a fountain to purify from sin and uncleanness.

The word of the Lord. All: **Thanks be to God.**

Responsorial Psalm 63

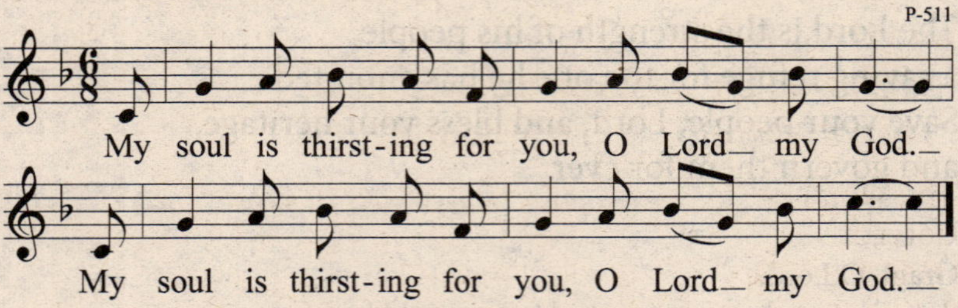

Psalm 63:2, 3-4, 5-6, 8-9

℟. (2b) **My soul is thirsting for you, O Lord my God.**

O God, you are my God whom I seek;
for you my flesh pines and my soul thirsts
like the earth, parched, lifeless and without water. ℟.

Thus have I gazed toward you in the sanctuary
to see your power and your glory,
for your kindness is a greater good than life;
my lips shall glorify you. ℟.

Thus will I bless you while I live;
lifting up my hands, I will call upon your name.
As with the riches of a banquet shall my soul be satisfied,
and with exultant lips my mouth shall praise you. ℟.

You are my help,
and in the shadow of your wings I shout for joy.
My soul clings fast to you;
your right hand upholds me. ℟.

Reading II (Galatians 3:26-29)

A reading from the Letter of Saint Paul to the Galatians

All of you who were baptized have clothed yourselves with Christ.

Brothers and sisters:
Through faith you are all children of God in Christ Jesus.
For all of you who were baptized into Christ
have clothed yourselves with Christ.
There is neither Jew nor Greek,
there is neither slave nor free person,
there is not male and female;

for you are all one in Christ Jesus.
And if you belong to Christ,
then you are Abraham's descendant,
heirs according to the promise.

The word of the Lord. All: Thanks be to God.

GOSPEL (Luke 9:18-24)
ALLELUIA (John 10:27)

℣. Alleluia, alleluia. ℟. **Alleluia, alleluia.**
℣. My sheep hear my voice, says the Lord;
I know them, and they follow me. ℟.

✠ **A reading from the holy Gospel according to Luke**

All: **Glory to you, O Lord.**

You are the Christ of God. The Son of Man must suffer greatly.

Once when Jesus was praying in solitude,
and the disciples were with him,
he asked them, "Who do the crowds say that I am?"
They said in reply, "John the Baptist;
others, Elijah;
still others, 'One of the ancient prophets has arisen.' "
Then he said to them, "But who do you say that I am?"
Peter said in reply, "The Christ of God."
He rebuked them
and directed them not to tell this to anyone.

He said, "The Son of Man must suffer greatly
and be rejected by the elders, the chief priests, and the scribes,
and be killed and on the third day be raised."

Then he said to all,
"If anyone wishes to come after me, he must deny himself
and take up his cross daily and follow me.
For whoever wishes to save his life will lose it,
but whoever loses his life for my sake will save it."

The Gospel of the Lord. All: Praise to you, Lord Jesus Christ.

Prayer over the Offerings
Receive, O Lord, the sacrifice of conciliation and praise
and grant that, cleansed by its action,
we may make offering of a heart pleasing to you.
Through Christ our Lord. All: **Amen.**

Communion Antiphon (Psalm 145[144]:15)
The eyes of all look to you, Lord,
and you give them their food in due season.

Or:

(John 10:11, 15)
I am the Good Shepherd,
and I lay down my life for my sheep, says the Lord.

Prayer after Communion
Renewed and nourished
by the Sacred Body and Precious Blood of your Son,
we ask of your mercy, O Lord,
that what we celebrate with constant devotion
may be our sure pledge of redemption.
Through Christ our Lord. All: **Amen.**

Thirteenth Sunday in Ordinary Time

June 26, 2016

Reflection on the Gospel

Following Jesus requires much more than simply walking with him from village to village. Following Jesus calls for being "resolutely determined" to journey all the way with him to Jerusalem—and beyond. Any excuses, no matter how seemingly legitimate, keep us from letting go of where we are and embracing where we must go. To be on this journey requires total self-surrender to what Jerusalem holds as well as to "being taken up" into what is "beyond" Jerusalem: the new Jerusalem, "the kingdom of God" fulfilled.

- *What do I need to do to follow Jesus? . . .*

—Living Liturgy™, *Thirteenth Sunday in Ordinary Time 2016*

ENTRANCE ANTIPHON (Psalm 47[46]:2)
All peoples, clap your hands.
Cry to God with shouts of joy!

COLLECT
O God, who through the grace of adoption
chose us to be children of light,
grant, we pray,
that we may not be wrapped in the darkness of error
but always be seen to stand in the bright light of truth.
Through our Lord Jesus Christ, your Son,
who lives and reigns with you in the unity of the Holy Spirit,
one God, for ever and ever. All: **Amen.**

READING I (L 99-C) (1 Kings 19:16b, 19-21)
A reading from the first Book of Kings

Then Elisha left and followed Elijah as his attendant.

The LORD said to Elijah:
"You shall anoint Elisha, son of Shaphat of Abel-meholah,
as prophet to succeed you."

Elijah set out and came upon Elisha, son of Shaphat,
as he was plowing with twelve yoke of oxen;
he was following the twelfth.
Elijah went over to him and threw his cloak over him.
Elisha left the oxen, ran after Elijah, and said,
"Please, let me kiss my father and mother goodbye,
and I will follow you."
Elijah answered, "Go back!
Have I done anything to you?"
Elisha left him and, taking the yoke of oxen, slaughtered them;
he used the plowing equipment for fuel to boil their flesh,
and gave it to his people to eat.
Then Elisha left and followed Elijah as his attendant.

The word of the Lord. All: **Thanks be to God.**

Responsorial Psalm 16

P-512

Psalm 16:1-2, 5, 7-8, 9-10, 11

℟. (*See* 5a) **You are my inheritance, O Lord.**

Keep me, O God, for in you I take refuge;
I say to the LORD, "My Lord are you.
O LORD, my allotted portion and my cup,
you it is who hold fast my lot." ℟.

I bless the LORD who counsels me;
even in the night my heart exhorts me.
I set the LORD ever before me;
with him at my right hand I shall not be disturbed. ℟.

Therefore my heart is glad and my soul rejoices,
my body, too, abides in confidence
because you will not abandon my soul to the netherworld,
nor will you suffer your faithful one to undergo corruption. ℟.

You will show me the path to life,
fullness of joys in your presence,
the delights at your right hand forever. ℟.

Reading II (Galatians 5:1, 13-18)

A reading from the Letter of Saint Paul to the Galatians

You were called for freedom.

Brothers and sisters:
For freedom Christ set us free;
so stand firm and do not submit again to the yoke of slavery.

For you were called for freedom, brothers and sisters.
But do not use this freedom
as an opportunity for the flesh;
rather, serve one another through love.

For the whole law is fulfilled in one statement,
namely, *You shall love your neighbor as yourself.*
But if you go on biting and devouring one another,
beware that you are not consumed by one another.

I say, then: live by the Spirit
and you will certainly not gratify the desire of the flesh.
For the flesh has desires against the Spirit,
and the Spirit against the flesh;
these are opposed to each other,
so that you may not do what you want.
But if you are guided by the Spirit, you are not under the law.

The word of the Lord. All: **Thanks be to God.**

GOSPEL (Luke 9:51-62)

ALLELUIA (1 Samuel 3:9; John 6:68c)

℣. Alleluia, alleluia. ℟. **Alleluia, alleluia.**
℣. Speak, Lord, your servant is listening;
you have the words of everlasting life. ℟.

✠ **A reading from the holy Gospel according to Luke**

All: **Glory to you, O Lord.**

He resolutely determined to journey to Jerusalem. I will follow you wherever you go.

When the days for Jesus' being taken up were fulfilled,
he resolutely determined to journey to Jerusalem,
and he sent messengers ahead of him.
On the way they entered a Samaritan village
to prepare for his reception there,
but they would not welcome him
because the destination of his journey was Jerusalem.
When the disciples James and John saw this they asked,
"Lord, do you want us to call down fire from heaven
to consume them?"
Jesus turned and rebuked them, and they journeyed to another village.

As they were proceeding on their journey someone said to him,
"I will follow you wherever you go."
Jesus answered him,
"Foxes have dens and birds of the sky have nests,
but the Son of Man has nowhere to rest his head."

And to another he said, "Follow me."
But he replied, "Lord, let me go first and bury my father."
But he answered him, "Let the dead bury their dead.
But you, go and proclaim the kingdom of God."
And another said, "I will follow you, Lord,
but first let me say farewell to my family at home."
To him Jesus said, "No one who sets a hand to the plow and looks to what was left behind is fit for the kingdom of God."

The Gospel of the Lord. All: **Praise to you, Lord Jesus Christ.**

PRAYER OVER THE OFFERINGS

O God, who graciously accomplish
the effects of your mysteries,
grant, we pray,
that the deeds by which we serve you
may be worthy of these sacred gifts.
Through Christ our Lord. All: **Amen.**

COMMUNION ANTIPHON (Cf. Psalm 103[102]:1)

Bless the Lord, O my soul,
and all within me, his holy name.

Or:

(John 17:20-21)

O Father, I pray for them, that they may be one in us,
that the world may believe that you have sent me,
says the Lord.

PRAYER AFTER COMMUNION

May this divine sacrifice we have offered and received
fill us with life, O Lord, we pray,
so that, bound to you in lasting charity,
we may bear fruit that lasts for ever.
Through Christ our Lord. All: **Amen.**

Fourteenth Sunday in Ordinary Time

July 3, 2016

Reflection on the Gospel

When Jesus sends disciples forth as "laborers for his harvest," he predicts two responses to their presence. Either disciples will be welcomed and able to minister fruitfully, or they will be rejected and their ministry becomes judgment against the unwelcoming town. In either case, however, the "kingdom of God is at hand." How so? Whether accepted or rejected, disciples "harvest" the "kingdom of God" by their very presence, by their very proclamation of Jesus' name, by their very fidelity to Jesus' mission.

- *If I know the kingdom of God is at hand, how do I proclaim Jesus? . . .*

—Living Liturgy™, *Fourteenth Sunday in Ordinary Time 2016*

ENTRANCE ANTIPHON (Cf. Psalm 48[47]:10-11)

Your merciful love, O God,
we have received in the midst of your temple.
Your praise, O God, like your name,
reaches the ends of the earth;
your right hand is filled with saving justice.

COLLECT

O God, who in the abasement of your Son
have raised up a fallen world,
fill your faithful with holy joy,
for on those you have rescued from slavery to sin
you bestow eternal gladness.
Through our Lord Jesus Christ, your Son,
who lives and reigns with you in the unity of the Holy Spirit,
one God, for ever and ever. All: **Amen.**

READING I (L 102-C) (Isaiah 66:10-14c)

A reading from the Book of the Prophet Isaiah

Behold, I will spread prosperity over her like a river.

Thus says the Lord:
Rejoice with Jerusalem and be glad because of her,
all you who love her;
exult, exult with her,
all you who were mourning over her!
Oh, that you may suck fully
of the milk of her comfort,
that you may nurse with delight
at her abundant breasts!
For thus says the Lord:
Lo, I will spread prosperity over Jerusalem like a river,
and the wealth of the nations like an overflowing torrent.
As nurslings, you shall be carried in her arms,
and fondled in her lap;
as a mother comforts her child,
so will I comfort you;
in Jerusalem you shall find your comfort.

When you see this, your heart shall rejoice
and your bodies flourish like the grass;
the Lord's power shall be known to his servants.

The word of the Lord. All: **Thanks be to God.**

Responsorial Psalm 66

P-513

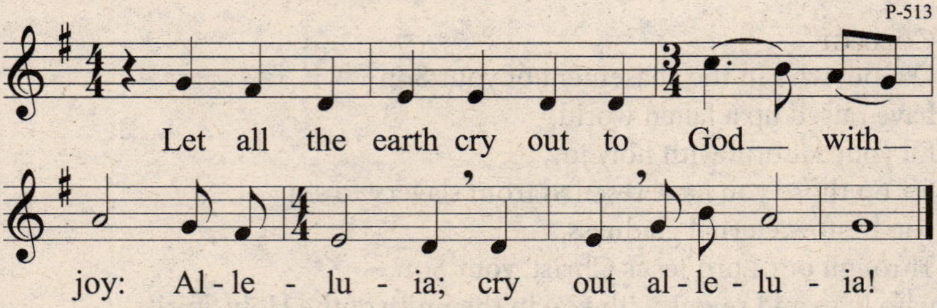

Psalm 66:1-3, 4-5, 6-7, 16, 20

℟. (1) **Let all the earth cry out to God with joy.**

Shout joyfully to God, all the earth,
sing praise to the glory of his name;

proclaim his glorious praise.
Say to God, "How tremendous are your deeds!" ℟.

"Let all on earth worship and sing praise to you,
sing praise to your name!"
Come and see the works of God,
his tremendous deeds among the children of Adam. ℟.

He has changed the sea into dry land;
through the river they passed on foot.
Therefore let us rejoice in him.
He rules by his might forever. ℟.

Hear now, all you who fear God,
while I declare what he has done for me.
Blessed be God who refused me not
my prayer or his kindness! ℟.

Reading II (Galatians 6:14-18)

A reading from the Letter of Saint Paul to the Galatians

I bear the marks of Jesus on my body.

Brothers and sisters:
May I never boast except in the cross of our Lord Jesus Christ,
through which the world has been crucified to me,
and I to the world.
For neither does circumcision mean anything, nor does uncircumcision,
but only a new creation.
Peace and mercy be to all who follow this rule
and to the Israel of God.

From now on, let no one make troubles for me;
for I bear the marks of Jesus on my body.

The grace of our Lord Jesus Christ be with your spirit,
brothers and sisters. Amen.

The word of the Lord. All: **Thanks be to God.**

GOSPEL (Luke 10:1-12, 17-20) *or* Shorter Form [ ] (Luke 10:1-9)

ALLELUIA (Colossians 3:15a, 16a)

℣. Alleluia, alleluia. ℟. **Alleluia, alleluia.**
℣. Let the peace of Christ control your hearts;
let the word of Christ dwell in you richly. ℟.

✠ A reading from the holy Gospel according to Luke

All: **Glory to you, O Lord.**

Your peace will rest on that person.

[At that time the Lord appointed seventy-two others
whom he sent ahead of him in pairs
to every town and place he intended to visit.
He said to them,
"The harvest is abundant but the laborers are few;
so ask the master of the harvest
to send out laborers for his harvest.
Go on your way;
behold, I am sending you like lambs among wolves.
Carry no money bag, no sack, no sandals;
and greet no one along the way.
Into whatever house you enter, first say,
'Peace to this household.'
If a peaceful person lives there,
your peace will rest on him;
but if not, it will return to you.
Stay in the same house and eat and drink what is offered to you,
for the laborer deserves his payment.
Do not move about from one house to another.
Whatever town you enter and they welcome you,
eat what is set before you,
cure the sick in it and say to them,
'The kingdom of God is at hand for you.']

Whatever town you enter and they do not receive you,
go out into the streets and say,
'The dust of your town that clings to our feet,
even that we shake off against you.'

Yet know this: the kingdom of God is at hand.
I tell you,
it will be more tolerable for Sodom on that day than for that town."

The seventy-two returned rejoicing, and said,
"Lord, even the demons are subject to us because of your name."
Jesus said, "I have observed Satan fall like lightning from the sky.
Behold, I have given you the power to 'tread upon serpents' and scorpions
and upon the full force of the enemy and nothing will harm you.
Nevertheless, do not rejoice because the spirits are subject to you,
but rejoice because your names are written in heaven."

The Gospel of the Lord. All: **Praise to you, Lord Jesus Christ.**

Prayer over the Offerings

May this oblation dedicated to your name
purify us, O Lord,
and day by day bring our conduct
closer to the life of heaven.
Through Christ our Lord. All: **Amen.**

Communion Antiphon (Psalm 34[33]:9)

Taste and see that the Lord is good;
blessed the man who seeks refuge in him.

Or:

(Matthew 11:28)
Come to me, all who labor and are burdened,
and I will refresh you, says the Lord.

Prayer after Communion

Grant, we pray, O Lord,
that, having been replenished by such great gifts,
we may gain the prize of salvation
and never cease to praise you.
Through Christ our Lord. All: **Amen.**

Fifteenth Sunday in Ordinary Time

July 10, 2016

Reflection on the Gospel

The generosity of the Good Samaritan goes way beyond expected neighborliness and simple human compassion. He personally cares for the victim: tending to his wounds, carrying him on his own animal, caring for him at the inn. Yet even this is not enough: he leaves money for his continued care. By this parable Jesus teaches that to inherit "eternal life" we must go beyond who we love and how we love them. We must love as God loves: personally, extravagantly, continually.

- *I am like the Good Samaritan if/when I . . .*

—Living Liturgy™, *Fifteenth Sunday in Ordinary Time 2016*

ENTRANCE ANTIPHON (Cf. Psalm 17[16]:15)

As for me, in justice I shall behold your face;
I shall be filled with the vision of your glory.

COLLECT

O God, who show the light of your truth
to those who go astray,
so that they may return to the right path,
give all who for the faith they profess
are accounted Christians
the grace to reject whatever is contrary to the name of Christ
and to strive after all that does it honor.
Through our Lord Jesus Christ, your Son,
who lives and reigns with you in the unity of the Holy Spirit,
one God, for ever and ever. All: **Amen.**

READING I (L 105-C) (Deuteronomy 30:10-14)

A reading from the Book of Deuteronomy

The word is very near to you: you have only to carry it out.

Moses said to the people:
"If only you would heed the voice of the LORD, your God,

and keep his commandments and statutes
that are written in this book of the law,
when you return to the LORD, your God,
with all your heart and all your soul.

"For this command that I enjoin on you today
is not too mysterious and remote for you.
It is not up in the sky, that you should say,
'Who will go up in the sky to get it for us
and tell us of it, that we may carry it out?'
Nor is it across the sea, that you should say,
'Who will cross the sea to get it for us
and tell us of it, that we may carry it out?'
No, it is something very near to you,
already in your mouths and in your hearts;
you have only to carry it out."

The word of the Lord. All: **Thanks be to God.**

RESPONSORIAL PSALM 69 or 19

P-514

1. Psalm 69:14, 17, 30-31, 33-34, 36, 37

℟. (*See* 33) **Turn to the Lord in your need, and you will live.**

I pray to you, O LORD,
for the time of your favor, O God!
In your great kindness answer me
with your constant help.
Answer me, O LORD, for bounteous is your kindness:
in your great mercy turn toward me. ℟.

I am afflicted and in pain;
let your saving help, O God, protect me.
I will praise the name of God in song,
and I will glorify him with thanksgiving. ℟.

"See, you lowly ones, and be glad;
you who seek God, may your hearts revive!
For the LORD hears the poor,
and his own who are in bonds he spurns not." ℟.

For God will save Zion
and rebuild the cities of Judah.
The descendants of his servants shall inherit it,
and those who love his name shall inhabit it. ℟.

Or:

2. Psalm 19:8, 9, 10, 11

℟. (9a) **Your words, Lord, are Spirit and life.**

The law of the LORD is perfect,
refreshing the soul;
the decree of the LORD is trustworthy,
giving wisdom to the simple. ℟.

The precepts of the LORD are right,
rejoicing the heart;
the command of the LORD is clear,
enlightening the eye. ℟.

The fear of the LORD is pure,
enduring forever;
the ordinances of the LORD are true,
all of them just. ℟.

They are more precious than gold,
than a heap of purest gold;
sweeter also than syrup
or honey from the comb. ℟.

Reading II (Colossians 1:15-20)

A reading from the Letter of Saint Paul to the Colossians

All things were created through him and for him.

Christ Jesus is the image of the invisible God,
the firstborn of all creation.
For in him were created all things in heaven and on earth,
the visible and the invisible,
whether thrones or dominions or principalities or powers;
all things were created through him and for him.
He is before all things,
and in him all things hold together.
He is the head of the body, the church.
He is the beginning, the firstborn from the dead,
that in all things he himself might be preeminent.
For in him all the fullness was pleased to dwell,
and through him to reconcile all things for him,
making peace by the blood of his cross
through him, whether those on earth or those in heaven.

The word of the Lord. All: **Thanks be to God.**

Gospel (Luke 10:25-37)

Alleluia (*See* John 6:63c, 68c)

℣. Alleluia, alleluia. ℟. **Alleluia, alleluia.**
℣. Your words, Lord, are Spirit and life;
you have the words of everlasting life. ℟.

✠ **A reading from the holy Gospel according to Luke**

All: **Glory to you, O Lord.**

Who is my neighbor?

There was a scholar of the law who stood up to test Jesus and said,
"Teacher, what must I do to inherit eternal life?"
Jesus said to him, "What is written in the law?
How do you read it?"

He said in reply,
"You shall love the Lord, your God,
with all your heart,
with all your being,
with all your strength,
and with all your mind,
and your neighbor as yourself."
He replied to him, "You have answered correctly;
do this and you will live."

But because he wished to justify himself, he said to Jesus,
"And who is my neighbor?"
Jesus replied,
"A man fell victim to robbers
as he went down from Jerusalem to Jericho.
They stripped and beat him and went off leaving him half-dead.
A priest happened to be going down that road,
but when he saw him, he passed by on the opposite side.
Likewise a Levite came to the place,
and when he saw him, he passed by on the opposite side.
But a Samaritan traveler who came upon him
was moved with compassion at the sight.
He approached the victim,
poured oil and wine over his wounds and bandaged them.
Then he lifted him up on his own animal,
took him to an inn, and cared for him.
The next day he took out two silver coins
and gave them to the innkeeper with the instruction,
'Take care of him.
If you spend more than what I have given you,
I shall repay you on my way back.'
Which of these three, in your opinion,
was neighbor to the robbers' victim?"

He answered, "The one who treated him with mercy." Jesus said to him, "Go and do likewise."

The Gospel of the Lord. All: **Praise to you, Lord Jesus Christ.**

PRAYER OVER THE OFFERINGS
Look upon the offerings of the Church, O Lord,
as she makes her prayer to you,
and grant that, when consumed by those who believe,
they may bring ever greater holiness.
Through Christ our Lord. All: **Amen.**

COMMUNION ANTIPHON (Cf. Psalm 84[83]:4-5)
The sparrow finds a home,
and the swallow a nest for her young:
by your altars, O Lord of hosts, my King and my God.
Blessed are they who dwell in your house,
for ever singing your praise.

Or:

(John 6:57)
Whoever eats my flesh and drinks my blood
remains in me and I in him, says the Lord.

PRAYER AFTER COMMUNION
Having consumed these gifts, we pray, O Lord,
that, by our participation in this mystery,
its saving effects upon us may grow.
Through Christ our Lord. All: **Amen.**

Sixteenth Sunday in Ordinary Time

July 17, 2016

Reflection on the Gospel

Jesus tells Martha in this gospel that there "is need of only one thing." What is it? On the surface, the answer would seem to be "listening to him speak," as Mary is doing. However, we must also heed how Jesus judges Martha: "you are anxious and worried about many things." The "one thing" is to be single-minded, single-hearted, open-minded, open-hearted. The "one thing" is to surrender ourselves to Jesus' Presence, whether sitting or standing, resting or working, receiving or giving.

- *I can surrender to the Presence of Jesus by . . .*

—Living Liturgy™, *Sixteenth Sunday in Ordinary Time 2016*

ENTRANCE ANTIPHON (Psalm 54[53]:6, 8)

See, I have God for my help.
The Lord sustains my soul.
I will sacrifice to you with willing heart,
and praise your name, O Lord, for it is good.

COLLECT

Show favor, O Lord, to your servants
and mercifully increase the gifts of your grace,
that, made fervent in hope, faith and charity,
they may be ever watchful in keeping your commands.
Through our Lord Jesus Christ, your Son,
who lives and reigns with you in the unity of the Holy Spirit,
one God, for ever and ever. All: **Amen.**

READING I (L 108-C) (Genesis 18:1-10a)

A reading from the Book of Genesis

Lord, do not go on past your servant.

The LORD appeared to Abraham by the terebinth of Mamre,
as he sat in the entrance of his tent,
while the day was growing hot.

Looking up, Abraham saw three men standing nearby.
When he saw them, he ran from the entrance of the tent to greet them;
and bowing to the ground, he said:
"Sir, if I may ask you this favor,
please do not go on past your servant.
Let some water be brought, that you may bathe your feet,
and then rest yourselves under the tree.
Now that you have come this close to your servant,
let me bring you a little food, that you may refresh yourselves;
and afterward you may go on your way."
The men replied, "Very well, do as you have said."

Abraham hastened into the tent and told Sarah,
"Quick, three measures of fine flour! Knead it and make rolls."
He ran to the herd, picked out a tender, choice steer,
and gave it to a servant, who quickly prepared it.
Then Abraham got some curds and milk,
as well as the steer that had been prepared,
and set these before the three men;
and he waited on them under the tree while they ate.

They asked Abraham, "Where is your wife Sarah?"
He replied, "There in the tent."
One of them said, "I will surely return to you about this time next year,
and Sarah will then have a son."

The word of the Lord. All: Thanks be to God.

Responsorial Psalm 15

P-516

Psalm 15:2-3, 3-4, 5

℟. (1a) **He who does justice will live in the presence of the Lord.**

One who walks blamelessly and does justice;
who thinks the truth in his heart
and slanders not with his tongue. ℟.

Who harms not his fellow man,
nor takes up a reproach against his neighbor;
by whom the reprobate is despised,
while he honors those who fear the LORD. ℟.

Who lends not his money at usury
and accepts no bribe against the innocent.
One who does these things
shall never be disturbed. ℟.

READING II (Colossians 1:24-28)

A reading from the Letter of Saint Paul to the Colossians

The mystery hidden from ages has now been manifested to his holy ones.

Brothers and sisters:
Now I rejoice in my sufferings for your sake,
and in my flesh I am filling up
what is lacking in the afflictions of Christ
on behalf of his body, which is the church,
of which I am a minister
in accordance with God's stewardship given to me
to bring to completion for you the word of God,
the mystery hidden from ages and from generations past.
But now it has been manifested to his holy ones,
to whom God chose to make known the riches of the glory
of this mystery among the Gentiles;
it is Christ in you, the hope for glory.
It is he whom we proclaim,
admonishing everyone and teaching everyone with all wisdom,
that we may present everyone perfect in Christ.

The word of the Lord. All: **Thanks be to God.**

Gospel (Luke 10:38-42)

Alleluia (*See* Luke 8:15)

℣. Alleluia, alleluia. ℟. **Alleluia, alleluia.**
℣. Blessed are they who have kept the word with a generous heart
and yield a harvest through perseverance. ℟.

✠ **A reading from the holy Gospel according to Luke**

All: **Glory to you, O Lord.**

Martha welcomed him. Mary has chosen the better part.

Jesus entered a village
where a woman whose name was Martha welcomed him.
She had a sister named Mary
who sat beside the Lord at his feet listening to him speak.
Martha, burdened with much serving, came to him and said,
"Lord, do you not care
that my sister has left me by myself to do the serving?
Tell her to help me."
The Lord said to her in reply,
"Martha, Martha, you are anxious and worried about many things.
There is need of only one thing.
Mary has chosen the better part
and it will not be taken from her."

The Gospel of the Lord. All: **Praise to you, Lord Jesus Christ.**

Prayer over the Offerings

O God, who in the one perfect sacrifice
brought to completion varied offerings of the law,
accept, we pray, this sacrifice from your faithful servants
and make it holy, as you blessed the gifts of Abel,
so that what each has offered to the honor of your majesty
may benefit the salvation of all.
Through Christ our Lord. All: **Amen.**

COMMUNION ANTIPHON (Psalm 111[110]:4-5)
The Lord, the gracious, the merciful,
has made a memorial of his wonders;
he gives food to those who fear him.

Or:

(Revelation 3:20)
Behold, I stand at the door and knock, says the Lord.
If anyone hears my voice and opens the door to me,
I will enter his house and dine with him, and he with me.

PRAYER AFTER COMMUNION
Graciously be present to your people, we pray, O Lord,
and lead those you have imbued with heavenly mysteries
to pass from former ways to newness of life.
Through Christ our Lord. All: **Amen.**

Seventeenth Sunday in Ordinary Time

July 24, 2016

Reflection on the Gospel

Jesus' disciples want him to teach them to pray "just as John taught his disciples." Jesus couldn't teach them the prayer of John, however, because he was not John. Jesus' prayer to his Father flows from who he is—the One who praises, intercedes, forgives, reconciles, and protects. In the end, his prayer is for his Father to "give the Holy Spirit." Then, no request is too great, no seeking is unrewarded, no door is locked.

- *Do I know how powerful prayer really is? . . .*

—Living Liturgy™, *Seventeenth Sunday in Ordinary Time 2016*

ENTRANCE ANTIPHON (Cf. Psalm 68[67]:6-7, 36)
God is in his holy place,
God who unites those who dwell in his house;
he himself gives might and strength to his people.

COLLECT

O God, protector of those who hope in you,
without whom nothing has firm foundation, nothing is holy,
bestow in abundance your mercy upon us
and grant that, with you as our ruler and guide,
we may use the good things that pass
in such a way as to hold fast even now
to those that ever endure.
Through our Lord Jesus Christ, your Son,
who lives and reigns with you in the unity of the Holy Spirit,
one God, for ever and ever. All: **Amen.**

READING I (L 111-C) (Genesis 18:20-32)

A reading from the Book of Genesis

Let not my Lord grow angry if I speak.

In those days, the LORD said: "The outcry against Sodom and Gomorrah is so great,
and their sin so grave,
that I must go down and see whether or not their actions
fully correspond to the cry against them that comes to me.
I mean to find out."

While Abraham's visitors walked on farther toward Sodom,
the LORD remained standing before Abraham.
Then Abraham drew nearer and said:
"Will you sweep away the innocent with the guilty?
Suppose there were fifty innocent people in the city;
would you wipe out the place, rather than spare it
for the sake of the fifty innocent people within it?
Far be it from you to do such a thing,
to make the innocent die with the guilty
so that the innocent and the guilty would be treated alike!
Should not the judge of all the world act with justice?"
The LORD replied,
"If I find fifty innocent people in the city of Sodom,
I will spare the whole place for their sake."

Abraham spoke up again:
"See how I am presuming to speak to my Lord,
though I am but dust and ashes!
What if there are five less than fifty innocent people?
Will you destroy the whole city because of those five?"
He answered, "I will not destroy it, if I find forty-five there."
But Abraham persisted, saying, "What if only forty are found there?"
He replied, "I will forbear doing it for the sake of the forty."
Then Abraham said, "Let not my Lord grow impatient if I go on.
What if only thirty are found there?"
He replied, "I will forbear doing it if I can find but thirty there."
Still Abraham went on,
"Since I have thus dared to speak to my Lord,
what if there are no more than twenty?"
The LORD answered, "I will not destroy it, for the sake of the twenty."
But he still persisted:
"Please, let not my Lord grow angry if I speak up this last time.
What if there are at least ten there?"
He replied, "For the sake of those ten, I will not destroy it."

The word of the Lord. All: **Thanks be to God.**

RESPONSORIAL PSALM 138

P-517

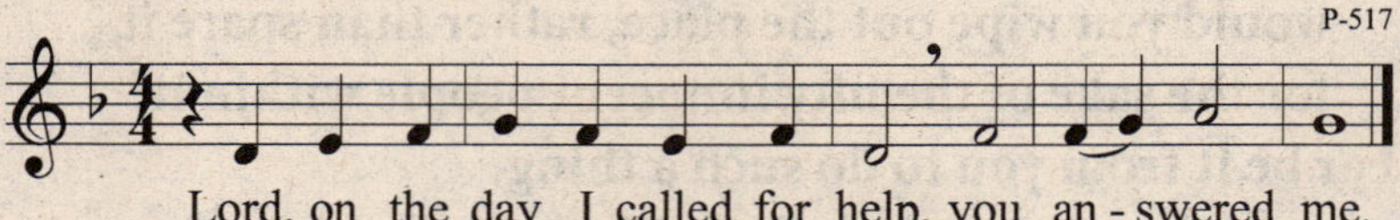

Psalm 138:1-2, 2-3, 6-7, 7-8

℟. (3a) **Lord, on the day I called for help, you answered me.**

I will give thanks to you, O LORD, with all my heart,
for you have heard the words of my mouth;
in the presence of the angels I will sing your praise;

I will worship at your holy temple
and give thanks to your name. ℟.

Because of your kindness and your truth;
for you have made great above all things
your name and your promise.
When I called you answered me;
you built up strength within me. ℟.

The LORD is exalted, yet the lowly he sees,
and the proud he knows from afar.
Though I walk amid distress, you preserve me;
against the anger of my enemies you raise your hand. ℟.

Your right hand saves me.
The LORD will complete what he has done for me;
your kindness, O LORD, endures forever;
forsake not the work of your hands. ℟.

READING II (Colossians 2:12-14)

A reading from the Letter of Saint Paul to the Colossians

God has brought you to life along with Christ, having forgiven us all our transgressions.

Brothers and sisters:
You were buried with him in baptism,
in which you were also raised with him
through faith in the power of God,
who raised him from the dead.
And even when you were dead
in transgressions and the uncircumcision of your flesh,
he brought you to life along with him,
having forgiven us all our transgressions;
obliterating the bond against us, with its legal claims,
which was opposed to us,
he also removed it from our midst, nailing it to the cross.

The word of the Lord. All: **Thanks be to God.**

GOSPEL (Luke 11:1-13)

ALLELUIA (Romans 8:15bc)

℣. Alleluia, alleluia. ℟. **Alleluia, alleluia.**
℣. You have received a Spirit of adoption,
through which we cry, Abba, Father. ℟.

✠ **A reading from the holy Gospel according to Luke**

All: **Glory to you, O Lord.**

Ask and you will receive.

Jesus was praying in a certain place, and when he had finished,
one of his disciples said to him,
"Lord, teach us to pray just as John taught his disciples."
He said to them, "When you pray, say:
Father, hallowed be your name,
your kingdom come.
Give us each day our daily bread
and forgive us our sins
for we ourselves forgive everyone in debt to us,
and do not subject us to the final test."

And he said to them, "Suppose one of you has a friend
to whom he goes at midnight and says,
'Friend, lend me three loaves of bread,
for a friend of mine has arrived at my house from a journey
and I have nothing to offer him,'
and he says in reply from within,
'Do not bother me; the door has already been locked
and my children and I are already in bed.
I cannot get up to give you anything.'
I tell you,
if he does not get up to give the visitor the loaves
because of their friendship,
he will get up to give him whatever he needs
because of his persistence.

"And I tell you, ask and you will receive;
seek and you will find;
knock and the door will be opened to you.
For everyone who asks, receives;
and the one who seeks, finds;
and to the one who knocks, the door will be opened.
What father among you would hand his son a snake
when he asks for a fish?
Or hand him a scorpion when he asks for an egg?
If you then, who are wicked,
know how to give good gifts to your children,
how much more will the Father in heaven
give the Holy Spirit to those who ask him?"

The Gospel of the Lord. All: **Praise to you, Lord Jesus Christ.**

Prayer over the Offerings

Accept, O Lord, we pray, the offerings
which we bring from the abundance of your gifts,
that through the powerful working of your grace
these most sacred mysteries may sanctify our present way of life
and lead us to eternal gladness.
Through Christ our Lord. All: **Amen.**

Communion Antiphon (Psalm 103[102]:2)

Bless the Lord, O my soul,
and never forget all his benefits.

Or:

(Matthew 5:7-8)
Blessed are the merciful, for they shall receive mercy.
Blessed are the clean of heart, for they shall see God.

Prayer after Communion

We have consumed, O Lord, this divine Sacrament,
the perpetual memorial of the Passion of your Son;
grant, we pray, that this gift,
which he himself gave us with love beyond all telling,
may profit us for salvation.
Through Christ our Lord. All: **Amen.**

Eighteenth Sunday in Ordinary Time

July 31, 2016

Reflection on the Gospel

The rich man in the gospel thinks building bigger barns to hold a boon of "grain and other goods" will give him enough security that he can "rest, eat, drink, be merry." He is misguided about the bigger barn he really needs to build. In the end, what "matters to God" is a "barn" full of what only God can give: life, love, holiness, fidelity, generosity, compassion, Life. No barn can ever be big enough to hold these.

• *Real treasure for eternal life is . . .*

—Living Liturgy™, *Eighteenth Sunday in Ordinary Time 2016*

Entrance Antiphon (Psalm 70[69]:2, 6)

O God, come to my assistance;
O Lord, make haste to help me!
You are my rescuer, my help;
O Lord, do not delay.

Collect

Draw near to your servants, O Lord,
and answer their prayers with unceasing kindness,
that, for those who glory in you as their Creator and guide,
you may restore what you have created
and keep safe what you have restored.
Through our Lord Jesus Christ, your Son,
who lives and reigns with you in the unity of the Holy Spirit,
one God, for ever and ever. All: **Amen.**

Reading I (L 114-C) (Ecclesiastes 1:2; 2:21-23)

A reading from the Book of Ecclesiastes

What profit comes to a man from all his toil?

**Vanity of vanities, says Qoheleth,
vanity of vanities! All things are vanity!**

Here is one who has labored with wisdom and knowledge and skill,

and yet to another who has not labored over it,
he must leave property.
This also is vanity and a great misfortune.
For what profit comes to man from all the toil and anxiety of heart
with which he has labored under the sun?
All his days sorrow and grief is his occupation;
even at night his mind is not at rest.
This also is vanity.

The word of the Lord. All: **Thanks be to God.**

Responsorial Psalm 90

P-518

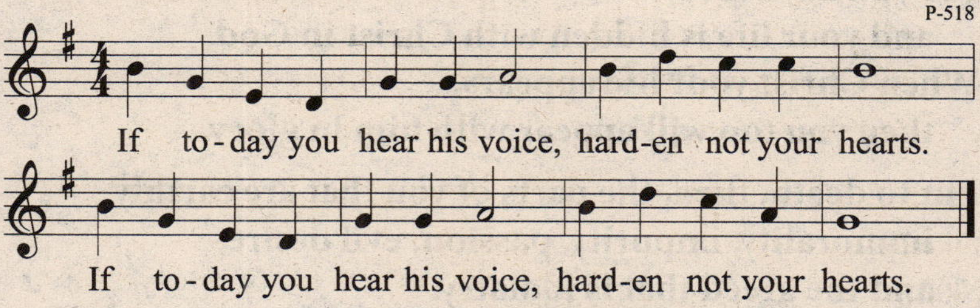

Psalm 90:3-4, 5-6, 12-13

℟. (8) **If today you hear his voice, harden not your hearts.**

You turn man back to dust,
saying, "Return, O children of men."
For a thousand years in your sight
are as yesterday, now that it is past,
or as a watch of the night. ℟.

You make an end of them in their sleep;
the next morning they are like the changing grass,
which at dawn springs up anew,
but by evening wilts and fades. ℟.

Teach us to number our days aright,
that we may gain wisdom of heart.
Return, O Lord! How long?
Have pity on your servants! ℟.

Fill us at daybreak with your kindness,
that we may shout for joy and gladness all our days.

(continued)

And may the gracious care of the LORD our God be ours;
prosper the work of our hands for us!
Prosper the work of our hands! ℟.

READING II (Colossians 3:1-5, 9-11)

A reading from the Letter of Saint Paul to the Colossians

Seek what is above, where Christ is.

Brothers and sisters:
If you were raised with Christ, seek what is above,
where Christ is seated at the right hand of God.
Think of what is above, not of what is on earth.
For you have died,
and your life is hidden with Christ in God.
When Christ your life appears,
then you too will appear with him in glory.

Put to death, then, the parts of you that are earthly:
immorality, impurity, passion, evil desire,
and the greed that is idolatry.
Stop lying to one another,
since you have taken off the old self with its practices
and have put on the new self,
which is being renewed, for knowledge,
in the image of its creator.
Here there is not Greek and Jew,
circumcision and uncircumcision,
barbarian, Scythian, slave, free;
but Christ is all and in all.

The word of the Lord. All: **Thanks be to God.**

GOSPEL (Luke 12:13-21)

ALLELUIA (Matthew 5:3)

℣. Alleluia, alleluia. ℟. **Alleluia, alleluia.**
℣. Blessed are the poor in spirit,
for theirs is the kingdom of heaven. ℟.

✠ **A reading from the holy Gospel according to Luke**

All: **Glory to you, O Lord.**

The things you have prepared, to whom will they belong?

Someone in the crowd said to Jesus,
"Teacher, tell my brother to share the inheritance with me."
He replied to him,
"Friend, who appointed me as your judge and arbitrator?"
Then he said to the crowd,
"Take care to guard against all greed,
for though one may be rich,
one's life does not consist of possessions."

Then he told them a parable.
"There was a rich man whose land produced a bountiful harvest.
He asked himself, 'What shall I do,
for I do not have space to store my harvest?'
And he said, 'This is what I shall do:
I shall tear down my barns and build larger ones.
There I shall store all my grain and other goods
and I shall say to myself, "Now as for you,
you have so many good things stored up for many years,
rest, eat, drink, be merry!"'
But God said to him,
'You fool, this night your life will be demanded of you;
and the things you have prepared, to whom will they belong?'
Thus will it be for all who store up treasure for themselves
but are not rich in what matters to God."

The Gospel of the Lord. All: **Praise to you, Lord Jesus Christ.**

PRAYER OVER THE OFFERINGS
Graciously sanctify these gifts, O Lord, we pray,
and, accepting the oblation of this spiritual sacrifice,
make of us an eternal offering to you.
Through Christ our Lord. All: **Amen.**

COMMUNION ANTIPHON (Wisdom 16:20)
You have given us, O Lord, bread from heaven,
endowed with all delights and sweetness in every taste.

Or:

(John 6:35)
I am the bread of life, says the Lord;
whoever comes to me will not hunger
and whoever believes in me will not thirst.

PRAYER AFTER COMMUNION
Accompany with constant protection, O Lord,
those you renew with these heavenly gifts
and, in your never-failing care for them,
make them worthy of eternal redemption.
Through Christ our Lord. All: **Amen.**

Nineteenth Sunday in Ordinary Time

August 7, 2016

Reflection on the Gospel

In both of these parables about a master's absence, the critical issue is what the servants do while the master is away. They must be vigilant for the "master's return" and faithful in doing "the master's will." Even when the master is absent, servants who have appropriated his way of life will act as if the master were present. To belong to Jesus' household—God's kingdom—we must appropriate Jesus' way of life. We are to be his living, saving Presence. In us, he is never absent.

- *As I . . . Jesus is always present and . . .*

—Living Liturgy™, *Nineteenth Sunday in Ordinary Time 2016*

ENTRANCE ANTIPHON (Cf. Psalm 74[73]:20, 19, 22, 23)
Look to your covenant, O Lord,
and forget not the life of your poor ones for ever.
Arise, O God, and defend your cause,
and forget not the cries of those who seek you.

COLLECT
Almighty ever-living God,
whom, taught by the Holy Spirit,
we dare to call our Father,

bring, we pray, to perfection in our hearts
the spirit of adoption as your sons and daughters,
that we may merit to enter into the inheritance
which you have promised.
Through our Lord Jesus Christ, your Son,
who lives and reigns with you in the unity of the Holy Spirit,
one God, for ever and ever. All: **Amen.**

Reading I (L 117-C) (Wisdom 18:6-9)

A reading from the Book of Wisdom

Just as you punished our adversaries, you glorified us whom you had summoned.

The night of the passover was known beforehand to our fathers,
that, with sure knowledge of the oaths in which they put their faith,
they might have courage.
Your people awaited the salvation of the just
and the destruction of their foes.
For when you punished our adversaries,
in this you glorified us whom you had summoned.
For in secret the holy children of the good were offering sacrifice
and putting into effect with one accord the divine institution.

The word of the Lord. All: **Thanks be to God.**

Responsorial Psalm 33

P-519

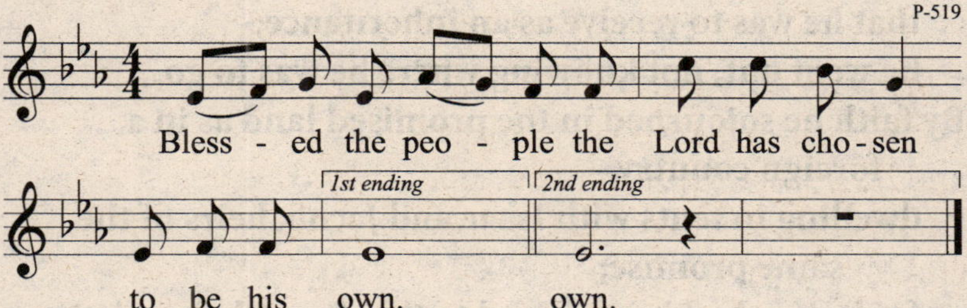

Psalm 33:1, 12, 18-19, 20-22

℟. (12b) **Blessed the people the Lord has chosen to be his own.**

Exult, you just, in the LORD;
praise from the upright is fitting.
Blessed the nation whose God is the LORD,
the people he has chosen for his own inheritance. ℟.

See, the eyes of the Lord are upon those who fear him,
upon those who hope for his kindness,
to deliver them from death
and preserve them in spite of famine. ℟.

Our soul waits for the LORD,
who is our help and our shield.
May your kindness, O LORD, be upon us
who have put our hope in you. ℟.

READING II (Hebrews 11:1-2, 8-19) *or* Shorter Form [ ]
(Hebrews 11:1-2, 8-12)

A reading from the Letter to the Hebrews

Abraham looked forward to the city whose architect and maker is God.

[**Brothers and sisters:**
Faith is the realization of what is hoped for
and evidence of things not seen.
Because of it the ancients were well attested.

By faith Abraham obeyed when he was called to go out to a place
that he was to receive as an inheritance;
he went out, not knowing where he was to go.
By faith he sojourned in the promised land as in a foreign country,
dwelling in tents with Isaac and Jacob, heirs of the same promise;
for he was looking forward to the city with foundations,
whose architect and maker is God.
By faith he received power to generate,
even though he was past the normal age

—and Sarah herself was sterile—
for he thought that the one who had made the promise was trustworthy.
So it was that there came forth from one man,
himself as good as dead,
descendants as numerous as the stars in the sky
and as countless as the sands on the seashore.]

All these died in faith.
They did not receive what had been promised
but saw it and greeted it from afar
and acknowledged themselves to be strangers and aliens on earth,
for those who speak thus show that they are seeking a homeland.
If they had been thinking of the land from which they had come,
they would have had opportunity to return.
But now they desire a better homeland, a heavenly one.
Therefore, God is not ashamed to be called their God,
for he has prepared a city for them.

By faith Abraham, when put to the test, offered up Isaac,
and he who had received the promises was ready to offer his only son,
of whom it was said,
"Through Isaac descendants shall bear your name."
He reasoned that God was able to raise even from the dead,
and he received Isaac back as a symbol.

The word of the Lord. All: **Thanks be to God.**

GOSPEL (Luke 12:32-48) *or* Shorter Form [ ] (Luke 12:35-40)
ALLELUIA (Matthew 24:42a, 44)

℣. Alleluia, alleluia. ℟. **Alleluia, alleluia.**
℣. Stay awake and be ready!
For you do not know on what day your Lord will come. ℟.

✠ **A reading from the holy Gospel according to Luke**

All: **Glory to you, O Lord.**

You also must be prepared.

[Jesus said to his disciples:]
"Do not be afraid any longer, little flock,
for your Father is pleased to give you the kingdom.
Sell your belongings and give alms.
Provide money bags for yourselves that do not wear out,
an inexhaustible treasure in heaven
that no thief can reach nor moth destroy.
For where your treasure is, there also will your heart be.

["Gird your loins and light your lamps
and be like servants who await their master's return from a wedding,
ready to open immediately when he comes and knocks.
Blessed are those servants
whom the master finds vigilant on his arrival.
Amen, I say to you, he will gird himself,
have them recline at table, and proceed to wait on them.
And should he come in the second or third watch
and find them prepared in this way,
blessed are those servants.
Be sure of this:
if the master of the house had known the hour
when the thief was coming,
he would not have let his house be broken into.
You also must be prepared, for at an hour you do not expect,
the Son of Man will come."]

Then Peter said,
"Lord, is this parable meant for us or for everyone?"
And the Lord replied,
"Who, then, is the faithful and prudent steward
whom the master will put in charge of his servants
to distribute the food allowance at the proper time?

Blessed is that servant whom his master on arrival finds doing so.
Truly, I say to you, the master will put the servant in charge of all his property.
But if that servant says to himself,
'My master is delayed in coming,'
and begins to beat the menservants and the maidservants,
to eat and drink and get drunk,
then that servant's master will come
on an unexpected day and at an unknown hour
and will punish the servant severely
and assign him a place with the unfaithful.
That servant who knew his master's will
but did not make preparations nor act in accord with his will
shall be beaten severely;
and the servant who was ignorant of his master's will
but acted in a way deserving of a severe beating
shall be beaten only lightly.
Much will be required of the person entrusted with much,
and still more will be demanded of the person entrusted with more."

The Gospel of the Lord. All: **Praise to you, Lord Jesus Christ.**

PRAYER OVER THE OFFERINGS

Be pleased, O Lord, to accept the offerings of your Church,
for in your mercy you have given them to be offered
and by your power you transform them
into the mystery of our salvation.
Through Christ our Lord. All: **Amen.**

COMMUNION ANTIPHON (Psalm 147:12, 14)

O Jerusalem, glorify the Lord,
who gives you your fill of finest wheat.

Or:

(Cf. John 6:51)

The bread that I will give, says the Lord,
is my flesh for the life of the world.

Prayer after Communion

May the communion in your Sacrament
that we have consumed, save us, O Lord,
and confirm us in the light of your truth.
Through Christ our Lord. All: **Amen.**

Twentieth Sunday in Ordinary Time

August 14, 2016

Reflection on the Gospel

This is a bad news, good news gospel. The bad news is that Jesus' coming throws the world headlong into fire, anguish, division. The good news is that, in spite of Jesus speaking to the contrary, he does grant peace—to his disciples after his resurrection. His gift of peace, however, does not eliminate the fire, anguish, and division. These painful consequences of faithful living sharpen the choice each of us must make: to be "baptized" with Jesus into his death—and risen Life.

- *Jesus comes not to bring freedom from suffering but . . .*

—Living Liturgy™, *Twentieth Sunday in Ordinary Time 2016*

Entrance Antiphon (Psalm 84[83]:10-11)

Turn your eyes, O God, our shield;
and look on the face of your anointed one;
one day within your courts
is better than a thousand elsewhere.

Collect

O God, who have prepared for those who love you
good things which no eye can see,
fill our hearts, we pray, with the warmth of your love,
so that, loving you in all things and above all things,
we may attain your promises,
which surpass every human desire.
Through our Lord Jesus Christ, your Son,
who lives and reigns with you in the unity of the Holy Spirit,
one God, for ever and ever. All: **Amen.**

READING I (L 120-C) (Jeremiah 38:4-6, 8-10)

A reading from the Book of the Prophet Jeremiah

A man of strife and contention to all the land.

In those days, the princes said to the king:
"Jeremiah ought to be put to death;
he is demoralizing the soldiers who are left in this city,
and all the people, by speaking such things to them;
he is not interested in the welfare of our people,
but in their ruin."
King Zedekiah answered: "He is in your power";
for the king could do nothing with them.
And so they took Jeremiah
and threw him into the cistern of Prince Malchiah,
which was in the quarters of the guard,
letting him down with ropes.
There was no water in the cistern, only mud,
and Jeremiah sank into the mud.

Ebed-melech, a court official,
went there from the palace and said to him:
"My lord king,
these men have been at fault
in all they have done to the prophet Jeremiah,
casting him into the cistern.
He will die of famine on the spot,
for there is no more food in the city."
Then the king ordered Ebed-melech the Cushite
to take three men along with him,
and draw the prophet Jeremiah out of the cistern before
he should die.

The word of the Lord. All: **Thanks be to God.**

Responsorial Psalm 40

P-520

Psalm 40:2, 3, 4, 18

℟. (14b) **Lord, come to my aid!**

I have waited, waited for the Lord,
  and he stooped toward me. ℟.

The Lord heard my cry.
He drew me out of the pit of destruction,
  out of the mud of the swamp;
he set my feet upon a crag;
  he made firm my steps. ℟.

And he put a new song into my mouth,
  a hymn to our God.
Many shall look on in awe
  and trust in the Lord. ℟.

Though I am afflicted and poor,
  yet the Lord thinks of me.
You are my help and my deliverer;
  O my God, hold not back! ℟.

Reading II (Hebrews 12:1-4)

A reading from the Letter to the Hebrews

Let us persevere in running the race that lies before us.

Brothers and sisters:
Since we are surrounded by so great a cloud of witnesses,
let us rid ourselves of every burden and sin that clings to us
and persevere in running the race that lies before us
while keeping our eyes fixed on Jesus,
the leader and perfecter of faith.
For the sake of the joy that lay before him
he endured the cross, despising its shame,
and has taken his seat at the right of the throne of God.

Consider how he endured such opposition from sinners,
in order that you may not grow weary and lose heart.
In your struggle against sin
you have not yet resisted to the point of shedding blood.

The word of the Lord. All: Thanks be to God.

Gospel (Luke 12:49-53)

Alleluia (John 10:27)

℣. Alleluia, alleluia. ℟. **Alleluia, alleluia.**
℣. My sheep hear my voice, says the Lord;
I know them, and they follow me. ℟.

✠ **A reading from the holy Gospel according to Luke**

All: **Glory to you, O Lord.**

I have come not to establish peace, but rather division.

Jesus said to his disciples:
"I have come to set the earth on fire,
and how I wish it were already blazing!
There is a baptism with which I must be baptized,
and how great is my anguish until it is accomplished!
Do you think that I have come to establish peace on the earth?
No, I tell you, but rather division.
From now on a household of five will be divided,
three against two and two against three;
a father will be divided against his son
and a son against his father,
a mother against her daughter
and a daughter against her mother,
a mother-in-law against her daughter-in-law
and a daughter-in-law against her mother-in-law."

The Gospel of the Lord. All: **Praise to you, Lord Jesus Christ.**

Prayer over the Offerings

Receive our oblation, O Lord,
by which is brought about a glorious exchange,
that, by offering what you have given,
we may merit to receive your very self.
Through Christ our Lord. All: **Amen.**

Communion Antiphon (Psalm 130[129]:7)

With the Lord there is mercy;
in him is plentiful redemption.

Or:

(John 6:51-52)

I am the living bread that came down from heaven,
 says the Lord.
Whoever eats of this bread will live for ever.

Prayer after Communion

Made partakers of Christ through these Sacraments,
we humbly implore your mercy, Lord,
that, conformed to his image on earth,
we may merit also to be his coheirs in heaven.
Who lives and reigns for ever and ever. All: **Amen.**

The Assumption of the Blessed Virgin Mary

AT THE VIGIL MASS

August 14, 2016

The Mass of the Vigil of the Assumption is to be used at evening Masses.

Reflection on the Gospel

What a greeting Mary gave Elizabeth that the infant in her womb "leaped for joy"! This could not have been any ordinary greeting. Hers was a greeting begotten by belief, by yes, by encounter. Hers was a greeting that proclaimed God's mighty deeds then and now. Hers was a greeting that announced the Presence of the dawning of salvation. Hers is a greeting still spoken and being fulfilled today. Hers is a greeting we must hear. Do we hear the greeting? Are we leaping for joy?

- *Salvation dawns, coming into the presence of Jesus I . . .*

—Living Liturgy™, *Assumption 2016*

ENTRANCE ANTIPHON

Glorious things are spoken of you, O Mary,
who today were exalted above the choirs of Angels
into eternal triumph with Christ.

COLLECT

O God, who, looking on the lowliness of the Blessed Virgin Mary,
raised her to this grace,
that your Only Begotten Son was born of her according to the flesh
and that she was crowned this day with surpassing glory,
grant through her prayers,
that, saved by the mystery of your redemption,
we may merit to be exalted by you on high.
Through our Lord Jesus Christ, your Son,
who lives and reigns with you in the unity of the Holy Spirit,
one God, for ever and ever. All: **Amen.**

READING I (L 621) (1 Chronicles 15:3-4, 15-16; 16:1-2)

A reading from the first Book of Chronicles

They brought in the ark of God and set it within the tent which David had pitched for it.

David assembled all Israel in Jerusalem to bring the ark of the LORD
to the place which he had prepared for it.
David also called together the sons of Aaron and the Levites.

The Levites bore the ark of God on their shoulders with poles,
as Moses had ordained according to the word of the LORD.

David commanded the chiefs of the Levites
to appoint their kinsmen as chanters,
to play on musical instruments, harps, lyres, and cymbals,
to make a loud sound of rejoicing.

They brought in the ark of God and set it within the tent which David had pitched for it.
Then they offered up burnt offerings and peace offerings to God.

When David had finished offering up the burnt offerings
and peace offerings,
he blessed the people in the name of the LORD.

The word of the Lord. All: **Thanks be to God.**

RESPONSORIAL PSALM 132

P-181

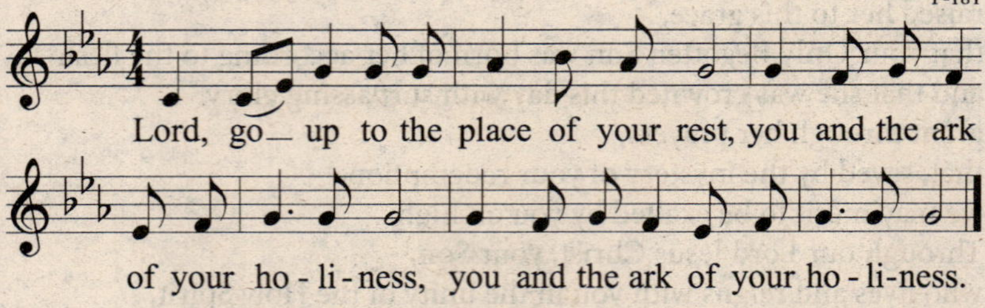

Psalm 132:6-7, 9-10, 13-14

℟. (8) **Lord, go up to the place of your rest, you and the ark of your holiness.**

Behold, we heard of it in Ephrathah;
we found it in the fields of Jaar.
Let us enter into his dwelling,
let us worship at his footstool. ℟.

May your priests be clothed with justice;
let your faithful ones shout merrily for joy.
For the sake of David your servant,
reject not the plea of your anointed. ℟.

For the LORD has chosen Zion;
he prefers her for his dwelling.
"Zion is my resting place forever;
in her will I dwell, for I prefer her." ℟.

READING II (1 Corinthians 15:54b-57)

A reading from the first Letter of Saint Paul to the Corinthians

God gave us victory through Jesus Christ.

Brothers and sisters:
When that which is mortal clothes itself with immortality,
then the word that is written shall come about:

> ***Death is swallowed up in victory.***
> ***Where, O death, is your victory?***
> ***Where, O death, is your sting?***

The sting of death is sin,
and the power of sin is the law.
But thanks be to God who gives us the victory
through our Lord Jesus Christ.

The word of the Lord. All: **Thanks be to God.**

GOSPEL (Luke 11:27-28)

ALLELUIA (Luke 11:28)

℣. Alleluia, alleluia. ℟. **Alleluia, alleluia.**
℣. Blessed are they who hear the word of God
and observe it. ℟.

✠ **A reading from the holy Gospel according to Luke**

All: **Glory to you, O Lord.**

Blessed is the womb that carried you!

While Jesus was speaking,
a woman from the crowd called out and said to him,
"Blessed is the womb that carried you
and the breasts at which you nursed."
He replied,
"Rather, blessed are those
who hear the word of God and observe it."

The Gospel of the Lord. All: **Praise to you, Lord Jesus Christ.**

PRAYER OVER THE OFFERINGS

Receive, we pray, O Lord,
the sacrifice of conciliation and praise,
which we celebrate on the Assumption of the holy Mother of God,
that it may lead us to your pardon
and confirm us in perpetual thanksgiving.
Through Christ our Lord. All: **Amen.**

COMMUNION ANTIPHON (Cf. Luke 11:27)

Blessed is the womb of the Virgin Mary,
which bore the Son of the eternal Father.

PRAYER AFTER COMMUNION
Having partaken of this heavenly table,
we beseech your mercy, Lord our God,
that we, who honor the Assumption of the Mother of God,
may be freed from every threat of harm.
Through Christ our Lord. All: **Amen.**

August 15

AT THE MASS DURING THE DAY

ENTRANCE ANTIPHON (Cf. Revelation 12:1)
A great sign appeared in heaven:
a woman clothed with the sun, and the moon beneath her feet,
and on her head a crown of twelve stars.

Or:

Let us all rejoice in the Lord,
as we celebrate the feast day in honor of the Virgin Mary,
at whose Assumption the Angels rejoice
and praise the Son of God.

COLLECT
Almighty ever-living God,
who assumed the Immaculate Virgin Mary, the Mother of your Son,
body and soul into heavenly glory,
grant, we pray,
that, always attentive to the things that are above,
we may merit to be sharers of her glory.
Through our Lord Jesus Christ, your Son,
who lives and reigns with you in the unity of the Holy Spirit,
one God, for ever and ever. All: **Amen.**

READING I (L 622) (Revelation 11:19a; 12:1-6a, 10ab)

A reading from the Book of Revelation

A woman clothed with the sun, with the moon beneath her feet.

God's temple in heaven was opened,
and the ark of his covenant could be seen in the temple.

A great sign appeared in the sky, a woman clothed with the sun,
with the moon under her feet,
and on her head a crown of twelve stars.

She was with child and wailed aloud in pain as she labored to give birth.
Then another sign appeared in the sky;
it was a huge red dragon, with seven heads and ten horns,
and on its heads were seven diadems.
Its tail swept away a third of the stars in the sky
and hurled them down to the earth.
Then the dragon stood before the woman about to give birth,
to devour her child when she gave birth.
She gave birth to a son, a male child,
destined to rule all the nations with an iron rod.
Her child was caught up to God and his throne.
The woman herself fled into the desert
where she had a place prepared by God.

Then I heard a loud voice in heaven say:
"Now have salvation and power come,
and the Kingdom of our God
and the authority of his Anointed One."

The word of the Lord. All: **Thanks be to God.**

Responsorial Psalm 45

P-182

Psalm 45:10bc, 11, 12ab, 16

℟. (10bc) **The queen stands at your right hand, arrayed in gold.**

The queen takes her place at your right hand in gold of Ophir. ℟.

Hear, O daughter, and see; turn your ear,
forget your people and your father's house. ℟.

So shall the king desire your beauty;
for he is your lord. ℟.

(continued)

They are borne in with gladness and joy;
they enter the palace of the king. ℟.

READING II (1 Corinthians 15:20-27)

A reading from the first Letter of Saint Paul to the Corinthians

Christ, the firstfruits; then those who belong to him.

Brothers and sisters:
Christ has been raised from the dead,
the firstfruits of those who have fallen asleep.
For since death came through man,
the resurrection of the dead came also through man.
For just as in Adam all die,
so too in Christ shall all be brought to life,
but each one in proper order:
Christ the firstfruits;
then, at his coming, those who belong to Christ;
then comes the end,
when he hands over the Kingdom to his God and Father,
when he has destroyed every sovereignty
and every authority and power.
For he must reign until he has put all his enemies under his feet.
The last enemy to be destroyed is death,
for "he subjected everything under his feet."

The word of the Lord. All: **Thanks be to God.**

GOSPEL (Luke 1:39-56)

ALLELUIA

℣. Alleluia, alleluia. ℟. **Alleluia, alleluia.**
℣. Mary is taken up to heaven;
a chorus of angels exults. ℟.

✠ **A reading from the holy Gospel according to Luke**

All: **Glory to you, O Lord.**

The Almighty has done great things for me; he has raised up the lowly.

Mary set out
and traveled to the hill country in haste
to a town of Judah,
where she entered the house of Zechariah
and greeted Elizabeth.
When Elizabeth heard Mary's greeting,
the infant leaped in her womb,
and Elizabeth, filled with the Holy Spirit,
cried out in a loud voice and said,
"Blessed are you among women,
and blessed is the fruit of your womb.
And how does this happen to me,
that the mother of my Lord should come to me?
For at the moment the sound of your greeting reached my ears,
the infant in my womb leaped for joy.
Blessed are you who believed
that what was spoken to you by the Lord
would be fulfilled."

And Mary said:
"My soul proclaims the greatness of the Lord;
my spirit rejoices in God my Savior
for he has looked with favor on his lowly servant.
From this day all generations will call me blessed:
the Almighty has done great things for me
and holy is his Name.
He has mercy on those who fear him
in every generation.
He has shown the strength of his arm,
and has scattered the proud in their conceit.
He has cast down the mighty from their thrones,
and has lifted up the lowly.
He has filled the hungry with good things,
and the rich he has sent away empty.

He has come to the help of his servant Israel
for he has remembered his promise of mercy,
the promise he made to our fathers,
to Abraham and his children forever."

Mary remained with her about three months
and then returned to her home.

The Gospel of the Lord. All: **Praise to you, Lord Jesus Christ.**

Prayer over the Offerings

May this oblation, our tribute of homage,
rise up to you, O Lord,
and, through the intercession of the most Blessed Virgin Mary,
whom you assumed into heaven,
may our hearts, aflame with the fire of love,
constantly long for you.
Through Christ our Lord. All: **Amen.**

Communion Antiphon (Luke 1:48-49)

All generations will call me blessed,
for he who is mighty has done great things for me.

Prayer after Communion

Having received the Sacrament of salvation,
we ask you to grant, O Lord,
that, through the intercession of the Blessed Virgin Mary,
whom you assumed into heaven,
we may be brought to the glory of the resurrection.
Through Christ our Lord. All: **Amen.**

Twenty-First Sunday in Ordinary Time

August 21, 2016

Reflection on the Gospel

What strength is needed to enter "through the narrow gate," the locked door? The strength that comes from living so that the "master of the house" knows us and opens to us. The strength that comes from faith-

fully living "in the kingdom of God." This strength only comes from God who offers it to everyone. Because of this strength we choose to journey "to Jerusalem," we choose to pass through death to Life.

- *With Jesus I journey to Jerusalem as I . . .*

—Living Liturgy™, *Twenty-First Sunday in Ordinary Time 2016*

ENTRANCE ANTIPHON (Cf. Psalm 86[85]:1-3)

Turn your ear, O Lord, and answer me;
save the servant who trusts in you, my God.
Have mercy on me, O Lord, for I cry to you all the day long.

COLLECT

O God, who cause the minds of the faithful
to unite in a single purpose,
grant your people to love what you command
and to desire what you promise,
that, amid the uncertainties of this world,
our hearts may be fixed on that place
where true gladness is found.
Through our Lord Jesus Christ, your Son,
who lives and reigns with you in the unity of the Holy Spirit,
one God, for ever and ever. All: **Amen.**

READING I (L 123-C) (Isaiah 66:18-21)

A reading from the Book of the Prophet Isaiah

They shall bring all your brothers and sisters from all the nations.

Thus says the LORD:
I know their works and their thoughts,
and I come to gather nations of every language;
they shall come and see my glory.
I will set a sign among them;
from them I will send fugitives to the nations:
to Tarshish, Put and Lud, Mosoch, Tubal and Javan,
to the distant coastlands
that have never heard of my fame, or seen my glory;
and they shall proclaim my glory among the nations.
They shall bring all your brothers and sisters from all the nations
as an offering to the LORD,

on horses and in chariots, in carts, upon mules and dromedaries,
to Jerusalem, my holy mountain, says the LORD,
just as the Israelites bring their offering
to the house of the LORD in clean vessels.
Some of these I will take as priests and Levites, says the LORD.

The word of the Lord. All: **Thanks be to God.**

RESPONSORIAL PSALM 117

P-521

Psalm 117:1, 2

℟. (Mark 16:15) **Go out to all the world and tell the good news.** *or:* ℟. **Alleluia.**

Praise the LORD, all you nations;
glorify him, all you peoples! ℟.

For steadfast is his kindness toward us,
and the fidelity of the LORD endures forever. ℟.

READING II (Hebrews 12:5-7, 11-13)

A reading from the Letter to the Hebrews

Those whom the Lord loves, he disciplines.

Brothers and sisters,
You have forgotten the exhortation addressed to you as children:
"My son, do not disdain the discipline of the Lord
or lose heart when reproved by him;
for whom the Lord loves, he disciplines;
he scourges every son he acknowledges."
Endure your trials as "discipline";
God treats you as sons.
For what "son" is there whom his father does not discipline?

At the time,
all discipline seems a cause not for joy but for pain,
yet later it brings the peaceful fruit of righteousness
to those who are trained by it.

So strengthen your drooping hands and your weak knees.
Make straight paths for your feet,
that what is lame may not be disjointed but healed.

The word of the Lord. All: **Thanks be to God.**

GOSPEL (Luke 13:22-30)
ALLELUIA (John 14:6)

℣. Alleluia, alleluia. ℟. **Alleluia, alleluia.**
℣. I am the way, the truth and the life, says the Lord;
no one comes to the Father, except through me. ℟.

✠ **A reading from the holy Gospel according to Luke**

All: **Glory to you, O Lord.**

They will come from east and west and recline at table in the kingdom of God.

Jesus passed through towns and villages,
teaching as he went and making his way to Jerusalem.
Someone asked him,
"Lord, will only a few people be saved?"
He answered them,
"Strive to enter through the narrow gate,
for many, I tell you, will attempt to enter
but will not be strong enough.
After the master of the house has arisen and locked the door,
then will you stand outside knocking and saying,
'Lord, open the door for us.'
He will say to you in reply,
'I do not know where you are from.'
And you will say,
'We ate and drank in your company and you taught in our streets.'

Then he will say to you,
'I do not know where you are from.
Depart from me, all you evildoers!'
And there will be wailing and grinding of teeth
when you see Abraham, Isaac, and Jacob
and all the prophets in the kingdom of God
and you yourselves cast out.
And people will come from the east and the west
and from the north and the south
and will recline at table in the kingdom of God.
For behold, some are last who will be first,
and some are first who will be last."

The Gospel of the Lord. All: **Praise to you, Lord Jesus Christ.**

Prayer over the Offerings

O Lord, who gained for yourself a people by adoption
through the one sacrifice offered once for all,
bestow graciously on us, we pray,
the gifts of unity and peace in your Church.
Through Christ our Lord. All: **Amen.**

Communion Antiphon (Cf. Psalm 104[103]:13-15)

The earth is replete with the fruits of your work, O Lord;
you bring forth bread from the earth
and wine to cheer the heart.

Or:

(Cf. John 6:54)
Whoever eats my flesh and drinks my blood
has eternal life, says the Lord,
and I will raise him up on the last day.

Prayer after Communion

Complete within us, O Lord, we pray,
the healing work of your mercy
and graciously perfect and sustain us,
so that in all things we may please you.
Through Christ our Lord. All: **Amen.**

Twenty-Second Sunday in Ordinary Time

August 28, 2016

Reflection on the Gospel

At Jesus' "wedding banquet" all *who hear and heed Jesus' admonition to humility, inclusivity, and generosity sit in the* one *"place of honor." This "place of honor" is not a limited space, a single seat, a physical arrangement of host and guests one to another. It is a spacious relationship to the risen Jesus that is a share in his divine Life. It is given to "the righteous," all those who have chosen to live and act as Jesus the Host. How blessed are they!*

- *I can be counted among the righteous by . . .*

—Living Liturgy™, *Twenty-Second Sunday in Ordinary Time 2016*

Entrance Antiphon (Cf. Psalm 86[85]:3, 5)

Have mercy on me, O Lord, for I cry to you all the day long.
O Lord, you are good and forgiving,
full of mercy to all who call to you.

Collect

God of might, giver of every good gift,
put into our hearts the love of your name,
so that, by deepening our sense of reverence,
you may nurture in us what is good
and, by your watchful care,
keep safe what you have nurtured.
Through our Lord Jesus Christ, your Son,
who lives and reigns with you in the unity of the Holy Spirit,
one God, for ever and ever. All: **Amen.**

Reading I (L 126-C) (Sirach 3:17-18, 20, 28-29)

A reading from the Book of Sirach

Humble yourself and you will find favor with God.

My child, conduct your affairs with humility,
and you will be loved more than a giver of gifts.
Humble yourself the more, the greater you are,
and you will find favor with God.

What is too sublime for you, seek not,
into things beyond your strength search not.
The mind of a sage appreciates proverbs,
and an attentive ear is the joy of the wise.
Water quenches a flaming fire,
and alms atone for sins.

The word of the Lord. All: **Thanks be to God.**

Responsorial Psalm 68

P-522

Psalm 68:4-5, 6-7, 10-11

℞. (*See* 11b) **God, in your goodness, you have made a home for the poor.**

The just rejoice and exult before God;
they are glad and rejoice.
Sing to God, chant praise to his name;
whose name is the LORD. ℞.

The father of orphans and the defender of widows
is God in his holy dwelling.
God gives a home to the forsaken;
he leads forth prisoners to prosperity. ℞.

A bountiful rain you showered down, O God, upon your inheritance;
you restored the land when it languished;
your flock settled in it;
in your goodness, O God, you provided it for the needy. ℞.

Reading II (Hebrews 12:18-19, 22-24a)

A reading from the Letter to the Hebrews

You have approached Mount Zion and the city of the living God.

Brothers and sisters:
You have not approached that which could be touched
and a blazing fire and gloomy darkness
and storm and a trumpet blast
and a voice speaking words such that those who heard
begged that no message be further addressed to them.
No, you have approached Mount Zion
and the city of the living God, the heavenly Jerusalem,
and countless angels in festal gathering,
and the assembly of the firstborn enrolled in heaven,
and God the judge of all,
and the spirits of the just made perfect,
and Jesus, the mediator of a new covenant,
and the sprinkled blood that speaks more eloquently
than that of Abel.

The word of the Lord. All: **Thanks be to God.**

GOSPEL (Luke 14:1, 7-14)

ALLELUIA (Matthew 11:29ab)

℣. Alleluia, alleluia. ℟. **Alleluia, alleluia.**
℣. Take my yoke upon you, says the Lord,
and learn from me, for I am meek and humble of
heart. ℟.

✠ **A reading from the holy Gospel according to Luke**

All: **Glory to you, O Lord.**

Everyone who exalts himself will be humbled, everyone who humbles himself will be exalted.

On a sabbath Jesus went to dine
at the home of one of the leading Pharisees,
and the people there were observing him carefully.

He told a parable to those who had been invited,
noticing how they were choosing the places of honor
at the table.
"When you are invited by someone to a wedding banquet,
do not recline at table in the place of honor.

A more distinguished guest than you may have been invited by him,
and the host who invited both of you may approach you and say,
'Give your place to this man,'
and then you would proceed with embarrassment
to take the lowest place.
Rather, when you are invited,
go and take the lowest place
so that when the host comes to you he may say,
'My friend, move up to a higher position.'
Then you will enjoy the esteem of your companions at the table.
For everyone who exalts himself will be humbled,
but the one who humbles himself will be exalted."
Then he said to the host who invited him,
"When you hold a lunch or a dinner,
do not invite your friends or your brothers
or your relatives or your wealthy neighbors,
in case they may invite you back and you have repayment.
Rather, when you hold a banquet,
invite the poor, the crippled, the lame, the blind;
blessed indeed will you be because of their inability to repay you.
For you will be repaid at the resurrection of the righteous."

The Gospel of the Lord. All: **Praise to you, Lord Jesus Christ.**

Prayer over the Offerings

May this sacred offering, O Lord,
confer on us always the blessing of salvation,
that what it celebrates in mystery
it may accomplish in power.
Through Christ our Lord. All: **Amen.**

Communion Antiphon (Psalm 31[30]:20)

How great is the goodness, Lord,
that you keep for those who fear you.

Or:

(Matthew 5:9-10)

Blessed are the peacemakers,
for they shall be called children of God.
Blessed are they who are persecuted for the sake of
righteousness,
for theirs is the Kingdom of Heaven.

Prayer after Communion

Renewed by this bread from the heavenly table,
we beseech you, Lord,
that, being the food of charity,
it may confirm our hearts
and stir us to serve you in our neighbor.
Through Christ our Lord. All: **Amen.**

Twenty-Third Sunday in Ordinary Time

September 4, 2016

Reflection on the Gospel

Jesus forewarns the "great crowds" traveling with him that they must "calculate the cost" and the risk of journeying with him to Jerusalem. Even family relationships cannot come before the demands of following him. However, we really cannot calculate the cost of discipleship. Yes, we must follow Jesus with eyes wide open. The cost of discipleship? Everything we have and are. The reward of discipleship? Everything God has and is.

- *The cost/reward of discipleship is . . .*

—Living Liturgy™, *Twenty-Third Sunday in Ordinary Time 2016*

Entrance Antiphon (Psalm 119[118]:137, 124)

You are just, O Lord, and your judgment is right;
treat your servant in accord with your merciful love.

Collect

O God, by whom we are redeemed and receive adoption,
look graciously upon your beloved sons and daughters,
that those who believe in Christ
may receive true freedom
and an everlasting inheritance.
Through our Lord Jesus Christ, your Son,
who lives and reigns with you in the unity of the Holy Spirit,
one God, for ever and ever. All: **Amen.**

Reading I (L 129-C) (Wisdom 9:13-18a)

A reading from the Book of Wisdom

Who can conceive what the Lord intends?

Who can know God's counsel,
or who can conceive what the Lord intends?
For the deliberations of mortals are timid,
and unsure are our plans.
For the corruptible body burdens the soul
and the earthen shelter weighs down the mind that has many concerns.
And scarce do we guess the things on earth,
and what is within our grasp we find with difficulty;
but when things are in heaven, who can search them out?
Or who ever knew your counsel, except you had given wisdom
and sent your holy spirit from on high?
And thus were the paths of those on earth made straight.

The word of the Lord. All: **Thanks be to God.**

Responsorial Psalm 90

P-523

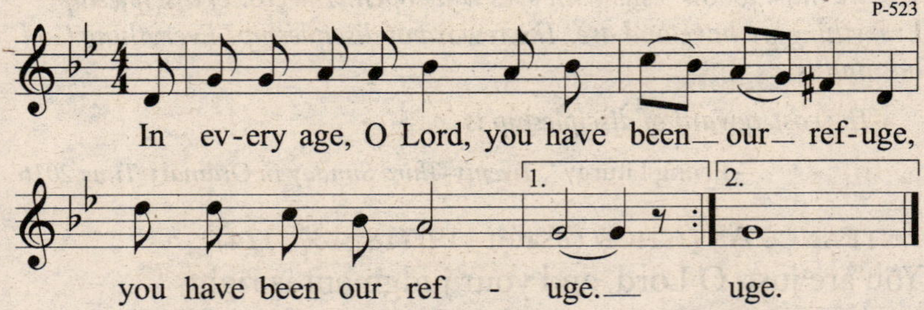

Psalm 90:3-4, 5-6, 12-13, 14 and 17

℟. (1) **In every age, O Lord, you have been our refuge.**

You turn man back to dust,
saying, "Return, O children of men."
For a thousand years in your sight
are as yesterday, now that it is past,
or as a watch of the night. ℟.

You make an end of them in their sleep;
the next morning they are like the changing grass,
which at dawn springs up anew,
but by evening wilts and fades. ℟.

Teach us to number our days aright,
that we may gain wisdom of heart.
Return, O Lord! How long?
Have pity on your servants! ℟.

Fill us at daybreak with your kindness,
that we may shout for joy and gladness all our days.
And may the gracious care of the Lord our God be ours;
prosper the work of our hands for us!
Prosper the work of our hands! ℟.

Reading II (Philemon 9-10, 12-17)

A reading from the Letter of Saint Paul to Philemon

Receive him no longer as a slave but as a beloved brother.

I, Paul, an old man,
and now also a prisoner for Christ Jesus,
urge you on behalf of my child Onesimus,
whose father I have become in my imprisonment;
I am sending him, that is, my own heart, back to you.
I should have liked to retain him for myself,
so that he might serve me on your behalf
in my imprisonment for the gospel,
but I did not want to do anything without your consent,
so that the good you do might not be forced but voluntary.

Perhaps this is why he was away from you for a while,
that you might have him back forever,
no longer as a slave
but more than a slave, a brother,
beloved especially to me, but even more so to you,
as a man and in the Lord.
So if you regard me as a partner, welcome him as you would me.

The word of the Lord. All: **Thanks be to God.**

GOSPEL (Luke 14:25-33)

ALLELUIA (Psalm 119:135)

℣. Alleluia, alleluia. ℟. **Alleluia, alleluia.**
℣. Let your face shine upon your servant;
and teach me your laws. ℟.

✠ **A reading from the holy Gospel according to Luke**

All: **Glory to you, O Lord.**

Anyone of you who does not renounce all possessions cannot be my disciple.

Great crowds were traveling with Jesus,
and he turned and addressed them,
"If anyone comes to me without hating his father and mother,
wife and children, brothers and sisters,
and even his own life,
he cannot be my disciple.
Whoever does not carry his own cross and come after me
cannot be my disciple.
Which of you wishing to construct a tower
does not first sit down and calculate the cost
to see if there is enough for its completion?
Otherwise, after laying the foundation
and finding himself unable to finish the work
the onlookers should laugh at him and say,
'This one began to build but did not have the resources to finish.'

**Or what king marching into battle would not first sit down
and decide whether with ten thousand troops
he can successfully oppose another king
advancing upon him with twenty thousand troops?
But if not, while he is still far away,
he will send a delegation to ask for peace terms.
In the same way,
anyone of you who does not renounce all his
possessions
cannot be my disciple."**

The Gospel of the Lord. All: **Praise to you, Lord Jesus Christ.**

Prayer over the Offerings

O God, who give us the gift of true prayer and of peace,
graciously grant that, through this offering,
we may do fitting homage to your divine majesty
and, by partaking of the sacred mystery,
we may be faithfully united in mind and heart.
Through Christ our Lord. All: **Amen.**

Communion Antiphon (Cf. Psalm 42[41]:2-3)

Like the deer that yearns for running streams,
so my soul is yearning for you, my God;
my soul is thirsting for God, the living God.

Or:

(John 8:12)
I am the light of the world, says the Lord;
whoever follows me will not walk in darkness,
but will have the light of life.

Prayer after Communion

Grant that your faithful, O Lord,
whom you nourish and endow with life
through the food of your Word and heavenly Sacrament,
may so benefit from your beloved Son's great gifts
that we may merit an eternal share in his life.
Who lives and reigns for ever and ever. All: **Amen.**

Twenty-Fourth Sunday in Ordinary Time

September 11, 2016

Reflection on the Gospel

In this gospel tax collectors and sinners are "drawing near to listen to Jesus." Pharisees and scribes, on the other hand, observe what is happening and complain to Jesus. He answers their complaint with three parables that turn the table on their belief about who is really saved. Jesus invites everyone to his table—his feast of mercy. But not everyone chooses to come. Only those come who recognize their need to be found.

- *What is salvation? I recognize it as . . .*

—Living Liturgy™, *Twenty-Fourth Sunday in Ordinary Time 2016*

Entrance Antiphon (Cf. Sirach 36:18)

Give peace, O Lord, to those who wait for you,
that your prophets be found true.
Hear the prayers of your servant,
and of your people Israel.

Collect

Look upon us, O God,
Creator and ruler of all things,
and, that we may feel the working of your mercy,
grant that we may serve you with all our heart.
Through our Lord Jesus Christ, your Son,
who lives and reigns with you in the unity of the Holy Spirit,
one God, for ever and ever. All: **Amen.**

Reading I (L 132-C) (Exodus 32:7-11, 13-14)

A reading from the Book of Exodus

The Lord relented in the punishment he had threatened to inflict on his people.

The LORD said to Moses,
"Go down at once to your people,
whom you brought out of the land of Egypt,
for they have become depraved.
They have soon turned aside from the way I pointed out to them,
making for themselves a molten calf and worshiping it,
sacrificing to it and crying out,
'This is your God, O Israel,
who brought you out of the land of Egypt!'
I see how stiff-necked this people is," continued the LORD to Moses.
"Let me alone, then,
that my wrath may blaze up against them to consume them.
Then I will make of you a great nation."

But Moses implored the LORD, his God, saying,
"Why, O LORD, should your wrath blaze up against your own people,
whom you brought out of the land of Egypt
with such great power and with so strong a hand?
Remember your servants Abraham, Isaac, and Israel,
and how you swore to them by your own self, saying,
'I will make your descendants as numerous as the stars in the sky;
and all this land that I promised,
I will give your descendants as their perpetual heritage.' "
So the LORD relented in the punishment
he had threatened to inflict on his people.

The word of the Lord. All: Thanks be to God.

Responsorial Psalm 51

P-524

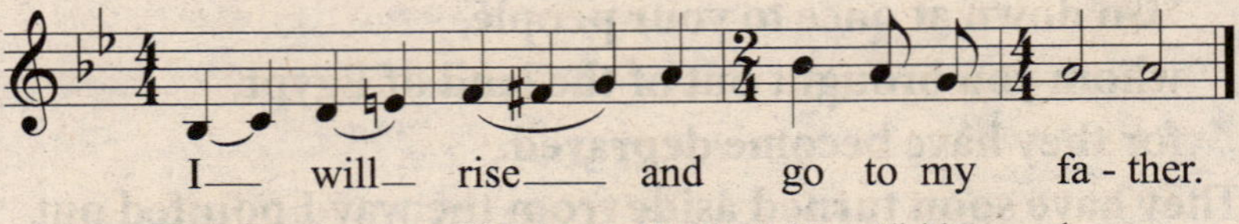

Psalm 51:3-4, 12-13, 17, 19

℟. (Luke 15:18) **I will rise and go to my father.**

Have mercy on me, O God, in your goodness;
in the greatness of your compassion wipe out my offense.
Thoroughly wash me from my guilt
and of my sin cleanse me. ℟.

A clean heart create for me, O God,
and a steadfast spirit renew within me.
Cast me not out from your presence,
and your Holy Spirit take not from me. ℟.

O Lord, open my lips,
and my mouth shall proclaim your praise.
My sacrifice, O God, is a contrite spirit;
a heart contrite and humbled, O God, you will not spurn. ℟.

Reading II (1 Timothy 1:12-17)

A reading from the first Letter of Saint Paul to Timothy

Christ came to save sinners.

Beloved:
I am grateful to him who has strengthened me, Christ Jesus our Lord,
because he considered me trustworthy
in appointing me to the ministry.
I was once a blasphemer and a persecutor and arrogant,
but I have been mercifully treated
because I acted out of ignorance in my unbelief.
Indeed, the grace of our Lord has been abundant,
along with the faith and love that are in Christ Jesus.

This saying is trustworthy and deserves full acceptance:
Christ Jesus came into the world to save sinners.
Of these I am the foremost.
But for that reason I was mercifully treated,
so that in me, as the foremost,
Christ Jesus might display all his patience as an example
for those who would come to believe in him for everlasting life.
To the king of ages, incorruptible, invisible, the only God,
honor and glory forever and ever. Amen.

The word of the Lord. All: **Thanks be to God.**

GOSPEL (Luke 15:1-32) *or* Shorter Form [ ] (Luke 15:1-10)
ALLELUIA (2 Corinthians 5:19)

℣. Alleluia, alleluia. ℟. **Alleluia, alleluia.**
℣. God was reconciling the world to himself in Christ
and entrusting to us the message of reconciliation. ℟.

✠ **A reading from the holy Gospel according to Luke**

All: **Glory to you, O Lord.**

There will be great joy in heaven over one sinner who repents.

[Tax collectors and sinners were all drawing near to listen to Jesus,
but the Pharisees and scribes began to complain, saying,
"This man welcomes sinners and eats with them."
So to them he addressed this parable.
"What man among you having a hundred sheep and losing one of them
would not leave the ninety-nine in the desert
and go after the lost one until he finds it?
And when he does find it,
he sets it on his shoulders with great joy
and, upon his arrival home,
he calls together his friends and neighbors and says to them,

'Rejoice with me because I have found my lost sheep.'
I tell you, in just the same way
there will be more joy in heaven over one sinner who repents
than over ninety-nine righteous people
who have no need of repentance.

"Or what woman having ten coins and losing one
would not light a lamp and sweep the house,
searching carefully until she finds it?
And when she does find it,
she calls together her friends and neighbors
and says to them,
'Rejoice with me because I have found the coin that I lost.'
In just the same way, I tell you,
there will be rejoicing among the angels of God
over one sinner who repents."]

Then he said,
"A man had two sons, and the younger son said to his father,
'Father give me the share of your estate that should come to me.'
So the father divided the property between them.
After a few days, the younger son collected all his belongings
and set off to a distant country
where he squandered his inheritance on a life of dissipation.
When he had freely spent everything,
a severe famine struck that country,
and he found himself in dire need.
So he hired himself out to one of the local citizens
who sent him to his farm to tend the swine.
And he longed to eat his fill of the pods on which the swine fed,
but nobody gave him any.

Coming to his senses he thought,
'How many of my father's hired workers
have more than enough food to eat,
but here am I, dying from hunger.
I shall get up and go to my father and I shall say to him,
"Father, I have sinned against heaven and against you.
I no longer deserve to be called your son;
treat me as you would treat one of your hired workers."'
So he got up and went back to his father.
While he was still a long way off,
his father caught sight of him,
and was filled with compassion.
He ran to his son, embraced him and kissed him.
His son said to him,
'Father, I have sinned against heaven and against you;
I no longer deserve to be called your son.'
But his father ordered his servants,
'Quickly bring the finest robe and put it on him;
put a ring on his finger and sandals on his feet.
Take the fattened calf and slaughter it.
Then let us celebrate with a feast,
because this son of mine was dead, and has come to life again;
he was lost, and has been found.'
Then the celebration began.
Now the older son had been out in the field
and, on his way back, as he neared the house,
he heard the sound of music and dancing.
He called one of the servants and asked what this might mean.
The servant said to him,
'Your brother has returned
and your father has slaughtered the fattened calf
because he has him back safe and sound.'

He became angry,
and when he refused to enter the house,
his father came out and pleaded with him.
He said to his father in reply,
'Look, all these years I served you
and not once did I disobey your orders;
yet you never gave me even a young goat to feast on with my friends. But when your son returns,
who swallowed up your property with prostitutes,
for him you slaughter the fattened calf.'
He said to him,
'My son, you are here with me always;
everything I have is yours.
But now we must celebrate and rejoice,
because your brother was dead and has come to life again;
he was lost and has been found.'"

The Gospel of the Lord. All: **Praise to you, Lord Jesus Christ.**

Prayer over the Offerings

Look with favor on our supplications, O Lord,
and in your kindness accept these, your servants' offerings,
that what each has offered to the honor of your name
may serve the salvation of all.
Through Christ our Lord. All: **Amen.**

Communion Antiphon (Cf. Psalm 36[35]:8)

How precious is your mercy, O God!
The children of men seek shelter in the shadow of your wings.

Or:

(Cf. 1 Corinthians 10:16)
The chalice of blessing that we bless
is a communion in the Blood of Christ;
and the bread that we break
is a sharing in the Body of the Lord.

Prayer after Communion

May the working of this heavenly gift, O Lord, we pray,
take possession of our minds and bodies,
so that its effects, and not our own desires,
may always prevail in us.
Through Christ our Lord. All: **Amen.**

Twenty-Fifth Sunday in Ordinary Time

September 18, 2016

Reflection on the Gospel

This gospel puts to us a basic question: Whom do we serve? The wily steward is clearly self-serving and decisive in doing what he thinks necessary for his own immediate well-being. But by acting in this way, he risks squandering his eternal well-being ("eternal dwellings"). To secure this, he needed to choose to serve God rather than self. The irony is that had he chosen to serve God and God alone, he would have chosen to serve himself in the best way possible.

- *I best serve myself when I . . .*

—Living Liturgy™, *Twenty-Fifth Sunday in Ordinary Time 2016*

Entrance Antiphon

I am the salvation of the people, says the Lord.
Should they cry to me in any distress,
I will hear them, and I will be their Lord for ever.

Collect

O God, who founded all the commands of your sacred Law
upon love of you and of our neighbor,
grant that, by keeping your precepts,
we may merit to attain eternal life.
Through our Lord Jesus Christ, your Son,
who lives and reigns with you in the unity of the Holy Spirit,
one God, for ever and ever. All: **Amen.**

Reading I (L 135-C) (Amos 8:4-7)

A reading from the Book of the Prophet Amos

Against those who buy the poor for money.

Hear this, you who trample upon the needy
and destroy the poor of the land!
"When will the new moon be over," you ask,
"that we may sell our grain,
and the sabbath, that we may display the wheat?
We will diminish the ephah,
add to the shekel,
and fix our scales for cheating!
We will buy the lowly for silver,
and the poor for a pair of sandals;
even the refuse of the wheat we will sell!"
The Lord has sworn by the pride of Jacob:
Never will I forget a thing they have done!

The word of the Lord. All: **Thanks be to God.**

Responsorial Psalm 113

P-525

Psalm 113:1-2, 4-6, 7-8

℟. (*See* 1a, 7b) **Praise the Lord, who lifts up the poor.**
or: ℟. **Alleluia.**

Praise, you servants of the Lord,
praise the name of the Lord.
Blessed be the name of the Lord
both now and forever. ℟.

High above all nations is the Lord;
above the heavens is his glory.
Who is like the Lord, our God, who is enthroned on high
and looks upon the heavens and the earth below? ℟.

He raises up the lowly from the dust;
  from the dunghill he lifts up the poor
to seat them with princes,
  with the princes of his own people. ℟.

READING II (1 Timothy 2:1-8)

A reading from the first Letter of Saint Paul to Timothy

Let prayers be offered for everyone to God who wills everyone to be saved.

Beloved:
First of all, I ask that supplications, prayers,
  petitions, and thanksgivings be offered for everyone,
  for kings and for all in authority,
  that we may lead a quiet and tranquil life
  in all devotion and dignity.
This is good and pleasing to God our savior,
  who wills everyone to be saved
  and to come to knowledge of the truth.
    For there is one God.
    There is also one mediator between God and men,
      the man Christ Jesus,
    who gave himself as ransom for all.
This was the testimony at the proper time.
For this I was appointed preacher and apostle
  —I am speaking the truth, I am not lying—,
  teacher of the Gentiles in faith and truth.

It is my wish, then, that in every place the men should pray,
  lifting up holy hands, without anger or argument.

The word of the Lord. All: **Thanks be to God.**

GOSPEL (Luke 16:1-13) *or* Shorter Form [ ] (Luke 16:10-13)
ALLELUIA (*See* 2 Corinthians 8:9)

℣. Alleluia, alleluia. ℟. **Alleluia, alleluia.**
℣. Though our Lord Jesus Christ was rich, he became poor,
  so that by his poverty you might become rich. ℟.

✠ **A reading from the holy Gospel according to Luke**

All: **Glory to you, O Lord.**

You cannot serve both God and mammon.

[Jesus said to his disciples:]
"A rich man had a steward
who was reported to him for squandering his property.
He summoned him and said,
'What is this I hear about you?
Prepare a full account of your stewardship,
because you can no longer be my steward.'
The steward said to himself, 'What shall I do,
now that my master is taking the position of steward away from me?
I am not strong enough to dig and I am ashamed to beg.
I know what I shall do so that,
when I am removed from the stewardship,
they may welcome me into their homes.'
He called in his master's debtors one by one.
To the first he said,
'How much do you owe my master?'
He replied, 'One hundred measures of olive oil.'
He said to him, 'Here is your promissory note.
Sit down and quickly write one for fifty.'
Then to another the steward said, 'And you, how much do you owe?'
He replied, 'One hundred kors of wheat.'
The steward said to him, 'Here is your promissory note;
write one for eighty.'
And the master commended that dishonest steward for acting prudently.

"For the children of this world
are more prudent in dealing with their own generation
than are the children of light.

I tell you, make friends for yourselves with dishonest wealth,
so that when it fails, you will be welcomed into eternal dwellings.
[The person who is trustworthy in very small matters
is also trustworthy in great ones;
and the person who is dishonest in very small matters
is also dishonest in great ones.
If, therefore, you are not trustworthy with dishonest wealth,
who will trust you with true wealth?
If you are not trustworthy with what belongs to another,
who will give you what is yours?
No servant can serve two masters.
He will either hate one and love the other,
or be devoted to one and despise the other.
You cannot serve both God and mammon."]

The Gospel of the Lord. All: **Praise to you, Lord Jesus Christ.**

Prayer over the Offerings

Receive with favor, O Lord, we pray,
the offerings of your people,
that what they profess with devotion and faith
may be theirs through these heavenly mysteries.
Through Christ our Lord. All: **Amen.**

Communion Antiphon (Psalm 119[118]:4-5)

You have laid down your precepts to be carefully kept;
may my ways be firm in keeping your statutes.

Or:

(John 10:14)
I am the Good Shepherd, says the Lord;
I know my sheep, and mine know me.

Prayer after Communion

Graciously raise up, O Lord,
those you renew with this Sacrament,
that we may come to possess your redemption
both in mystery and in the manner of our life.
Through Christ our Lord. All: **Amen.**

Twenty-Sixth Sunday in Ordinary Time

September 25, 2016

Reflection on the Gospel

The rich man in torment begs Abraham to send "someone from the dead" to warn his five brothers to repent and change their way of living. In fact, during his earthly life, the rich man had *"someone from the dead" warning him to repent and change—the sick, suffering, starving Lazarus "lying at his door" who was as good as "dead" to the rich man. Indeed, "someone from the dead"* has *come to warn us, too. Who? Do we listen?*

- *Jesus has the word of eternal life, so I . . .*

—Living Liturgy™, *Twenty-Sixth Sunday in Ordinary Time 2016*

Entrance Antiphon (Daniel 3:31, 29, 30, 43, 42)

All that you have done to us, O Lord,
you have done with true judgment,
for we have sinned against you
and not obeyed your commandments.
But give glory to your name
and deal with us according to the bounty of your mercy.

Collect

O God, who manifest your almighty power
above all by pardoning and showing mercy,
bestow, we pray, your grace abundantly upon us
and make those hastening to attain your promises
heirs to the treasures of heaven.
Through our Lord Jesus Christ, your Son,
who lives and reigns with you in the unity of the Holy Spirit,
one God, for ever and ever. All: **Amen.**

Reading I (L 138-C) (Amos 6:1a, 4-7)

A reading from the Book of the Prophet Amos

Their wanton revelry shall be done away with.

Thus says the Lord, the God of hosts:
Woe to the complacent in Zion!
Lying upon beds of ivory,
stretched comfortably on their couches,
they eat lambs taken from the flock,
and calves from the stall!
Improvising to the music of the harp,
like David, they devise their own accompaniment.
They drink wine from bowls
and anoint themselves with the best oils;
yet they are not made ill by the collapse of Joseph!
Therefore, now they shall be the first to go into exile,
and their wanton revelry shall be done away with.

The word of the Lord. All: Thanks be to God.

Responsorial Psalm 146

Psalm 146:7, 8-9, 9-10

℟. (1b) **Praise the Lord, my soul!** *or:* **℟. Alleluia.**

Blessed is he who keeps faith forever,
secures justice for the oppressed,
gives food to the hungry.
The Lord sets captives free. ℟.

The Lord gives sight to the blind.
The Lord raises up those who were bowed down;
the Lord loves the just.
The Lord protects strangers. ℟.

The fatherless and the widow he sustains,
but the way of the wicked he thwarts.
The Lord shall reign forever;
your God, O Zion, through all generations. Alleluia. ℟.

READING II (1 Timothy 6:11-16)

A reading from the first Letter of Saint Paul to Timothy

Keep the commandment until the appearance of the Lord Jesus Christ.

But you, man of God, pursue righteousness,
devotion, faith, love, patience, and gentleness.
Compete well for the faith.
Lay hold of eternal life, to which you were called
when you made the noble confession in the presence
of many witnesses.
I charge you before God, who gives life to all things,
and before Christ Jesus,
who gave testimony under Pontius Pilate for the
noble confession,
to keep the commandment without stain or reproach
until the appearance of our Lord Jesus Christ
that the blessed and only ruler
will make manifest at the proper time,
the King of kings and Lord of lords,
who alone has immortality, who dwells in
unapproachable light,
and whom no human being has seen or can see.
To him be honor and eternal power. Amen.

The word of the Lord. All: **Thanks be to God.**

GOSPEL (Luke 16:19-31)

ALLELUIA (*See* 2 Corinthians 8:9)

℣. Alleluia, alleluia. ℟. **Alleluia, alleluia.**
℣. Though our Lord Jesus Christ was rich, he became poor,
so that by his poverty you might become rich. ℟.

✠ **A reading from the holy Gospel according to Luke**

All: **Glory to you, O Lord.**

You received what was good, Lazarus what was bad; now he is comforted, whereas you are tormented.

Jesus said to the Pharisees:
"There was a rich man who dressed in purple garments and fine linen
and dined sumptuously each day.
And lying at his door was a poor man named Lazarus, covered with sores,
who would gladly have eaten his fill of the scraps
that fell from the rich man's table.
Dogs even used to come and lick his sores.
When the poor man died,
he was carried away by angels to the bosom of Abraham.
The rich man also died and was buried,
and from the netherworld, where he was in torment,
he raised his eyes and saw Abraham far off
and Lazarus at his side.
And he cried out, 'Father Abraham, have pity on me.
Send Lazarus to dip the tip of his finger in water and cool my tongue,
for I am suffering torment in these flames.'
Abraham replied,
'My child, remember that you received
what was good during your lifetime
while Lazarus likewise received what was bad;
but now he is comforted here, whereas you are tormented.
Moreover, between us and you a great chasm is established
to prevent anyone from crossing who might wish to go
from our side to yours or from your side to ours.'
He said, 'Then I beg you, father,
send him to my father's house, for I have five brothers,
so that he may warn them,
lest they too come to this place of torment.'
But Abraham replied, 'They have Moses and the prophets.
Let them listen to them.'

He said, 'Oh no, father Abraham,
but if someone from the dead goes to them, they will repent.'
Then Abraham said, 'If they will not listen to Moses and the prophets,
neither will they be persuaded if someone should rise from the dead.' "

The Gospel of the Lord. All: **Praise to you, Lord Jesus Christ.**

Prayer over the Offerings

Grant us, O merciful God,
that this our offering may find acceptance with you
and that through it the wellspring of all blessing
may be laid open before us.
Through Christ our Lord. All: **Amen.**

Communion Antiphon (Cf. Psalm 119[118]:49-50)

Remember your word to your servant, O Lord,
by which you have given me hope.
This is my comfort when I am brought low.

Or:

(1 John 3:16)
By this we came to know the love of God:
that Christ laid down his life for us;
so we ought to lay down our lives for one another.

Prayer after Communion

May this heavenly mystery, O Lord,
restore us in mind and body,
that we may be coheirs in glory with Christ,
to whose suffering we are united
whenever we proclaim his Death.
Who lives and reigns for ever and ever. All: **Amen.**

Twenty-Seventh Sunday in Ordinary Time

October 2, 2016

Reflection on the Gospel

Jesus says that even faith "the size of a mustard seed" is enough to do great things. The "unprofitable servants" of Jesus' gospel teaching simply do what they are commanded—they do not go beyond normal expectations; they cannot uproot a mulberry tree. To go beyond expectations, we must risk doing the impossible and thereby become profitable servants. In this we align ourselves with God, become able to do as God does. Being aligned with God: this is faith.

- *My faith can be profitable if I but . . .*

—Living Liturgy™, *Twenty-Seventh Sunday in Ordinary Time 2016*

Entrance Antiphon (Cf. Esther 4:17)

Within your will, O Lord, all things are established,
and there is none that can resist your will.
For you have made all things, the heaven and the earth,
and all that is held within the circle of heaven;
you are the Lord of all.

Collect

Almighty ever-living God,
who in the abundance of your kindness
surpass the merits and the desires of those who entreat you,
pour out your mercy upon us
to pardon what conscience dreads
and to give what prayer does not dare to ask.
Through our Lord Jesus Christ, your Son,
who lives and reigns with you in the unity of the Holy Spirit,
one God, for ever and ever. All: **Amen.**

Reading I (L 141-C) (Habakkuk 1:2-3; 2:2-4)

A reading from the Book of the Prophet Habakkuk

The just one, because of his faith, shall live.

How long, O Lord? I cry for help
but you do not listen!
I cry out to you, "Violence!"
but you do not intervene.
Why do you let me see ruin;
why must I look at misery?
Destruction and violence are before me;
there is strife, and clamorous discord.
Then the Lord answered me and said:
Write down the vision clearly upon the tablets,
so that one can read it readily.
For the vision still has its time,
presses on to fulfillment, and will not disappoint;
if it delays, wait for it,
it will surely come, it will not be late.
The rash one has no integrity;
but the just one, because of his faith, shall live.

The word of the Lord. All: **Thanks be to God.**

Responsorial Psalm 95

P-527

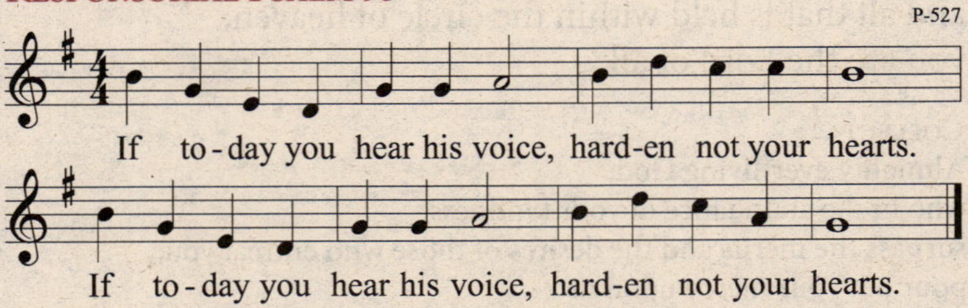

Psalm 95:1-2, 6-7, 8-9

℟. (8) **If today you hear his voice, harden not your hearts.**

Come, let us sing joyfully to the Lord;
let us acclaim the Rock of our salvation.

Let us come into his presence with thanksgiving;
let us joyfully sing psalms to him. ℟.

Come, let us bow down in worship;
let us kneel before the LORD who made us.
For he is our God,
and we are the people he shepherds, the flock he guides. ℟.

Oh, that today you would hear his voice:
"Harden not your hearts as at Meribah,
as in the day of Massah in the desert,
where your fathers tempted me;
they tested me though they had seen my works." ℟.

READING II (2 Timothy 1:6-8, 13-14)

A reading from the second Letter of Saint Paul to Timothy

Do not be ashamed of your testimony to our Lord.

Beloved:
I remind you to stir into flame
the gift of God that you have through the imposition of my hands.
For God did not give us a spirit of cowardice
but rather of power and love and self-control.
So do not be ashamed of your testimony to our Lord,
nor of me, a prisoner for his sake;
but bear your share of hardship for the gospel
with the strength that comes from God.

Take as your norm the sound words that you heard from me,
in the faith and love that are in Christ Jesus.
Guard this rich trust with the help of the Holy Spirit
that dwells within us.

The word of the Lord. All: Thanks be to God.

Gospel (Luke 17:5-10)

Alleluia (1 Peter 1:25)

℣. Alleluia, alleluia. ℟. **Alleluia, alleluia.**
℣. The word of the Lord remains forever.
This is the word that has been proclaimed to you. ℟.

✠ **A reading from the holy Gospel according to Luke**

All: **Glory to you, O Lord.**

If you have faith!

The apostles said to the Lord, "Increase our faith."
The Lord replied,
"If you have faith the size of a mustard seed,
you would say to this mulberry tree,
'Be uprooted and planted in the sea,' and it would obey you.

"Who among you would say to your servant
who has just come in from plowing or tending sheep in the field,
'Come here immediately and take your place at table'?
Would he not rather say to him,
'Prepare something for me to eat.
Put on your apron and wait on me while I eat and drink.
You may eat and drink when I am finished'?
Is he grateful to that servant because he did what was commanded?
So should it be with you.
When you have done all you have been commanded,
say, 'We are unprofitable servants;
we have done what we were obliged to do.' "

The Gospel of the Lord. All: **Praise to you, Lord Jesus Christ.**

Prayer over the Offerings

Accept, O Lord, we pray,
the sacrifices instituted by your commands
and, through the sacred mysteries,
which we celebrate with dutiful service,
graciously complete the sanctifying work

by which you are pleased to redeem us.
Through Christ our Lord. All: **Amen.**

Communion Antiphon (Lamentations 3:25)

The Lord is good to those who hope in him,
to the soul that seeks him.

Or:

(Cf. 1 Corinthians 10:17)
Though many, we are one bread, one body,
for we all partake of the one Bread and one Chalice.

Prayer after Communion

Grant us, almighty God,
that we may be refreshed and nourished
by the Sacrament which we have received,
so as to be transformed into what we consume.
Through Christ our Lord. All: **Amen.**

Twenty-Eighth Sunday in Ordinary Time

October 9, 2016

Reflection on the Gospel

The ten lepers were all outcasts. Jesus, on his journey to Jerusalem which would end in salvation for all, healed them all. For Jesus, there are no outcasts. Yet only one of the ten demonstrates that being saved is being healed, is returning to the Healer, is glorifying God, is falling at the feet of Jesus, is giving thanks. Only one shows us how *faith saves. Faith is not static; it is dynamic, unfolding in various daily activities.*

- *I return to "the Healer" when I . . .*

—Living Liturgy™, *Twenty-Eighth Sunday in Ordinary Time 2016*

Entrance Antiphon (Psalm 130[129]:3-4)

If you, O Lord, should mark iniquities,
Lord, who could stand?
But with you is found forgiveness,
O God of Israel.

Collect

May your grace, O Lord, we pray,
at all times go before us and follow after
and make us always determined
to carry out good works.
Through our Lord Jesus Christ, your Son,
who lives and reigns with you in the unity of the Holy Spirit,
one God, for ever and ever. All: **Amen.**

Reading I (L 144-C) (2 Kings 5:14-17)

A reading from the second Book of Kings

Naaman returned to the man of God and acknowledged the Lord.

Naaman went down and plunged into the Jordan seven times
at the word of Elisha, the man of God.
His flesh became again like the flesh of a little child,
and he was clean of his leprosy.

Naaman returned with his whole retinue to the man of God.
On his arrival he stood before Elisha and said,
"Now I know that there is no God in all the earth,
except in Israel.
Please accept a gift from your servant."

Elisha replied, "As the LORD lives whom I serve, I will not take it";
and despite Naaman's urging, he still refused.
Naaman said: "If you will not accept,
please let me, your servant, have two mule-loads of earth,
for I will no longer offer holocaust or sacrifice
to any other god except to the LORD."

The word of the Lord. All: **Thanks be to God.**

Responsorial Psalm 98

Psalm 98:1, 2-3, 3-4

℟. (*See* 2b) **The Lord has revealed to the nations his saving power.**

Sing to the Lord a new song,
for he has done wondrous deeds;
his right hand has won victory for him,
his holy arm. ℟.

The Lord has made his salvation known:
in the sight of the nations he has revealed his justice.
He has remembered his kindness and his faithfulness
toward the house of Israel. ℟.

All the ends of the earth have seen
the salvation by our God.
Sing joyfully to the Lord, all you lands:
break into song; sing praise. ℟.

Reading II (2 Timothy 2:8-13)

A reading from the second Letter of Saint Paul to Timothy

If we persevere we shall also reign with Christ.

Beloved:
Remember Jesus Christ, raised from the dead, a descendant of David:
such is my gospel, for which I am suffering,
even to the point of chains, like a criminal.
But the word of God is not chained.
Therefore, I bear with everything for the sake of those who are chosen,
so that they too may obtain the salvation that is in Christ Jesus,
together with eternal glory.

This saying is trustworthy:
If we have died with him
we shall also live with him;
if we persevere
we shall also reign with him.
But if we deny him
he will deny us.
If we are unfaithful
he remains faithful,
for he cannot deny himself.

The word of the Lord. All: **Thanks be to God.**

GOSPEL (Luke 17:11-19)
ALLELUIA (1 Thessalonians 5:18)

℣. Alleluia, alleluia. ℟. **Alleluia, alleluia.**
℣. In all circumstances, give thanks,
for this is the will of God for you in Christ Jesus. ℟.

✠ **A reading from the holy Gospel according to Luke**

All: **Glory to you, O Lord.**

None but this foreigner has returned to give thanks to God.

As Jesus continued his journey to Jerusalem,
he traveled through Samaria and Galilee.
As he was entering a village, ten lepers met him.
They stood at a distance from him and raised their voices, saying,
"Jesus, Master! Have pity on us!"
And when he saw them, he said,
"Go show yourselves to the priests."
As they were going they were cleansed.
And one of them, realizing he had been healed,
returned, glorifying God in a loud voice;
and he fell at the feet of Jesus and thanked him.
He was a Samaritan.
Jesus said in reply,
"Ten were cleansed, were they not?

Where are the other nine?
Has none but this foreigner returned to give thanks to God?"
Then he said to him, "Stand up and go;
your faith has saved you."

The Gospel of the Lord. All: **Praise to you, Lord Jesus Christ.**

Prayer over the Offerings

Accept, O Lord, the prayers of your faithful
with the sacrificial offerings,
that, through these acts of devotedness,
we may pass over to the glory of heaven.
Through Christ our Lord. All: **Amen.**

Communion Antiphon (Cf. Psalm 34[33]:11)

The rich suffer want and go hungry,
but those who seek the Lord lack no blessing.

Or:

(1 John 3:2)
When the Lord appears, we shall be like him,
for we shall see him as he is.

Prayer after Communion

We entreat your majesty most humbly, O Lord,
that, as you feed us with the nourishment
which comes from the most holy Body and Blood of your Son,
so you may make us sharers of his divine nature.
Who lives and reigns for ever and ever. All: **Amen.**

Twenty-Ninth Sunday in Ordinary Time

October 16, 2016

(World Mission Sunday)

Reflection on the Gospel

The widow seeks justice out of need; the judge renders justice out of exasperation; God bestows justice out of love for God's "chosen ones/who call out to him day and night." The widow had a legal relationship with the judge that ended the moment he rendered a decision. We, however, have a personal relationship with God that continually deepens as we "pray always," that reveals we are God's "chosen ones" who are in right relationship with God.

- *Praying always means I . . .*

—Living Liturgy™, *Twenty-Ninth Sunday in Ordinary Time 2016*

Entrance Antiphon (Cf. Psalm 17[16]:6, 8)

To you I call; for you will surely heed me, O God;
turn your ear to me; hear my words.
Guard me as the apple of your eye;
in the shadow of your wings protect me.

Collect

Almighty ever-living God,
grant that we may always conform our will to yours
and serve your majesty in sincerity of heart.
Through our Lord Jesus Christ, your Son,
who lives and reigns with you in the unity of the Holy Spirit,
one God, for ever and ever. All: **Amen.**

Reading I (L 147-C) (Exodus 17:8-13)

A reading from the Book of Exodus

As long as Moses kept his hands raised up, Israel had the better of the fight.

In those days, Amalek came and waged war against Israel.
Moses, therefore, said to Joshua,
"Pick out certain men,
and tomorrow go out and engage Amalek in battle.
I will be standing on top of the hill
with the staff of God in my hand."
So Joshua did as Moses told him:
he engaged Amalek in battle
after Moses had climbed to the top of the hill with Aaron and Hur.

As long as Moses kept his hands raised up,
Israel had the better of the fight,
but when he let his hands rest,
Amalek had the better of the fight.
Moses' hands, however, grew tired;
so they put a rock in place for him to sit on.
Meanwhile Aaron and Hur supported his hands,
one on one side and one on the other,
so that his hands remained steady till sunset.
And Joshua mowed down Amalek and his people
with the edge of the sword.

The word of the Lord. All: **Thanks be to God.**

RESPONSORIAL PSALM 121

P-529

Psalm 121:1-2, 3-4, 5-6, 7-8

℟. (*See* 2) **Our help is from the Lord, who made heaven and earth.**

I lift up my eyes toward the mountains;
whence shall help come to me?
My help is from the LORD,
who made heaven and earth. ℟.

(continued)

May he not suffer your foot to slip;
  may he slumber not who guards you:
indeed he neither slumbers nor sleeps,
  the guardian of Israel. ℟.

The LORD is your guardian; the LORD is your shade;
  he is beside you at your right hand.
The sun shall not harm you by day,
  nor the moon by night. ℟.

The LORD will guard you from all evil;
  he will guard your life.
The LORD will guard your coming and your going,
  both now and forever. ℟.

READING II (2 Timothy 3:14—4:2)

A reading from the second Letter of Saint Paul to Timothy

One who belongs to God may be competent, equipped for every good work.

Beloved:
Remain faithful to what you have learned and believed,
because you know from whom you learned it,
and that from infancy you have known the sacred Scriptures,
which are capable of giving you wisdom for salvation
through faith in Christ Jesus.
All Scripture is inspired by God
and is useful for teaching, for refutation, for correction,
and for training in righteousness,
so that one who belongs to God may be competent,
equipped for every good work.

I charge you in the presence of God and of Christ Jesus,
who will judge the living and the dead,
and by his appearing and his kingly power:
proclaim the word;
be persistent whether it is convenient or inconvenient;

convince, reprimand, encourage through all patience and teaching.

The word of the Lord. All: **Thanks be to God.**

GOSPEL (Luke 18:1-8)

ALLELUIA (Hebrews 4:12)

℣. Alleluia, alleluia. ℟. **Alleluia, alleluia.**

℣. The word of God is living and effective,
discerning reflections and thoughts of the heart. ℟.

✠ **A reading from the holy Gospel according to Luke**

All: **Glory to you, O Lord.**

God will secure the rights of his chosen ones who call out to him.

Jesus told his disciples a parable
about the necessity for them to pray always without becoming weary.
He said, "There was a judge in a certain town
who neither feared God nor respected any human being.
And a widow in that town used to come to him and say,
'Render a just decision for me against my adversary.'
For a long time the judge was unwilling, but eventually he thought,
'While it is true that I neither fear God nor respect any human being,
because this widow keeps bothering me
I shall deliver a just decision for her
lest she finally come and strike me.' "
The Lord said, "Pay attention to what the dishonest judge says.
Will not God then secure the rights of his chosen ones
who call out to him day and night?
Will he be slow to answer them?
I tell you, he will see to it that justice is done for them speedily.
But when the Son of Man comes, will he find faith on earth?"

The Gospel of the Lord. All: **Praise to you, Lord Jesus Christ.**

Prayer over the Offerings

Grant us, Lord, we pray,
a sincere respect for your gifts,
that, through the purifying action of your grace,
we may be cleansed by the very mysteries we serve.
Through Christ our Lord. All: **Amen.**

Communion Antiphon (Cf. Psalm 33[32]:18-19)

Behold, the eyes of the Lord
are on those who fear him,
who hope in his merciful love,
to rescue their souls from death,
to keep them alive in famine.

Or:

(Mark 10:45)
The Son of Man has come
to give his life as a ranson for many.

Prayer after Communion

Grant, O Lord, we pray,
that, benefiting from participation in heavenly things,
we may be helped by what you give in this present age
and prepared for the gifts that are eternal.
Through Christ our Lord. All: **Amen.**

Thirtieth Sunday in Ordinary Time

October 23, 2016

Reflection on the Gospel

Both the Pharisee and tax collector addressed God in prayer. The content of their prayer, however, differed greatly. The Pharisee's prayer was about himself and was turned toward self. The tax collector's prayer, by contrast, was turned toward God in the true self-knowledge of who he was. Jesus declared the tax collector justified, not the Pharisee. Justification—right relationship with God—comes only from knowing ourselves as God knows us. Paradoxically, true humility is exaltation—the gift received while being one's true self before God and others.

- *Prayer is effective and gives justification if . . .*

—Living Liturgy™, *Thirtieth Sunday in Ordinary Time 2016*

ENTRANCE ANTIPHON (Cf. Psalm 105[104]:3-4)

Let the hearts that seek the Lord rejoice;
turn to the Lord and his strength;
constantly seek his face.

COLLECT

Almighty ever-living God,
increase our faith, hope and charity,
and make us love what you command,
so that we may merit what you promise.
Through our Lord Jesus Christ, your Son,
who lives and reigns with you in the unity of the Holy Spirit,
one God, for ever and ever. All: **Amen.**

READING I (L 150-C) (Sirach 35:12-14, 16-18)

A reading from the Book of Sirach

The prayer of the lowly pierces the clouds.

The LORD is a God of justice,
who knows no favorites.

Though not unduly partial toward the weak,
yet he hears the cry of the oppressed.
The Lord is not deaf to the wail of the orphan,
nor to the widow when she pours out her complaint.
The one who serves God willingly is heard;
his petition reaches the heavens.
The prayer of the lowly pierces the clouds;
it does not rest till it reaches its goal,
nor will it withdraw till the Most High responds,
judges justly and affirms the right,
and the Lord will not delay.

The word of the Lord. All: **Thanks be to God.**

RESPONSORIAL PSALM 34

P-530

Psalm 34:2-3, 17-18, 19, 23

℟. (7a) **The Lord hears the cry of the poor.**

I will bless the LORD at all times;
his praise shall be ever in my mouth.
Let my soul glory in the LORD;
the lowly will hear me and be glad. ℟.

The LORD confronts the evildoers,
to destroy remembrance of them from the earth.
When the just cry out, the LORD hears them,
and from all their distress he rescues them. ℟.

The LORD is close to the brokenhearted;
and those who are crushed in spirit he saves.
The LORD redeems the lives of his servants;
no one incurs guilt who takes refuge in him. ℟.

READING II (2 Timothy 4:6-8, 16-18)

A reading from the second Letter of Saint Paul to Timothy

From now on, the crown of righteousness awaits me.

Beloved:
I am already being poured out like a libation,
and the time of my departure is at hand.
I have competed well; I have finished the race;
I have kept the faith.
From now on the crown of righteousness awaits me,
which the Lord, the just judge,
will award to me on that day, and not only to me,
but to all who have longed for his appearance.

At my first defense no one appeared on my behalf,
but everyone deserted me.
May it not be held against them!
But the Lord stood by me and gave me strength,
so that through me the proclamation might be completed
and all the Gentiles might hear it.
And I was rescued from the lion's mouth.
The Lord will rescue me from every evil threat
and will bring me safe to his heavenly kingdom.
To him be glory forever and ever. Amen.

The word of the Lord. All: Thanks be to God.

GOSPEL (Luke 18:9-14)

ALLELUIA (2 Corinthians 5:19)

℣. Alleluia, alleluia. ℟. **Alleluia, alleluia.**
℣. God was reconciling the world to himself in Christ,
and entrusting to us the message of salvation. ℟.

✠ **A reading from the holy Gospel according to Luke**

All: Glory to you, O Lord.

The tax collector, not the Pharisee, went home justified.

Jesus addressed this parable
to those who were convinced of their own righteousness
and despised everyone else.
"Two people went up to the temple area to pray;
one was a Pharisee and the other was a tax collector.

The Pharisee took up his position and spoke this prayer to himself,
'O God, I thank you that I am not like the rest of humanity—
greedy, dishonest, adulterous—or even like this tax collector.
I fast twice a week, and I pay tithes on my whole income.'
But the tax collector stood off at a distance
and would not even raise his eyes to heaven
but beat his breast and prayed,
'O God, be merciful to me a sinner.'
I tell you, the latter went home justified, not the former;
for whoever exalts himself will be humbled,
and the one who humbles himself will be exalted."

The Gospel of the Lord. All: **Praise to you, Lord Jesus Christ.**

Prayer over the Offerings

Look, we pray, O Lord,
on the offerings we make to your majesty,
that whatever is done by us in your service
may be directed above all to your glory.
Through Christ our Lord. All: **Amen.**

Communion Antiphon (Cf. Psalm 20[19]:6)

We will ring out our joy at your saving help
and exult in the name of our God.

Or:

(Ephesians 5:2)
Christ loved us and gave himself up for us,
as a fragrant offering to God.

Prayer after Communion

May your Sacraments, O Lord, we pray,
perfect in us what lies within them,
that what we now celebrate in signs
we may one day possess in truth.
Through Christ our Lord. All: **Amen.**

Thirty-First Sunday in Ordinary Time

October 30, 2016

Reflection on the Gospel

Zacchaeus's short stature kept him from seeing Jesus with his physical eyes. His ardent desire to encounter Jesus, however, indicates that he had already seen him with the eyes of his heart. Encountering Jesus does not depend upon the goodness of one's life, but encountering him can bring about conversion of life. Zacchaeus chooses to put his life in right order. For this does Zacchaeus come to salvation. We come to salvation when we see Jesus with the eyes of our own hearts wide open.

- *I can put my life in order by . . .*

—Living Liturgy™, *Thirty-First Sunday in Ordinary Time 2016*

Entrance Antiphon (Cf. Psalm 38[37]:22-23)

Forsake me not, O Lord, my God;
be not far from me!
Make haste and come to my help,
O Lord, my strong salvation!

Collect

Almighty and merciful God,
by whose gift your faithful offer you
right and praiseworthy service,
grant, we pray,
that we may hasten without stumbling
to receive the things you have promised.
Through our Lord Jesus Christ, your Son,
who lives and reigns with you in the unity of the Holy Spirit,
one God, for ever and ever. All: **Amen.**

Reading I (L 153-C) (Wisdom 11:22—12:2)

A reading from the Book of Wisdom

You have mercy on all because you love all things that are.

Before the Lord the whole universe is as a grain from
a balance
or a drop of morning dew come down upon the
earth.
But you have mercy on all, because you can do all things;
and you overlook people's sins that they may repent.
For you love all things that are
and loathe nothing that you have made;
for what you hated, you would not have fashioned.
And how could a thing remain, unless you willed it;
or be preserved, had it not been called forth by you?
But you spare all things, because they are yours,
O Lord and lover of souls,
for your imperishable spirit is in all things!
Therefore you rebuke offenders little by little,
warn them and remind them of the sins
they are committing,
that they may abandon their wickedness
and believe in you, O Lord!

The word of the Lord. All: **Thanks be to God.**

Responsorial Psalm 145

P-531

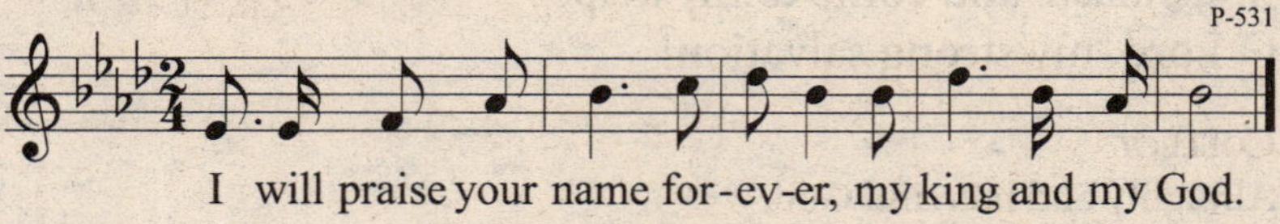

Psalm 145:1-2, 8-9, 10-11, 13, 14

℟. (*See* 1) **I will praise your name forever, my king and my God.**

I will extol you, O my God and King,
and I will bless your name forever and ever.
Every day will I bless you,
and I will praise your name forever and ever. ℟.

The Lord is gracious and merciful,
slow to anger and of great kindness.

The LORD is good to all
and compassionate toward all his works. ℟.

Let all your works give you thanks, O LORD,
and let your faithful ones bless you.
Let them discourse of the glory of your kingdom
and speak of your might. ℟.

The LORD is faithful in all his words
and holy in all his works.
The LORD lifts up all who are falling
and raises up all who are bowed down. ℟.

READING II (2 Thessalonians 1:11—2:2)

A reading from the second Letter of Saint Paul to the Thessalonians

May the name of Christ be glorified in you and you in him.

Brothers and sisters:
We always pray for you,
that our God may make you worthy of his calling
and powerfully bring to fulfillment every good purpose
and every effort of faith,
that the name of our Lord Jesus may be glorified in you,
and you in him,
in accord with the grace of our God and Lord Jesus Christ.

We ask you, brothers and sisters,
with regard to the coming of our Lord Jesus Christ
and our assembling with him,
not to be shaken out of your minds suddenly, or to be alarmed
either by a "spirit," or by an oral statement,
or by a letter allegedly from us
to the effect that the day of the Lord is at hand.

The word of the Lord. All: **Thanks be to God.**

GOSPEL (Luke 19:1-10)

ALLELUIA (John 3:16)

℣. Alleluia, alleluia. ℟. **Alleluia, alleluia.**

℣. God so loved the world that he gave his only Son,
so that everyone who believes in him might have eternal life. ℟.

✠ **A reading from the holy Gospel according to Luke**

All: **Glory to you, O Lord.**

The Son of Man has come to seek and to save what was lost.

At that time, Jesus came to Jericho and intended to pass through the town.
Now a man there named Zacchaeus,
who was a chief tax collector and also a wealthy man,
was seeking to see who Jesus was;
but he could not see him because of the crowd,
for he was short in stature.
So he ran ahead and climbed a sycamore tree in order to see Jesus,
who was about to pass that way.
When he reached the place, Jesus looked up and said,
"Zacchaeus, come down quickly,
for today I must stay at your house."
And he came down quickly and received him with joy.
When they all saw this, they began to grumble, saying,
"He has gone to stay at the house of a sinner."
But Zacchaeus stood there and said to the Lord,
"Behold, half of my possessions, Lord, I shall give to the poor,
and if I have extorted anything from anyone
I shall repay it four times over."
And Jesus said to him,
"Today salvation has come to this house
because this man too is a descendant of Abraham.
For the Son of Man has come to seek
and to save what was lost."

The Gospel of the Lord. All: **Praise to you, Lord Jesus Christ.**

Prayer over the Offerings

May these sacrificial offerings, O Lord,
become for you a pure oblation,
and for us a holy outpouring of your mercy.
Through Christ our Lord. All: **Amen.**

Communion Antiphon (Cf. Psalm 16[15]:11)

You will show me the path of life,
the fullness of joy in your presence, O Lord.

Or:

(John 6:58)

Just as the living Father sent me
and I have life because of the Father,
so whoever feeds on me
shall have life because of me, says the Lord.

Prayer after Communion

May the working of your power, O Lord,
increase in us, we pray,
so that, renewed by these heavenly Sacraments,
we may be prepared by your gift
for receiving what they promise.
Through Christ our Lord. All: **Amen.**

All Saints

November 1, 2016

Reflection on the Gospel

Jesus "began to teach" his disciples the Beatitudes, an ongoing way of living for his followers. Disciples' learning is not only in the hearing, but even more importantly in the daily living. The saints we honor today are those who took Jesus' Beatitudes to heart and lived them well. They now dwell in the land of inheritance—"the Kingdom of heaven" where they "see God" and know the fullness of what it means to be called "blessed."

- *With the "blessed," I daily journey with Jesus as I . . .*

—Living Liturgy™, *All Saints 2016*

Entrance Antiphon

Let us all rejoice in the Lord,
as we celebrate the feast day in honor of all the Saints,
at whose festival the Angels rejoice
and praise the Son of God.

Collect

Almighty ever-living God,
by whose gift we venerate in one celebration
the merits of all the Saints,
bestow on us, we pray,
through the prayers of so many intercessors,
an abundance of the reconciliation with you
for which we earnestly long.
Through our Lord Jesus Christ, your Son,
who lives and reigns with you in the unity of the Holy Spirit,
one God, for ever and ever. All: **Amen.**

Reading I (L 667) (Revelation 7:2-4, 9-14)

A reading from the Book of Revelation

I had a vision of a great multitude, which no one could count, from every nation, race, people and tongue.

I, John, saw another angel come up from the East,
holding the seal of the living God.
He cried out in a loud voice to the four angels
who were given power to damage the land and the sea,
"Do not damage the land or the sea or the trees
until we put the seal on the foreheads of the servants of our God."
I heard the number of those who had been marked with the seal,
one hundred and forty-four thousand marked
from every tribe of the children of Israel.

After this I had a vision of a great multitude,
which no one could count,
from every nation, race, people, and tongue.
They stood before the throne and before the Lamb,
wearing white robes and holding palm branches in their hands.
They cried out in a loud voice:

"Salvation comes from our God, who is seated on the throne,
and from the Lamb."

All the angels stood around the throne
and around the elders and the four living creatures.
They prostrated themselves before the throne,
worshiped God, and exclaimed:

"Amen. Blessing and glory, wisdom and thanksgiving,
honor, power, and might
be to our God forever and ever. Amen."

Then one of the elders spoke up and said to me,
"Who are these wearing white robes, and where did they come from?"
I said to him, "My lord, you are the one who knows."

He said to me,
"These are the ones who have survived the time of great distress;
they have washed their robes
and made them white in the Blood of the Lamb."

The word of the Lord. All: **Thanks be to God.**

Responsorial Psalm 24

P-184

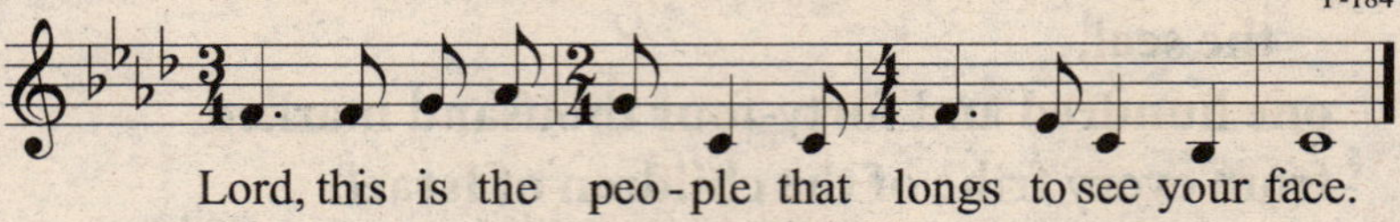

Psalm 24:1bc-2, 3-4ab, 5-6

℟. (*See* 6) **Lord, this is the people that longs to see your face.**

The LORD's are the earth and its fullness;
the world and those who dwell in it.
For he founded it upon the seas
and established it upon the rivers. ℟.

Who can ascend the mountain of the LORD?
or who may stand in his holy place?
One whose hands are sinless, whose heart is clean,
who desires not what is vain. ℟.

He shall receive a blessing from the LORD,
a reward from God his savior.
Such is the race that seeks him,
that seeks the face of the God of Jacob. ℟.

Reading II (1 John 3:1-3)

A reading from the first Letter of Saint John

We shall see God as he is.

Beloved:
See what love the Father has bestowed on us
that we may be called the children of God.
Yet so we are.
The reason the world does not know us
is that it did not know him.

Beloved, we are God's children now;
what we shall be has not yet been revealed.
We do know that when it is revealed we shall be like him,
for we shall see him as he is.
Everyone who has this hope based on him makes himself pure,
as he is pure.

The word of the Lord. All: **Thanks be to God.**

Gospel (Matthew 5:1-12a)

Alleluia (Matthew 11:28)

℣. Alleluia, alleluia. ℟. **Alleluia, alleluia.**
℣. Come to me, all you who labor and are burdened,
and I will give you rest, says the Lord. ℟.

✠ **A reading from the holy Gospel according to Matthew**

All: **Glory to you, O Lord.**

Rejoice and be glad, for your reward will be great in heaven.

When Jesus saw the crowds, he went up the mountain,
and after he had sat down, his disciples came to him.
He began to teach them, saying:

"Blessed are the poor in spirit,
for theirs is the Kingdom of heaven.
Blessed are they who mourn,
for they will be comforted.
Blessed are the meek,
for they will inherit the land.
Blessed are they who hunger and thirst for righteousness,
for they will be satisfied.
Blessed are the merciful,
for they will be shown mercy.
Blessed are the clean of heart,
for they will see God.
Blessed are the peacemakers,
for they will be called children of God.

Blessed are they who are persecuted for the sake of righteousness,
for theirs is the Kingdom of heaven.
Blessed are you when they insult you and persecute you
and utter every kind of evil against you falsely because of me.
Rejoice and be glad,
for your reward will be great in heaven."

The Gospel of the Lord. All: Praise to you, Lord Jesus Christ.

Prayer over the Offerings

May these offerings we bring in honor of all the Saints
be pleasing to you, O Lord,
and grant that, just as we believe the Saints
to be already assured of immortality,
so we may experience their concern for our salvation.
Through Christ our Lord. All: **Amen.**

Communion Antiphon (Matthew 5:8-10)

Blessed are the clean of heart, for they shall see God.
Blessed are the peacemakers,
for they shall be called children of God.
Blessed are they who are persecuted for the sake of righteousness,
for theirs is the Kingdom of Heaven.

Prayer after Communion

As we adore you, O God, who alone are holy
and wonderful in all your Saints,
we implore your grace,
so that, coming to perfect holiness in the fullness of your love,
we may pass from this pilgrim table
to the banquet of our heavenly homeland.
Through Christ our Lord. All: **Amen.**

Thirty-Second Sunday in Ordinary Time

November 6, 2016

Reflection of the Gospel

For the Sadducees, one's immortality was contingent on having progeny, the tradition and context of their argument about marrying and remarrying taken to extremes. Jesus answers them by asserting that there is no marriage and remarriage in heaven because there is no dying in heaven. In heaven, "all are alive," in perfect union with God. The proof of Jesus' truth is his own resurrection, his own perfect union with his Father. The promise of Jesus' truth is our resurrection, our perfect union with God.

- ***With Jesus I come into union with God as I . . .***

—Living Liturgy™, *Thirty-Second Sunday in Ordinary Time 2016*

Entrance Antiphon (Cf. Psalm 88[87]:3)

Let my prayer come into your presence.
Incline your ear to my cry for help, O Lord.

Collect

Almighty and merciful God,
graciously keep from us all adversity,
so that, unhindered in mind and body alike,
we may pursue in freedom of heart
the things that are yours.
Through our Lord Jesus Christ, your Son,
who lives and reigns with you in the unity of the Holy Spirit,
one God, for ever and ever. All: **Amen.**

Reading I (L 156-C) (2 Maccabees 7:1-2, 9-14)

A reading from the second Book of Maccabees

The King of the world will raise us up to live again forever.

It happened that seven brothers with their mother were arrested
and tortured with whips and scourges by the king,
to force them to eat pork in violation of God's law.
One of the brothers, speaking for the others, said:
"What do you expect to achieve by questioning us?
We are ready to die rather than transgress the laws of our ancestors."

At the point of death he said:
"You accursed fiend, you are depriving us of this present life,
but the King of the world will raise us up to live again forever.
It is for his laws that we are dying."
After him the third suffered their cruel sport.
He put out his tongue at once when told to do so,
and bravely held out his hands, as he spoke these noble words:
"It was from Heaven that I received these;
for the sake of his laws I disdain them;
from him I hope to receive them again."
Even the king and his attendants marveled at the young man's courage,
because he regarded his sufferings as nothing.

After he had died,
they tortured and maltreated the fourth brother in the same way.
When he was near death, he said,
"It is my choice to die at the hands of men
with the hope God gives of being raised up by him;
but for you, there will be no resurrection to life."

The word of the Lord. All: **Thanks be to God.**

Responsorial Psalm 17

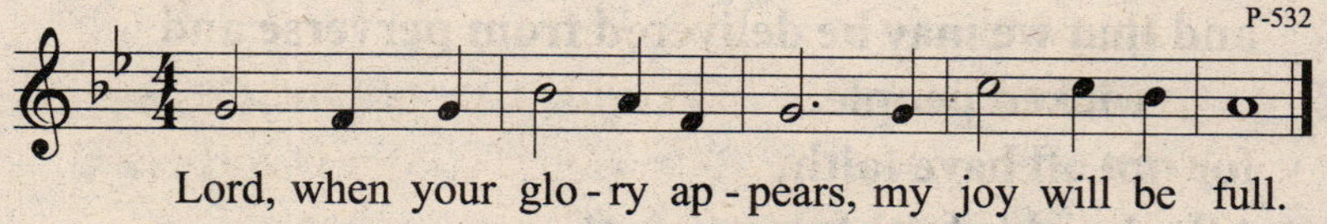

Psalm 17:1, 5-6, 8, 15

℟. (15b) **Lord, when your glory appears, my joy will be full.**

Hear, O Lord, a just suit;
attend to my outcry;
hearken to my prayer from lips without deceit. ℟.

My steps have been steadfast in your paths,
my feet have not faltered.
I call upon you, for you will answer me, O God;
incline your ear to me; hear my word. ℟.

Keep me as the apple of your eye,
hide me in the shadow of your wings.
But I in justice shall behold your face;
on waking I shall be content in your presence. ℟.

Reading II (2 Thessalonians 2:16—3:5)

A reading from the second Letter of Saint Paul to the Thessalonians

May the Lord encourage your hearts and strengthen them in every good deed and word.

Brothers and sisters:
May our Lord Jesus Christ himself and God our Father,
who has loved us and given us everlasting encouragement
and good hope through his grace,
encourage your hearts and strengthen them in every good deed and word.

Finally, brothers and sisters, pray for us,
so that the word of the Lord may speed forward and be glorified,

as it did among you,
and that we may be delivered from perverse and wicked people,
for not all have faith.
But the Lord is faithful;
he will strengthen you and guard you from the evil one.
We are confident of you in the Lord that what we instruct you,
you are doing and will continue to do.
May the Lord direct your hearts to the love of God
and to the endurance of Christ.

The word of the Lord. All: **Thanks be to God.**

GOSPEL (Luke 20:27-38) *or* Shorter Form [ ] (Luke 20:27, 34-38)
ALLELUIA (Revelation 1:5a, 6b)

℣. Alleluia, alleluia. ℟. **Alleluia, alleluia.**
℣. Jesus Christ is the firstborn of the dead;
to him be glory and power, forever and ever. ℟.

✠ **A reading from the holy Gospel according to Luke**

All: **Glory to you, O Lord.**

He is not God of the dead, but of the living.

[Some Sadducees, those who deny that there is a resurrection,
came forward] and put this question to Jesus, saying,
"Teacher, Moses wrote for us,
If someone's brother dies leaving a wife but no child,
his brother must take the wife
and raise up descendants for his brother.
Now there were seven brothers;
the first married a woman but died childless.
Then the second and the third married her,
and likewise all the seven died childless.
Finally the woman also died.
Now at the resurrection whose wife will that woman be?
For all seven had been married to her."

[Jesus said to them,
"The children of this age marry and remarry;
but those who are deemed worthy to attain to the coming age
and to the resurrection of the dead
neither marry nor are given in marriage.
They can no longer die,
for they are like angels;
and they are the children of God
because they are the ones who will rise.
That the dead will rise
even Moses made known in the passage about the bush,
when he called out 'Lord,'
the God of Abraham, the God of Isaac, and the God of Jacob;
and he is not God of the dead, but of the living,
for to him all are alive."]

The Gospel of the Lord. All: **Praise to you, Lord Jesus Christ.**

Prayer over the Offerings

Look with favor, we pray, O Lord,
upon the sacrificial gifts offered here,
that, celebrating in mystery the Passion of your Son,
we may honor it with loving devotion.
Through Christ our Lord. All: **Amen.**

Communion Antiphon (Cf. Psalm 23[22]:1-2)

The Lord is my shepherd; there is nothing I shall want.
Fresh and green are the pastures where he gives me repose,
near restful waters he leads me.

Or:

(Cf. Luke 24:35)

The disciples recognized the Lord Jesus in the breaking of bread.

Prayer after Communion

Nourished by this sacred gift, O Lord,
we give you thanks and beseech your mercy,
that, by the pouring forth of your Spirit,

the grace of integrity may endure
in those your heavenly power has entered.
Through Christ our Lord. All: **Amen.**

Thirty-Third Sunday in Ordinary Time

November 13, 2016

Reflection on the Gospel

In the beginning, all things came to be. At the end, things as we know them will cease to be. Does anything really last forever? Certainly not temples, not nations, not even the foundations of the earth. So, what does last forever? God, the wisdom of Jesus, divine Life. And, yes, the lives of those who persevere in fidelity to the name and mission of Jesus and who "will secure" a share in divine Life. At the end . . . a new beginning.

- *With Jesus in the wisdom of God I can . . .*

—Living Liturgy™, *Thirty-Third Sunday in Ordinary Time 2016*

Entrance Antiphon (Jeremiah 29:11, 12, 14)

The Lord said: I think thoughts of peace and not of affliction.
You will call upon me, and I will answer you,
and I will lead back your captives from every place.

Collect

Grant us, we pray, O Lord our God,
the constant gladness of being devoted to you,
for it is full and lasting happiness
to serve with constancy
the author of all that is good.
Through our Lord Jesus Christ, your Son,
who lives and reigns with you in the unity of the Holy Spirit,
one God, for ever and ever. All: **Amen.**

Reading I (L 159-C) (Malachi 3:19-20a)

A reading from the Book of the Prophet Malachi

The sun of justice will shine on you.

Lo, the day is coming, blazing like an oven,
when all the proud and all evildoers will be stubble,
and the day that is coming will set them on fire,
leaving them neither root nor branch,
says the Lord of hosts.
But for you who fear my name, there will arise
the sun of justice with its healing rays.

The word of the Lord. All: **Thanks be to God.**

Responsorial Psalm 98

P-533

Psalm 98:5-6, 7-8, 9

℟. (*See* 9) **The Lord comes to rule the earth with justice.**

Sing praise to the Lord with the harp,
with the harp and melodious song.
With trumpets and the sound of the horn
sing joyfully before the King, the Lord. ℟.

Let the sea and what fills it resound,
the world and those who dwell in it;
let the rivers clap their hands,
the mountains shout with them for joy. ℟.

Before the Lord, for he comes,
for he comes to rule the earth;
he will rule the world with justice
and the peoples with equity. ℟.

READING II (2 Thessalonians 3:7-12)

A reading from the second Letter of Saint Paul to the Thessalonians

If anyone is unwilling to work, neither should that one eat.

Brothers and sisters:
You know how one must imitate us.
For we did not act in a disorderly way among you,
nor did we eat food received free from anyone.
On the contrary, in toil and drudgery, night and day
we worked, so as not to burden any of you.
Not that we do not have the right.
Rather, we wanted to present ourselves as a model for you,
so that you might imitate us.
In fact, when we were with you,
we instructed you that if anyone was unwilling to work,
neither should that one eat.
We hear that some are conducting themselves among you in a disorderly way,
by not keeping busy but minding the business of others.
Such people we instruct and urge in the Lord Jesus Christ to work quietly
and to eat their own food.

The word of the Lord. All: **Thanks be to God.**

GOSPEL (Luke 21:5-19)

ALLELUIA (Luke 21:28)

℣. Alleluia, alleluia. ℟. **Alleluia, alleluia.**
℣. Stand erect and raise your heads
because your redemption is at hand. ℟.

✠ **A reading from the holy Gospel according to Luke**

All: **Glory to you, O Lord.**

By your perseverance you will secure your lives.

While some people were speaking about
how the temple was adorned with costly stones and votive offerings,
Jesus said, "All that you see here—
the days will come when there will not be left
a stone upon another stone that will not be thrown down."

Then they asked him,
"Teacher, when will this happen?
And what sign will there be when all these things are about to happen?"
He answered,
"See that you not be deceived,
for many will come in my name, saying,
'I am he,' and 'The time has come.'
Do not follow them!
When you hear of wars and insurrections,
do not be terrified; for such things must happen first,
but it will not immediately be the end."
Then he said to them,
"Nation will rise against nation, and kingdom against kingdom.
There will be powerful earthquakes, famines, and plagues
from place to place;
and awesome sights and mighty signs will come from the sky.

"Before all this happens, however,
they will seize and persecute you,
they will hand you over to the synagogues and to prisons,
and they will have you led before kings and governors
because of my name.
It will lead to your giving testimony.

Remember, you are not to prepare your defense beforehand,
for I myself shall give you a wisdom in speaking
that all your adversaries will be powerless to resist or refute.
You will even be handed over by parents, brothers, relatives, and friends,
and they will put some of you to death.
You will be hated by all because of my name,
but not a hair on your head will be destroyed.
By your perseverance you will secure your lives."

The Gospel of the Lord. All: **Praise to you, Lord Jesus Christ.**

Prayer over the Offerings

Grant, O Lord, we pray,
that what we offer in the sight of your majesty
may obtain for us the grace of being devoted to you
and gain us the prize of everlasting happiness.
Through Christ our Lord. All: **Amen.**

Communion Antiphon (Psalm 73[72]:28)

To be near God is my happiness,
to place my hope in God the Lord.

Or:

(Mark 11:23-24)
Amen, I say to you: Whatever you ask in prayer,
believe that you will receive,
and it shall be given to you, says the Lord.

Prayer after Communion

We have partaken of the gifts of this sacred mystery,
humbly imploring, O Lord,
that what your Son commanded us to do
in memory of him
may bring us growth in charity.
Through Christ our Lord. All: **Amen.**

Our Lord Jesus Christ, King of the Universe

November 20, 2016

Reflection on the Gospel

Three hang on crosses, suffering and dying. One reviles, one begs for salvation, One promises Paradise. Indeed, only One can promise Paradise. Who but "the Christ of God" could make such a promise? Who but a divine King could reach beyond his own suffering and dying to bestow Life on another? Who but One totally innocent of evil could draw goodness out of one who is "condemned justly"? Three hang on crosses. One remains condemned. One is redeemed. One will rise from the dead, King of the universe.

- *Who is this Jesus dying on a cross at Jerusalem? What does he mean for me? . . .*

—Living Liturgy™, *Christ the King 2016*

ENTRANCE ANTIPHON (Revelation 5:12; 1:6)

How worthy is the Lamb who was slain,
to receive power and divinity,
and wisdom and strength and honor.
To him belong glory and power for ever and ever.

COLLECT

Almighty ever-living God,
whose will is to restore all things
in your beloved Son, the King of the universe,
grant, we pray,
that the whole creation, set free from slavery,
may render your majesty service
and ceaselessly proclaim your praise.
Through our Lord Jesus Christ, your Son,
who lives and reigns with you in the unity of the Holy Spirit,
one God, for ever and ever. All: **Amen.**

READING I (L 162-C) (2 Samuel 5:1-3)

A reading from the second Book of Samuel

They anointed David king of Israel.

In those days, all the tribes of Israel came to David in
Hebron and said:
"Here we are, your bone and your flesh.
In days past, when Saul was our king,
it was you who led the Israelites out and brought
them back.
And the LORD said to you,
'You shall shepherd my people Israel
and shall be commander of Israel.'"
When all the elders of Israel came to David in Hebron,
King David made an agreement with them there
before the LORD,
and they anointed him king of Israel.

The word of the Lord. All: **Thanks be to God.**

RESPONSORIAL PSALM 122

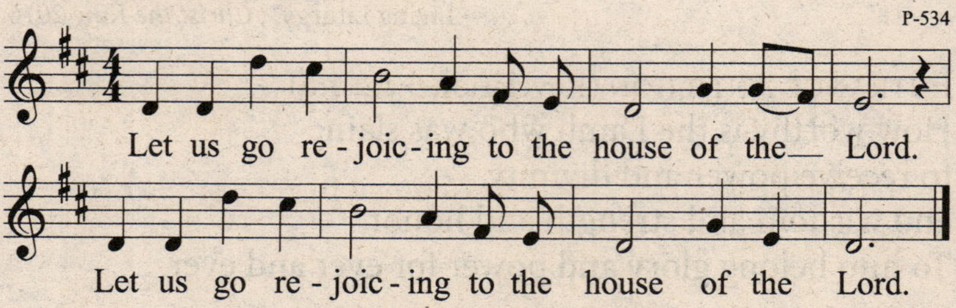

Psalm 122:1-2, 3-4, 4-5

℟. (*See* 1) **Let us go rejoicing to the house of the Lord.**

I rejoiced because they said to me,
"We will go up to the house of the LORD."
And now we have set foot
within your gates, O Jerusalem. ℟.

Jerusalem, built as a city
with compact unity.
To it the tribes go up,
the tribes of the LORD. ℟.

According to the decree for Israel,
  to give thanks to the name of the LORD.
In it are set up judgment seats,
  seats for the house of David. ℟.

READING II (Colossians 1:12-20)

A reading from the Letter of Saint Paul to the Colossians

He transferred us to the kingdom of his beloved Son.

Brothers and sisters:
Let us give thanks to the Father,
who has made you fit to share
in the inheritance of the holy ones in light.
He delivered us from the power of darkness
and transferred us to the kingdom of his beloved Son,
in whom we have redemption, the forgiveness of sins.

He is the image of the invisible God,
the firstborn of all creation.
For in him were created all things in heaven and on earth,
the visible and the invisible,
whether thrones or dominions or principalities or powers;
all things were created through him and for him.
He is before all things,
and in him all things hold together.
He is the head of the body, the church.
He is the beginning, the firstborn from the dead,
that in all things he himself might be preeminent.
For in him all the fullness was pleased to dwell,
and through him to reconcile all things for him,
making peace by the blood of his cross
through him, whether those on earth or those in heaven.

The word of the Lord. All: **Thanks be to God.**

GOSPEL (Luke 23:35-43)

ALLELUIA (Mark 11:9, 10)

℣. Alleluia, alleluia. ℟. **Alleluia, alleluia.**

℣. Blessed is he who comes in the name of the Lord!
Blessed is the kingdom of our father David that is to come! ℟.

✠ A reading from the holy Gospel according to Luke

All: **Glory to you, O Lord.**

Lord, remember me when you come into your kingdom.

The rulers sneered at Jesus and said,
"He saved others, let him save himself
if he is the chosen one, the Christ of God."
Even the soldiers jeered at him.
As they approached to offer him wine they called out,
"If you are King of the Jews, save yourself."
Above him there was an inscription that read,
"This is the King of the Jews."
Now one of the criminals hanging there reviled Jesus, saying,
"Are you not the Christ?
Save yourself and us."
The other, however, rebuking him, said in reply,
"Have you no fear of God,
for you are subject to the same condemnation?
And indeed, we have been condemned justly,
for the sentence we received corresponds to our crimes,
but this man has done nothing criminal."
Then he said,
"Jesus, remember me when you come into your kingdom."
He replied to him,
"Amen, I say to you,
today you will be with me in Paradise."

The Gospel of the Lord. All: **Praise to you, Lord Jesus Christ.**

Prayer over the Offerings

As we offer you, O Lord, the sacrifice
by which the human race is reconciled to you,
we humbly pray
that your Son himself may bestow on all nations
the gifts of unity and peace.
Through Christ our Lord. All: **Amen.**

Communion Antiphon (Psalm 29[28]:10-11)

The Lord sits as King for ever.
The Lord will bless his people with peace.

Prayer after Communion

Having received the food of immortality,
we ask, O Lord,
that, glorying in obedience
to the commands of Christ, the King of the universe,
we may live with him eternally in his heavenly Kingdom.
Who lives and reigns for ever and ever. All: **Amen.**

Eucharistic Prayer for Reconciliation I

Preface

It is truly right and just
that we should always give you thanks,
Lord, holy Father, almighty and eternal God.

For you do not cease to spur us on
to possess a more abundant life
and, being rich in mercy,
you constantly offer pardon
and call on sinners
to trust in your forgiveness alone.

Never did you turn away from us,
and, though time and again we have broken your covenant,
you have bound the human family to yourself
through Jesus your Son, our Redeemer,
with a new bond of love so tight
that it can never be undone.

Even now you set before your people
a time of grace and reconciliation,
and, as they turn back to you in spirit,
you grant them hope in Christ Jesus
and a desire to be of service to all,
while they entrust themselves
more fully to the Holy Spirit.

And so, filled with wonder,
we extol the power of your love,
and, proclaiming our joy
at the salvation that comes from you,
we join in the heavenly hymn of countless hosts,
as without end we acclaim:

Holy, Holy, Holy Lord God of hosts.
Heaven and earth are full of your glory.
Hosanna in the highest.
Blessed is he who comes in the name of the Lord.
Hosanna in the highest.

Priest:
You are indeed Holy, O Lord,
and from the world's beginning
are ceaselessly at work,
so that the human race may become holy,
just as you yourself are holy.
Look, we pray, upon your people's offerings
and pour out on them the power of your Spirit,
that they may become the Body and ✠ Blood
of your beloved Son, Jesus Christ,
in whom we, too, are your sons and daughters.
Indeed, though we once were lost
and could not approach you,
you loved us with the greatest love:
for your Son, who alone is just,
handed himself over to death,
and did not disdain to be nailed for our sake
to the wood of the Cross.

But before his arms were outstretched between heaven and earth,
to become the lasting sign of your covenant,
he desired to celebrate the Passover with his disciples.

As he ate with them,
he took bread
and, giving you thanks, he said the blessing,
broke the bread and gave it to them, saying:

TAKE THIS, ALL OF YOU, AND EAT OF IT,
FOR THIS IS MY BODY,
WHICH WILL BE GIVEN UP FOR YOU.

In a similar way, when supper was ended,
knowing that he was about to reconcile all things in himself
through his Blood to be shed on the Cross,
he took the chalice, filled with the fruit of the vine,
and once more giving you thanks,
handed the chalice to his disciples, saying:

TAKE THIS, ALL OF YOU, AND DRINK FROM IT,
FOR THIS IS THE CHALICE OF MY BLOOD,
THE BLOOD OF THE NEW AND ETERNAL COVENANT,
WHICH WILL BE POURED OUT FOR YOU AND FOR MANY
FOR THE FORGIVENESS OF SINS.

DO THIS IN MEMORY OF ME.

The mystery of faith.

People:

A **We proclaim your Death, O Lord,
and profess your Resurrection
until you come again.**

B **When we eat this Bread and drink this Cup,
we proclaim your Death, O Lord,
until you come again.**

C **Save us, Savior of the world,
for by your Cross and Resurrection
you have set us free.**

Priest:
Therefore, as we celebrate
the memorial of your Son Jesus Christ,
who is our Passover and our surest peace,
we celebrate his Death and Resurrection from the dead,
and looking forward to his blessed Coming,
we offer you, who are our faithful and merciful God,
this sacrificial Victim
who reconciles to you the human race.

Look kindly, most compassionate Father,
on those you unite to yourself
by the Sacrifice of your Son,
and grant that, by the power of the Holy Spirit,
as they partake of this one Bread and one Chalice,

they may be gathered into one Body in Christ,
who heals every division.

Be pleased to keep us always
in communion of mind and heart,
together with N. our Pope and N. our Bishop.*
Help us to work together
for the coming of your Kingdom,
until the hour when we stand before you,
Saints among the Saints in the halls of heaven,
with the Blessed Virgin Mary, Mother of God,
the blessed Apostles and all the Saints,
and with our deceased brothers and sisters,
whom we humbly commend to your mercy.

Then, freed at last from the wound of corruption
and made fully into a new creation,
we shall sing to you with gladness
the thanksgiving of Christ,
who lives for all eternity.

Through him, and with him, and in him,
O God, almighty Father,
in the unity of the Holy Spirit,
all glory and honor is yours,
for ever and ever.

People: **Amen.**

Then follows the Communion Rite, p. 23.

* Mention may be made here of the Coadjutor Bishop, or Auxiliary Bishops, as noted in the *General Instruction of the Roman Missal*, no. 149.